Classic Aircraft
Bombers

Classic Aircraft

Bombers

Bill Gunston

Optimum Books

Contents

Front end paper
An Italian Caproni of the Ca 46 family gets a once-over from a private of the US Army Air Service in 1918. Had the war continued into 1919, large numbers of Capronis would have been shipped from the United States

Opposite
An officer of the Italian Army gives scale to one of the large Caproni triplanes of the Ca 42 series. Up to 3197 lb of bombs could be released from the large container on the bottom wing

Back end paper
Much-modified over the past 15 years, this Hawker Siddeley Vulcan represents Britain's effective but microscopic airborne deterrent to war. Its unit is 44 Squadron, which in 1941 was the first to operate the Lancaster, built in the same factory

Acknowledgments

The publishers are grateful to the following individuals and organizations for the illustrations in this book: *Aeroplane Monthly*; Gordon Bain; John Batchelor Ltd; Chas Bowyer; Camera Press; Chris Ellis; *Flight International*; Bill Gunston; Kenneth McDonough; Novosty Press Agency (APN); Pilot Press; John W. R. Taylor; Phoebus Publishing Co; Michael Turner.

Copyright © 1978 The Hamlyn Publishing Group Limited
This edition published by Optimum Books 1981

ISBN 0 600 349969

Filmset by Filmtype Services Limited, Scarborough

Printed in Italy

Introduction

In this book twenty of the most famous bombers are described in words, pictures and cutaway drawings. Obviously the contrast between the earliest bombers and those of today is extreme; and so is the contrast between one cutaway and another. Some of the drawings were prepared forty or more years ago, when the aircraft depicted was new. In those days the technique of the cutaway was in its infancy, and in any case drawings had to be done for reproduction by the letterpress printing that was then almost universal. Today our artists, like our book publishers, can set a higher standard.

Of course new technology will give us new qualities, but it will cost money, both for books and for aircraft. Even when allowance is made for inflation – for example by reckoning all prices in 1918 values, or a similar yardstick – modern bombers are astronomically expensive. In 1918 the first bombers in this book cost approximately £2300, half of which was attributable to the engines. The last truly strategic American bomber, the cancelled Rockwell B–1, would have cost about £4 million in the same 1918 pounds sterling, though obviously, we are not comparing like with like.

The difference is highlighted by the cutaways. With early aircraft of the pre-1930 era there is little difficulty in creating a faithful and indeed complete cutaway that shows every significant part and item of equipment. There was not very much inside, and an artist could almost do a worthwhile drawing from a single clear photograph, using a bit of guesswork. But today no artist could hope to draw any cutaway significantly smaller than life size if it were to contain a majority of the parts or equipment. The number of items to be covered in a drawing depends on how they are reckoned. For example, does a large box containing a computer of fantastic complexity count as a single item? Probably it should, for whichever way they are counted the components of a modern bomber number hundreds of thousands. If electronic units were broken down into their own separate pieces the result would add up to hundreds of millions. This, while a problem for the artist, more importantly explains the soaring costs of modern bombers, where even seemingly simple items represent the very pinnacle of technology. For example, a single turbine blade from a modern engine, which looks like a simple sliver of metal which could be slipped into a pocket, may cost as much as an Arab ruler would pay for his most expensive motor car.

Thus, the challenge faced by today's technical artist depends almost entirely on the age of the bomber he is drawing. Some aircraft are so large that it is difficult to show interesting small details and still get the wing tips into the drawing, so that they need small inset enlargements to reveal special features of construction. The writer perhaps has an easier task; but he can be criticised for being partisan, too technical, not technical enough, or for any of a dozen other faults. One of the most obvious areas of possible debate is in his choice of bombers which will give a representative coverage.

This book certainly contains some great bombers; in fact the author tried to omit none which could be considered the very greatest of all, at the same time achieving an international balance. To include the B–47, B–36 or B–58 would have given an emphasis in favour of the United States. To include a Gotha or Staaken Giant would have been pleasant, but perhaps would have overdone the First World War period when the whole business of bombing was in its infancy. Again, one could argue that the balance would have been better with a chapter on a modern Soviet bomber, but we do not know enough about them to prepare an authoritative cutaway drawing. One of the questionable inclusions was the Martin Bomber, but probably no bomber in history has generated such technical interest, though quite a few have, like the Martin, been faster than contemporary fighters.

What about the bomber in the modern world? In the vast majority of cases the best answers lie in the use of missiles and the tactical attack aircraft. Existing long-range missiles are ideal for hitting anything in a fixed location, such as a city, an airfield or an underground silo housing an enemy missile. They are useless for things which move about, such as V/STOL aircraft bases, armies, navies and mobile defence installations. On the other hand tactical attack aircraft can accomplish far more than their modest size may suggest, and even the Jaguar – one of the smaller breed, with wing span ten feet less than a Spitfire – could have flown almost any of the missions of the four-engined heavy bombers that raided Germany in the Second World War. A slightly larger machine, the Tornado, is the RAF's replacement for the Vulcan. One can assume there is no lessening of effectiveness, but there is a startling difference in size and the number of crew needed to manage it, when comparing it to the older aircraft.

Sometimes even the experts get confused about bombers. Several modern attack aircraft have been described as fighters, though they carry no air-to-air radar or weapons and do their best to avoid combat. The outstanding example of this is the US Air Force's F–111, which actually received a fighter designation. Then a special long-range bomber version was built for Strategic Air Command, but instead of being called the B–1 or B–2 it was called FB–111A. Now the US Air Force may rebuild these aircraft so that they really fit the bomber role and to fly as many of the missions planned for the cancelled B–1 as possible. Eventually they will emerge, at a cost not far short of that of a B–1 as completely new aircraft, but they will still not receive bomber designations. The mass media usually take one look and, if the thing looks to them like a fighter, it is labelled as such. So the F–111 is invariably described as a 'tactical fighter'. The popular inference is that bombers are obsolete, but nothing could be further from the truth. The fact that they now drop much more sophisticated things than plain free-fall bombs does not mean we have to cease calling them bombers.

Caproni series, Ca1 to Ca5

More than a century ago bold fiction-writers described bombing attacks by 'aerial armies'. Most were conveyed in balloons, while a few came in terrifying winged machines like prehistoric birds of prey. At the time such an assault was beyond the available technology, but man flew a successful aeroplane in 1903 and dropped a bomb in 1910.

In 1911 light Blériot monoplanes were used as bombers in anger by the Italians in fighting near Tripoli. This campaign was the first in which aeroplanes were used as weapons. It set the Italians on a path of development which to us appears obvious, yet which had no parallel in any other country except Czarist Russia. At a time when the British and all other advanced nations saw no use for the aeroplane in warfare at all—except possibly as a reconnaissance platform—the Italians saw that aeroplanes could be used to drop bombs on enemies, and went ahead and created aircraft designed to do just this. Apart from the parallel Russian *Ilya Mourometz* series they were the world's first bombers.

These pioneer aircraft were the result of talks between the Italian Army and government and a millionaire industrialist, Count Gianni Caproni. He had formed an aircraft company in 1908, and in 1913 it had the experience to plan an aircraft which exceeded all others in carrying power. At that time there was no established arrangement for large aeroplanes. Caproni decided to use a short central nacelle and carry the tail on twin booms joined to the lower wing on each side. He put three engines in the nacelle, one behind the other. The rearmost engine drove a pusher screw at the back of the nacelle, while the other two engines drove tractor propellers at the front of each tail boom. He tried both chain drive and bevel-gear shafts. Having all three engines in the nacelle along with the crew of three was thought to allow

Biggest of the Caproni bombers were the Ca 40 (Ca 4) series triplanes. N–527, a Ca 42 photographed at the company aircraft assembly plant, served with the RAF in Italy in 1918 but was soon returned to the Italian Army. The tall vertical boxes above the Isotta engines were radiators

One of the best photographs of the best Caproni, the Ca 46 (Ca 5), which was the mainstay of the CAM bomber force at the end of the First World War. The 'mid-upper turret' is vacant

adjustments or repairs to be made, but in fact it was a poor arrangement. Although the Ca 30 flew successfully in 1913 it was soon replaced by the Ca 31 with direct-drive engines at the front of each boom. Until this time the engines had been 80 hp Gnome rotaries, some of the pusher engines being 90 hp water-cooled Curtiss types because the Gnomes overheated in this position. But with the Ca 32 of 1914 three Italian Fiat A–10 engines were used, rated at 100 hp each.

Caproni built 164 of these bombers, which entered service with the Corpo Aeronautica Militare in July 1915 as the Ca 2. Italy had declared war on Austria-Hungary on 25 May 1915, and at once set about something new in human experience: a campaign of strategic bombing. The only other forces that could consider such a campaign were the Czar's *Squadron of Flying Ships,* then being formed with *Ilya Mourometz* bombers, and the Imperial German Navy's Zeppelin airships.

On 20 August 1915 two Capronis took off from Pordenone and dropped bombs on Aisovizza. This was the first of many missions by Ca 2 and by the later Ca 3 (Ca 33) of which 269 were built in 1916–18. The Ca 3 equipped 18 CAM bomber squadrons; a torpedo squadron served with the Italian Navy, and French-built versions served with the Aviation Militaire. There were many variants, some of them built after the First World War and serving until 1928.

One can feel nothing but admiration for the stoicism of the crews who flew the Ca 2 and 3 on the world's first long bombing missions. On take-off the seemingly flimsy machines weighed about 8400 lb, of which 1000 lb was the externally hung bomb load. In the nacelle two pilots sat side-by-side, with a gunner immediately in front of them manning a 6·5 mm Revelli in a nose position. Just behind the upper wing was a second gun position where a rear gunner had one to three Revellis with a good arc of fire. But even if everything went well, a mission was no picnic. Some targets were 150 miles away, and at a cruising speed of around 60 mph this meant a round trip of not less than five hours. Most of the flights took the lumbering biplanes across parts of the Alps and other rugged mountains where a successful forced landing was out of the question (and the Caproni could not remain in the air on two engines). Even if the aircraft were to be put down safely, there was often little hope of the crew getting out of the wilderness of precipices and glaciers. Inevitably, the Austrian anti-aircraft and fighter defences multiplied to counter the Caproni threat.

There was no cockpit heating, and almost invariably the outside air temperature was below zero. The man whose perch was especially exposed was the rear gunner, who stood in an open cage directly above the rear engine and six inches in front of the rear propeller. Even in a thick leather coat, five hours in this deafening, freezing and highly dangerous position was all a man could stand. It was often difficult for the rear gunner to retain his senses, spot enemy fighters or aim his guns correctly.

In the later war years Caproni built small numbers of a much larger triplane bomber, the Ca 40 series (called Ca 4 in service). These monsters had three Isotta-Fraschini, Fiat or Liberty engines, each of 270 to 350 hp, and carried up to 3197 lb of bombs in a large box on the bottom wing between the sixteen landing wheels. Some had the pilots seated in tandem, and there were two rear gunners in protected cockpits in the tail booms. But they were slow and vulnerable, and soon used only at night (when it was even colder and navigation was difficult).

Caproni therefore returned to the biplane arrangement in his final wartime bombers, the excellent Ca 44 to 47, or Ca 5. Slightly smaller but much more powerful than the original machines, these were powered by three 300–375 hp engines of the same types as the giant triplanes, giving a speed of up to about 90 mph with a bomb load of 1188 lb. Altogether 255 of this family were built in Italy and small numbers in France and the United States. The total of at least 740 large Caproni bombers built in Italy before the end of the First World War is impressive, and a small number of additional machines of many sub-types were also built as prototypes or trials aircraft. Construction was not entirely by Caproni, although during the war that industrial empire expanded enormously. Many of the bombers were built in the factories of Bastianelli, Breda, Miani-Silvestri and Savigliano. The French licence-constructors were REP (Esnault-Pelterie) and Bessaneau, while the American builders were Fisher Body (General Motors) and Standard. It was the largest bomber programme of the First World War.

In detail unlike any Italian Caproni, this example was one of two completed by Standard Aero Corporation of New Jersey in 1918

Accurate in every detail, this modern cutaway was drawn by John Batchelor from original Caproni engineering references. Interesting features of this Ca 46 include the triple Revelli guns manned by the mid-upper gunner, the chain-driven engine camshafts, the location of the engine water radiators and the closed-loop control wires to the tail (which traversed empty space between the central nacelle and the tail booms)

SPECIFICATIONS
Types Ca 30 to Ca 47 (military designations)
(data for 33)
Engines: three 150 hp Isotta-Fraschini V–4B six-cylinder water cooled
Dimensions: span 72 ft 10 in (22·2 m); length 35 ft 9 in (10·9 m); height 12 ft 2 in (3·7 m)
Weights: empty, 5512 (2500 kg); loaded 7302 lb (3315 kg).
Performance: maximum speed 94 mph (151 km/h); service ceiling 13450 ft (4100 m), range with bomb load 280 miles (450 km).

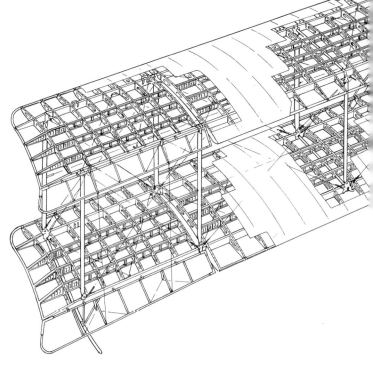

An excellent close-up of N–526, the Ca 42 triplane completed immediately ahead of that pictured on page 8. This was one of six in operational service with the RAF against the Austrians

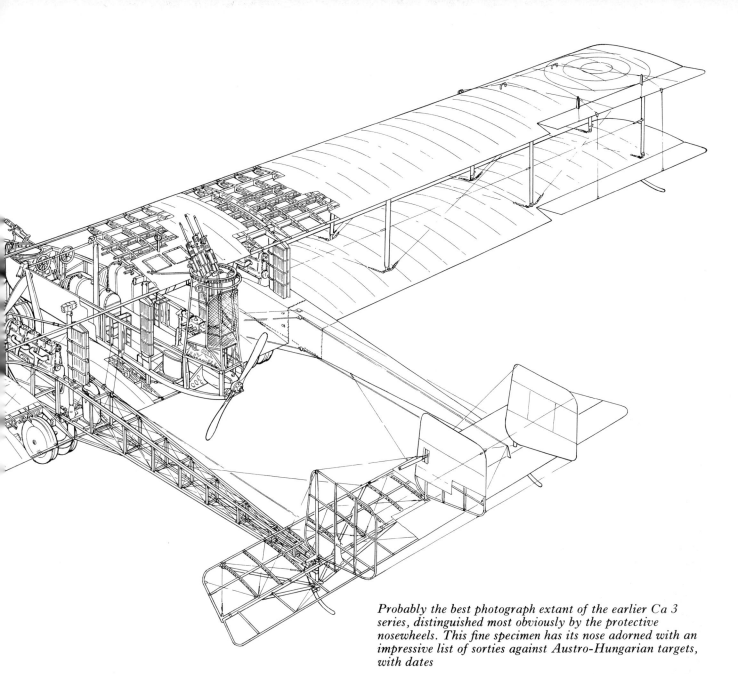

*Probably the best photograph extant of the earlier Ca 3
series, distinguished most obviously by the protective
nosewheels. This fine specimen has its nose adorned with an
impressive list of sorties against Austro-Hungarian targets,
with dates*

Handley Page O/400

For three decades *The Concise Oxford Dictionary* included the name (incorrectly hyphenated) 'Handley-Page' with the explanation 'type of large aeroplane'. It is doubtful that any other manufacturer has ever achieved such an entry, and it shows the way in which Sir Frederick Handley Page so dominated large aircraft prior to the Second World War that when one was seen overhead the uninitiated automatically ascribed it to him. But the credit for first listening to the young plane-maker's campaign on behalf of large aircraft belongs to the far-sighted Admiralty. In 1914, while the Army-led Royal Flying Corps disbelieved the whole notion of combat aircraft, the Admiralty Air Department, directed by Commodore (later Rear-Admiral) Murray Sueter, issued a specification for a patrol bomber able to carry six 112 lb bombs, with two engines and a speed of at least 72 mph. This was still short of the capability of the Capronis which then were already flying in Italy, but in the British environment it was revolutionary.

Frederick Handley Page responded with an impressive design powered by two 120 hp Beardmore engines, but when he took the drawings to the Admiralty in January 1915 Sueter knew he could set his sights much higher. The head of the Air Engine Section, Engineer-Commander W. Briggs, had towed a 1914 Mercedes Grand Prix racing car to Derby, left it with Rolls-Royce and instructed them to use its cylinder design as the basis for new aircraft engines. The famous car company could see at least 250 hp from a V–12 engine, and Sueter told 'HP' to go and scale up his bomber to fly on 500 hp. The plane-maker did not have a formal instruction what to do; merely the classic order by Sueter 'Go and build a bloody paralyser of an aeroplane'.

The result was the Handley Page O/100, forty of which were ordered in March 1915, the first taking the air on 18 December 1915. In every way it exceeded the Admiralty specification. With the 250 hp Rolls-Royce Eagle II engine it carried eight 250 lb or sixteen 112 lb bombs internally, had a crew of four (twice as many as requested) with up to five Lewis guns in the nose, dorsal and rear ventral positions, and a speed of almost 80 mph. Unlike other contemporary heavy bombers the entire bomb load was carried internally, the weapons being hung nose-up in bays fitted with doors on the underside. As each bomb was released, its cruciform tail pushed open the door of its cell, which then shut again under the influence of air load and a spring This considerably reduced drag on a long mission, making a significant difference to the range attainable. Fuel was housed in tanks in the rear of the engine nacelles, and the first prototype had 1200 lb of armour covering the nacelles and tanks and forward fuselage. Subsequent O/100 aircraft did not have armoured nacelles, although crew armour and bullet-proof glass was retained. To fit in the canvas Bessonneau hangar the wings could be folded back on each side, and four large landing wheels spread the weight of up to 14000 lb to permit safe operation from soft ground.

Although quaint to modern eyes, in fact the O/100 was a remarkably modern aircraft. Its appearance was in all essentials the same as that of most heavy bombers for the next 20 years. There were no nosewheels or skids to prevent damage in the event of nosing over, no skids under the wingtips and remarkably few excrescences of any sort. It was one of the first aircraft to establish the classic form for multi-engined machines, with a capacious fuselage in which the crew could walk about, tractor engines only and the whole load carried internally. In

Opposite, top: *Scale is lent this Handley Page (the first O/100 of the RNAS to land at Coudekirk on 4 March 1917) by a Nieuport and a Sopwith Triplane*

Centre, upper: *Take-off from Cricklewood of one of the impressive V/1500 longe-range giants of 1918*

Centre, lower: *Production O/400, with Eagle engines*

Bottom: *D9702 was an O/400 built by Clayton & Shuttleworth of Lincoln. Obviously, it went to the RNAS*

1 Twin 0·303-in (7,62-mm) Lewis guns
2 Rotatable Scarff ring
3 Gunner's cockpit (plywood construction)
4 Folding seat
5 Slat flooring
6 Entry hatch to gunner's cockpit
7 ASI pitot tube
8 Negative lens
9 Rudder pedals
10 Control wheel
11 Clear Pyralin windshield
12 Padded cockpit coaming
13 Pilot's seat
14 Observer's seat
15 Slat flooring
16 Light-bomb rack (manual)
17 Batteries
18 Trap-type forward entry door
19 Fabric lacing
20 Transparent panel
21 Plywood turtle-deck
22 Aluminium fairing
23 Steel propeller hub
24 Brass tip sheathing
25 Four-blade walnut propeller
26 Radiator filler cap
27 Radiator
28 360 hp Rolls-Royce Eagle VIII engine
29 Exhaust manifold
30 Nacelle bracing strut/control spar
31 Oil tank, 15 Imp gal (681 l) in each nacelle
32 Rigging lines
33 Streamlined steel struts
34 Double flying cable braces
35 Spruce/plywood inner strut
36 Double flying cable braces
37 Single landing cable brace
38 Single stagger cables
39 Spruce/plywood outer strut
40 Double flying braces
41 Outer aileron control horn
42 Cabane braces (four point)
43 Steel cabane
44 Inner aileron control horn
45 Solid end ribs
46 Wing dihedral break-line
47 Gravity-feed fuel tanks in leading edge, two of 12-Imp gal (54,5-l) capacity
48 Centre-section streamlined forward cabane strut
49 Centre-section streamlined aft cabane strut
50 Forward cylindrical fuel tank (held by web straps), capacity 130 Imp gal (591-l)
51 Filler cap
52 Cross member
53 Engine control pulley cluster
54 Centre-section main bomb-bay
55 Six volt wind-driven generator (port and starboard)
56 Perforated baffle plate
57 Air-driven fuel pumps
58 Aft fuel tank, capacity 130 Imp gal (591-l)
59 Solid rib at dihedral breakline
60 Upper gunner's seat
61 Transparent panels
62 Ammunition racks
63 Ventral gunner's hatch
64 Clear Pyralin panels
65 Gunner's slatted flooring
66 Plywood bulkheads
67 Single dorsal 0·303-in (7,62-mm) Lewis gun
68 Fabric lacing
69 Control cable pulleys
70 Fuselage frame
71 Multi-strand cable bracing
72 Elevator control cable
73 Interplane streamlined spruce strut
74 Starboard rudder
75 Fabric-covered upper tailplane
76 Elevator control horn
77 Fixed centre-section
78 Fabric-covered elevator
79 Port rudder spruce frame
80 Port lower elevator frame
81 Fabric-covered lower tailplane
82 Rudder hinge spar
83 Plywood tail covering
84 Rear navigation light
85 Interplane strut
86 Vertical stabilizer
87 Steel attachment point
88 Faired struts
89 Tailskid
90 Removable fabric panel
91 Lifting points (stations 10 and 12)
92 Port steel cabane
93 Rear upper mainplane spar
94 Forward upper mainplane spar
95 Plywood covering
96 Steel fitting
97 Solid drag strut
98 Wing structure
99 Port aileron structure
100 Port outer interplane struts (plywood-covered spruce)
101 Lower mainplane end rib
102 Wing structure
103 Leading-edge rib construction
104 Port inner interplane struts (plywood-covered spruce)
105 Hinge strut
106 Lower mainplane dihedral break-line
107 Steel tube engine nacelle support struts
108 Wing/fuselage attachment points
109 Wing root walkway
110 Fire extinguisher
111 Starboard undercarriage
112 Undercarriage forward strut
113 Port twin mainwheels
114 Faired rubber chord shock strut
115 Aft strut

This modern cutaway is believed to be the only one ever drawn of an O/400—and one could have done a better job with the machine available 60 years ago. With aircraft such as this, designers often had to learn as they went along. For example, at certain airspeeds the entire O/400 tail fluttered violently, oscillating in roll four times a second through an angle of 15°. The brilliant F. W. Lanchester worked out the cause. The upper and lower elevators on each side were joined by struts, but the left and right pairs were not linked except via the long cables which were joined at the cockpit. The answer was to add a metal tube to link the left and right elevators

Opposite: *This O/100 is one of the batch fitted with the powerful Sunbeam Cossack engine. The nacelles were longer than on the O/400 because the fuel tanks were behind the engines*

SPECIFICATIONS

Types H.P.11 0/100, H.P.12 0/400

Engines: (0/100) two 250 hp Rolls-Royce Eagle II vee-12 water-cooled (last six had 320 hp Sunbeam Cossack); (0/400) normally two 360 hp Rolls-Royce Eagle VIII, but alternatively two 350 hp Liberty 12–N, 260 hp Fiat A–12bis, 320 hp Sunbeam Cossack or 275 hp Sunbeam Maori.

Dimensions: span (0/100, 400) 100 ft (30·48 m); length (0/100, 400) 62 ft 10¼ in (19·16 m); height (0/100, 400) 22 ft (6·7 m).

Weights: empty (0/100) 8000 lb (3 629 kg); (0/400) 8502 lb (3857 kg); loaded (0/100) 14000 lb (6350 kg); (0/400) 13360 lb (6060 kg).

Performance: maximum speed (0/100) 76 mph (122 km/h); (0/400) 97 mph (156 km/h), service ceiling (0/100, 400) 8500 ft (2590 m); range with bomb load (0/100) 450 miles (724 km); (0/400) 650 miles (1046 km).

15

This O/400 was photographed whilst serving with 48 Sqn, RAF, probably in the occupation of Germany in the winter 1918–19

many respects it was remarkably similar to the great Handley Page airliners built for Imperial Airways in the early 1930s (although by that time biplanes of this character were obsolescent).

Handley Page Ltd had begun work at Barking, but to handle production of the great bomber a much larger establishment was built at Cricklewood, then on the northern outskirts of London. Here the forty bombers with the Eagle II were built in 1916, followed by a further six fitted with the most powerful engine then readily available, the 320 hp Sunbeam Cossack. Most of these 46 aircraft saw active service, initially with Royal Naval Air Service No 3 Wing on the Western Front from November 1916, two months after the first deliveries to a training squadron at Manston. Unfortunately, the third machine to fly to the Western Front became lost in unbroken cloud, let down near its destination, searched for an airfield and finally pulled off a good landing in a large field. The snag was, the field was 12 miles inside the German lines. The present was as welcome as Oberstleutnant Faber's arrival at RAF Pembrey in April 1942 in an Fw 190, or Lt Belenko's touchdown at Tokyo Hakodate in 1976 in a 'Foxbat'.

In the early months of 1917 the new Handley Pages flexed their muscles in offshore patrols, night bombing airfields in Germany and occupied territory, rail centres and U-boat bases,

and later anti-submarine sorties from Redcar to discourage the numerous U-boats off the Tyne and Tees. Two flew to Palestine—greatly impressing the Arabs—and undertook reconnaissance and bombing in support of the forces under General Allenby and T. E. Lawrence. Another operated from Mudros in the Aegean against Constantinople and many other targets, finally being lost through engine failure in September 1917 (the pilot, taken prisoner with the rest of the crew, was later to become Sir John Alcock after his pioneer Atlantic flight in 1919).

Extensive combat experience was rapidly fed back to the Admiralty and Handley Page. One of the major changes was a completely different fuel system. The tanks were moved from behind the engines into the fuselage, and a wind-driven pump on each side of the fuselage pumped fuel both direct to the carburettors and up to a pair of 14-gallon tanks in the leading edge of the upper wings to give gravity feed. The central fin was moved back, the dorsal gun position changed in shape, and the engines increased in power. The modified machine was designated O/400, and most were fitted with the outstanding Rolls-Royce Eagle VIII engine which allowed much higher speeds by raising maximum power to 360 hp. Some had the 275 hp Sunbeam Maori or 260 hp Fiat A–12bis, while examples made in the United States by Standard Aircraft had the

D8350 was the last of a batch of 50 O/400 bombers completed in 1918 by the British Caudron Co. Some of the Caudron-built aircraft had Sunbeam Maori or American

Liberty engines. The letter G on the tail indicates post-war use as a transport, the G (for Great Britain) subsequently becoming the national civil registration letter

350 hp Liberty 12–N fitted instead.

Production of the O/400 was on a large scale for so big a machine. By the Armistice at least 400 had been delivered by Handley Page, Birmingham Carriage, Metropolitan Waggon, Clayton & Shuttleworth, No 1 National Aircraft Factory and the Royal Aircraft Factory. Standard built 107 of the US Air Service order for 1500. It is ironic that the urgency behind the production programme was spurred by the German Gotha (widely, but erroneously, thought to be a copy of the British bomber).

In mid-1917 the Air Board was convinced that night bombing was inaccurate and that speed was better than a heavy load of bombs. On 23 July 1917 that august body decided to postpone all orders for heavy bombers, despite the success of the RNAS with the O/100. The outcry among people who had some knowledge of the subject was so great that an order for 100 of the new Handley Page was approved only a week later, and on 10 August a Royal Navy captain startled the Air Board by informing them that the RNAS Handley Pages had suffered fewer casualties than the day-bombing D.H.4s, and that in general night bombing by the O/100 had proved more accurate. On 2 September the Gothas began to bomb England, and so damaging were their attacks that the Air Board did not really need a letter sent by Sir Douglas Haig from the Western Front on 10 September,

asking that at least one-quarter of all future bomber squadrons should be night-equipped, to decide to order hundreds more of the hard-hitting O/400s.

In fact, while the O/100 switched to all-night work, the 98 mph O/400 often operated by day from its first appearance on the Western Front in April 1918 (the month in which RFC and RNAS units combined to form the RAF). From the summer of 1918 the O/400 was in action in impressive numbers, although never more than 40 were sent against one target. Some of the missions were truly daring, none more so than the attack on the great Badische Anilin chemical works at Mannheim on the night of 25 August. Two machines of RAF 215 Squadron came down to low level (one at 500 feet, the other at 200) to drop heavy bombs and spray the factory with machine-gun fire. Hundreds of workers watched spellbound as the great bombers droned apparently unscathed through a hail of anti-aircraft fire, brilliantly lit by searchlights whose beams were almost horizontal. A month later O/400s began to drop the monster 1650 lb bomb, the heaviest used in the First World War. When one fell on a target in Wiesbaden it caused so much damage the Germans thought a group of bombs had been dropped fastened together. The new Royal Air Force had in seven months convincingly demonstrated with the Handley Page the meaning of strategic bombing.

This painting shows a trio of Ca 3 bombers droning across the Austrian Alps on a long strategic mission. Having pioneered the use of bombers as early as 1911–12, Italy formed the Corpo Aereo Militare with no preconceived belief that aeroplanes had 'no role in warfare'. The Caproni bombers were a visible result

Tupolev TB-3

Certainly, the original design achievements of the Soviet Union in the years between the two world wars can be shown to exceed that of any country except the United States – and the same is probably true today. Even before 1930 a wealth of prototypes of extreme technical interest took off from the steppes and snows, while the Soviet economy and air fleets were underpinned by more pedestrian aircraft that were built in large numbers and gave faithful service. The

TB–3 was both an outstandingly advanced prototype and a valuable production machine, and it was by a wide margin the most capable bomber in the world in the long and important period from 1930 until the Second World War. The only aircraft that could rival it at the end of the 1930s was the Boeing B–17B, which entered service in mid-1939. The American bomber could fly slightly higher and much faster, but it carried much less than half the

Probably taken about 1933, this fine picture shows the first production version in operational service, flying an echelon formation parallel to a large river seen in the background. This was the first quantity-produced aircraft to have today's multi-engined monoplane configuration

bomb load. The very fact that it is reasonable to compare the TB–3 with the B–17 underlines the greatness of the TB–3's designers back in the 1920s.

Leader of the team was Andrei N. Tupolev. From the very beginning in 1922–23 he had inclined towards aircraft with cantilever monoplane wings and all-metal structures (although not yet with stressed-skin covering). The ruling material was Kolchug aluminium, named for the town where it was first produced just before the 1917 Revolution, which was in some respects superior to the German alloy duralumin. Tupolev spurred his engineers to solve a formidable number of problems in a short time, apparently without the guidance or collaboration of engineers from Junkers—which in 1922–24 had a team in the Soviet Union—which with several other German groups was dedicated to solving the same problems. The main gap in existing knowledge was calculating the stresses in a thick-section cantilever wing of light-alloy construction. The section of engineers and mathematicians that solved this problem was led by Vladimir M. Petlyakov, who managed the design of all Tupolev wings until the Second World War and not only gave his name to new versions of Tupolev aircraft (notably the TB–7 heavy bomber, which became the Pe–8) but also led the design of the Pe–2, the greatest light attack bomber of the Great Patriotic War.

Tupolev's first big cantilever monoplane was the ANT–4 of 1925, which had a span of 90 feet and served in numbers as the TB–1 bomber. One of its many claims to fame was the carriage of two of Tupolev's parasol-winged I–4 fighters on the wings in a bold experiment in fighter escort that went even further with the TB–3. The TB–1 was the first Soviet aircraft since the Sikorsky IM-class of the First World War to exceed the capability of foreign rivals. Comparison with, say, the Vimy or Martin MB–2 will show that a flight endurance of nine hours with a 2205 lb bomb load, or $2\frac{1}{2}$ hours with 6614 lb, was remarkable. The TB–1 provided a basis on which, from 1926, Tupolev planned a much larger bomber to meet a December 1925 requirement by the Ostechburo (Special Technical Bureau) for a strategic bomber with engines totalling 2000 hp. Tupolev followed exactly the same formula with the ANT–6 (TB–3) but used four engines. As in the earlier bomber, a corrugated Kolchug skin was used for virtually the entire airframe, but this does not mean—as Western periodicals claimed when they discovered the TB–3—that the whole aircraft was 'copied from Junkers designs'.

Mikhail Gromov, who had made the first

This 1939 picture shows paratroops, apparently signalled by the flag-waver in the bow, leaving a 1936-series TB–3

flights of many important Soviet aircraft, climbed aboard the first ANT–6 on 22 December 1930. The flight escaped disaster by a hair's breadth. It was a basic characteristic of the very wide and deep Tupolev wings that there was a substantial shift in centre of pressure as speed increased or decreased. On top of this, the prototype ANT–6 may have had its centre of gravity in the wrong position. Gromov opened the throttles of the four 600 hp engines—imported Curtiss Conquerors, the most powerful available—and found that, as speed built up, he had to use both hands on the control wheel to get the giant machine off the ground and climbing at a reasonable attitude (he was using all his strength and had to use both hands, but whether it was a pull or push is not recorded in available literature). In this situation, the throttles of the two starboard engines chose firmly to move towards the closed position. Gromov just managed to get the machine off the ground, with the aircraft banking to the right, and almost hit a hangar with the right wing. Gromov's shouts and the sudden realization of the situation by the co-pilot/engineer saved the day, the right-seat man having to keep his left hand on the right throttles until after the landing.

Apart from needing even higher control forces than the TB–1, the big new machine was very promising, and even in its first production form in 1932 it was the heaviest and most capable landplane in the world. At the May Day parade fly past in 1932 there were nine production TB–3 bombers; in the 1933 display there were fifty; in 1934 the number grew to 250 (there is no evidence to back up cynical suggestions that these were the same aircraft making repeated passes). By late 1937 the number built, in three major families and many minor variations, is estimated at at least 800. They were by far the most formidable strategic bombing force of the 1930s, and the world has only gradually learned

Top: *With the sudden switch to night bombing in 1940 the Luftwaffe hastily painted temporary black over most surfaces of the bombers involved. Later a thin but dense permanent black pigment was substituted, long-lasting and covering the centre-section and leading edges. This is an He 111P*
Above: *St.G.3 was the dominant Stukageschwader (dive-bomber wing) in the Mediterranean theatre, with three complete gruppen in action from mid-1941. A year later St.G.3 began to receive the better-looking Ju 87D–1/Trop, shown here*
Right: *Yellow gruppe and white staffel markings adorn this Ju 87B–2, probably of St.G.77, at rest on a Greek airfield in early 1941*

Top: *Two of the Type 1932 model. The usual colour was dark bluish-green*
Centre: *This Type 1932 has been re-engined with the AN-1 diesel, a little-known engine apparently of broad-arrow form with three banks of four cylinders*

Bottom: *The date which was stamped on this photograph, 1930, must be in error; it is probably several years later and shows a Type 1932, with external bomb racks, in the Arctic*

Above: *The ANT.42, flown in December 1936, led to the TB-7, later redesignated Pe-8, which succeeded the TB-3*

some of the TB-3's many accomplishments.

The Type 1932 was powered by four 730 hp M-17 engines (with friction locks on the throttles!), carried a normal bomb load of up to 4850 lb with an endurance of 13 hours, and had five gunners in the nose, left and right rear dorsal and two underwing positions, each with two DA machine guns. Each landing gear had tandem wire-spoked wheels on neat rocking frames, or alternatively large skis. Normal crew was nine, and there was space inside for 12 troops, who from 1934 onwards were often delivered in a neat stick by parachute. The TB-3 was the world's first paratroop transport, and the extremely impressive displays given in public spurred similar training in Germany (but not in Britain until German paratroops had proved the idea worked). Quite early in its career the TB-3 took part in long-range Arctic operations, usually in civil G-2 transport versions, flying missions no other aircraft in the world could hope to accomplish. They also carried light tanks slung under the fuselage, and on one memorable occasion no fewer than five parasite fighters on the wings and fuselage of one TB-3.

In 1933 the M-17 was replaced by the 830 hp M-34, and the following year the production bombers had the 970 hp M-34RN with reduction gear and supercharger. Propellers were still fixed-pitch, but the inboards often had four blades. The underwing guns were removed, and the wing skin (later also the tail) was made smooth with an overlay of fabric, which, with a new wing-root fairing, raised speed to about 180 mph. The rear fuselage was extended behind the tail to carry a rear gunner, and provision was made for internal and external racks for the remarkable bomb load of 12 800 lb for short ranges. The tailskid was replaced by a steerable wheel, and brakes fitted to the main wheels.

In the final (1936) series the corrugated skin was replaced by smooth metal, the tandem wheels were replaced by single larger wheels,

and the crew was reduced from ten to six, chiefly by using only three gunners, each with two of the new ShKAS machine guns firing 1800 rds/min. Large numbers of these powerful bombers were used in the border fighting against Japanese Manchuria in the Lake Hasan and River Khalkin-Gol areas in 1938–39 and against Finland in 1939–40. By June 1941 most had been relegated to transport and training duties, but some flew long-range bombing missions by night against Berlin until at least mid-1942. Beyond doubt, this was one of the greatest of strategic bombers. So were its crews, for 13 hours in an open cockpit with such heavy controls called for a Hero of the Soviet Union.

SPECIFICATIONS
ANT-6, TB-3 Types 1932, 1934 and 1936
Engines: four vee-12 liquid-cooled (1932) 730 hp M-17; (1934) 900 hp M-34R (derived from BMW VI); later 950–1280 hp M-34RN or RNF.
Dimensions: span 132 ft 10½ in (40.5 m); (1936) 137 ft 1½ in (41.8 m), length (early) 81 ft (24.69 m); (1934 onward) 82 ft 8¼ in (25.21 m); height, not available but about 18 ft.
Weights: empty, 22 000–26 450 lb (11 000–12 000 kg); maximum loaded (1932) 38 360 lb (17 500 kg); (1934) 41 021 lb (18 606 kg), (1936) 41 226 lb (18 700 kg), with overload of 54 020 lb (24 500 kg).
Performance: maximum speed (M-17, 1932) 134 mph (215 km/h); (M-34R, 1934) 144 mph (232 km/h); (M-34RN, 1936) 179 mph (288 km/h); initial climb, not available; service ceiling (1932) 12 467 ft (3800 m); (1934) 15 090 ft (4600 m); (1936) 25 365 ft (7750 m); range with bomb load (typical of all) 1550 miles (2500 km).

Below: *In 1941 combat missions were flown against Danube bridges by bomb-carrying I-16 fighters, which were conveyed near to their targets under Type 1936 TB-3 bombers*

Left: *This painting by Michael Turner depicts a summer scene over the Eastern Front. Lease-lend P–39 Airacobras (in fact, only later sub-types were supplied) are tearing into unescorted Ju 88s of KG 3, with red and yellow markings of II and III Gruppen, respectively*
Above: *Probably the finest painting of Stukas available, this action shot of three Ju 87B–2 dive-bombers over the Eastern Front captures the moment when the aircraft wing over in quick succession to begin their steep dive on to the target. Gruppe numbers are fictitious.*

Martin Bomber

Glenn L. Martin had been one of the select band of American pioneer constructor-pilots in the first decade of the twentieth century. After partnership with Wright he set up his own company in 1917 and soon became the undisputed king of US Air Service bombers. His first, the MB-1 flown in August 1918, was specifically designed to beat the Handley Page O/400, then being built by Standard at New Jersey. Just after the war the improved MB-2 appeared, and on 21 July 1921 General 'Billy' Mitchell went out with eight of them, each carrying two 1000 lb bombs, in a bid to sink the 'unsinkable' ex-German battleship *Ostfriesland*. It was the central act in a long and bitter political row with the US Navy which, three years later, was to lead to the intransigent Mitchell being court martialled, some said for believing in air power. What happened in 1921 was that, disobeying the Navy's rule that he use no bomb heavier than 660 lb, Mitchell and his men had let go seven of the bigger bombs when the great battleship rolled over and sank. The other nine bombs were dumped just offshore. It was the most memorable confrontation in history between those who believed in air power and those who did not. It also helped put Martin's name on the map.

Although there were many Martins in the ranks of the Army's bombers and the Navy's torpedo planes in the 1920s, the backbone of the heavy squadrons gradually became a make today almost forgotten: the Huff-Daland/Keystone. Then in November 1931 Boeing flew a radically new bomber with a cantilever monoplane wing, stressed-skin construction and semi-retractable landing gear. The new Boeing appeared in three models, which were evaluated by the Army Air Corps as the B-9. With a speed of 179-186 mph the new Boeings could outpace nearly all the Air Corps fighters, and still fly over 1000 miles with four 600 lb bombs. A large order would have been in the bag, but for one thing. Unasked, Martin had built the Martin Bomber, and it knocked everything else for six—including the new Boeing B-9. Almost always, when a good design team have been free to create a new aeroplane 'from a clean sheet of paper' it has outperformed rivals which had to meet detailed official specifications. It was certainly true in this case.

One of the clues to the Martin 123, to give it the maker's designation, was the new Wright R-1820 Cyclone engine, which began life at 600 hp and drove some of the first variable-pitch propellers to be released for regular use by Hamilton Standard. Smaller than the B-9, it reached 197 mph, faster than any Air Corps pursuit plane. It was delivered for Army trials on 20 March 1932 as the XB-907, and soon reached 207 mph after the fitting of 675 hp

This impressive line-up shows 'Hap' Arnold's Martins at Fairbanks in July 1934, during their great round trip to Alaska. The snag is that there are 11 bombers in the photograph, one more than were supposed to have taken part!

The prototype, then called XB–907A, with up-rated Cyclone engines in long-chord cowlings and the new front gun turret. Army colours were dark green fuselage and chrome-yellow wings and tail

F-series Cyclones and a then-novel glazed rotating turret for the front gunner. There were two further 0·30-in machine guns above and below at the rear, and a 2200 lb bomb load was housed in an internal bay that made the Martin appear pot-bellied. In overload condition a further 2000 lb could be hung on racks under the wings. The Army bought the aircraft as the XB–10, and on 17 January 1933 ordered 48 production B–10 bombers for the inventory. The new bomber got even greater newspaper coverage than Boeing's new 247 transport, and to make Martin's joy complete the Model 123 was awarded the 1933 Collier Trophy, which goes to 'the greatest achievement in aviation in America, the value of which has been proved

Top: *This Ju 88R–1 night fighter arrived out of the blue at RAF Dyce, now Aberdeen Airport, on the afternoon of Sunday, 9 May 1943. A defecting crew of II/NJG 3 brought this very welcome gift, which—complete with FuG 202 Lichtenstein BC radar—is today in pristine condition at RAF St Athan in South Wales*
Above: *The white theatre-band of the Eastern Front locates this yellow-gruppe Ju 88A (probably an A–5) with two external SC 500 (1102 lb) bombs*

Top: 1939–40 was a bitter winter, and keeping the Bomber Command stations in East Anglia operational was hard work. These Wellington ICs, beautifully portrayed by Michael Turner, went out on long and bitterly cold leaflet raids, as far as Czechoslovakia. Only when they began to drop bombs was it realised they could not find targets
Above: MF628 was a Mk X Wellington built at Squires Gate in the last year of the war. After 1948 it was rebuilt as a T.10, without a front turret; later it was changed from silver back to wartime colours for the RAF Museum

31

by actual use during the preceding year.'
Today the trophy seldom goes to bombers.

Production Martin B–10s, called Model 139 to denote their many small changes, reached the Air Corps from June 1934, and by the following year were operating with Bombardment Groups in the United States, Panama and Hawaii. In July 1935 the future Chief of the Air Corps, Colonel 'Hap' Arnold, led ten of the new bombers on an 18000-mile round trip from Washington DC to Alaska and back. In the primitive environment, with small grass fields, no navaids and no radio contact for much of the journey, it reflects well on the speedy Martin that the only untoward event was that one was ditched in Cooks Bay, Anchorage, and sank in 40 feet of water—to be promptly raised, dried out and flown on with the others!

In 1935–36 Martin delivered a further 103 B–10Bs with 775 hp Cyclones and 213 mph

SPECIFICATIONS

Model 123, 139 and 166, B–10, –12 and –14
Engines: (YB–10) two 775 hp Wright R–1820–25 Cyclone nine-cylinder radials, (YB–12) two 665 hp Pratt & Whitney R–1690–11 Hornet nine-cylinder radials; (XB–14) two 850 hp P & W R–1830–9 Twin Wasp 14-cylinder two-row radials; (most export 139) 750 hp Cyclone SGR–1820–F3S; (export 166) usually 850 hp Cyclone R–1820–G2, but some 900 hp Twin Wasp R–1830–SC3–G.
Dimensions: span 70 ft 6 in (21·48 m); length 44 ft 8¾ in (13·63 m); (XB–10) 45 ft; (B–12A) 45 ft 3 in; (export 166) 44 ft 2 in; height 11 ft (3·35 m); (XB–10) 10 ft 4 in; (B–10B) 15 ft 5 in; (export 166) 11 ft 7 in.
Weights: empty (typical B–10, 139) 8870–9000 lb; (166) 10900 lb (4944 kg); maximum loaded (XB–10) 12560 lb; (B–10B) 14600 lb (6622 kg); (B–12A) 14200 lb; (139) 14192 lb; (166) 15624 lb (Cyclone) or 16100 lb (Twin Wasp).
Performance: maximum speed (all B–10, 139, B–12) 207–213 mph (340 km/h); (166) 255 mph (W) or 268 mph (P & W); initial climb (all) 1290–1455 ft (about 410 m)/min; service ceiling (all) 24200–25200 ft (about 7500 m); range with bomb load (typical) 700 miles (1125 km); maximum range with extra fuel (early models) 1240 miles, (166) 2080 miles.

Top: *This USAAC squadron has the Hornet-powered B–12A, which also had increased fuel capacity*
Above: *A rare picture showing the pilot's cockpit in a US Army Martin B–10. Five prominent notices relate to the novel retractable landing gear, worked by the manual/electric change lever on the right console or (laboriously) by the crank-handle ahead of it*
Right: *The Martin Model 146 was an advanced B–10 version with Cyclone engines driving three-blade Hamilton propellers and with a much-enlarged flight deck. The roof was faired back into the rear cockpit, as in the Model 166 bought by the Netherlands East Indies. The nose badge is that of the Glenn L. Martin Company*

Top: *One of the small batch of YB–12 bombers converted as coast-defence seaplanes and used in this role by the USAAC in 1936–40*

Above: *B–10B bombers putting down 100 lb and 300 lb bombs from 14000 ft at the Army War College, Washington*

speed. By this time many of the original batch had various Cyclone, Hornet or Twin Wasp engines, and a few had become seaplanes used in the offshore 'coast defence' role for which the B–17 was at that time being designed. By 1936 the popular and tractable Martin had become obsolescent, the Boeing B–17 and Douglas B–18 demonstrating the rapidity of bomber progress. The Air Corps accordingly allowed Martin to fulfil some of the avalanche of export orders that had been arriving at the Baltimore plant ever since the first flight in 1932. Despite the lateness of the hour, Martin picked up a useful 189 overseas sales. The largest order was 117 for the Dutch East Indies, beginning with 39

Model 139W and going on to a modified model, the Martin 166, with a single long 'greenhouse' covering both the front and rear cockpits. All other export sales were of the 166 type, customers including Argentina (25), Turkey (20) and China (9). Although they weighed as much as 16100 lb loaded, almost 30 per cent more than the original 123, use of 850 hp Cyclones or 900 hp Twin Wasps with constant-speed propellers pushed speed up to 260 mph—well up to typical bomber speeds of the Second World War. Many of the East Indies bombers were in action against Japanese invasion fleets in the dark days of early 1942, while the Chinese aircraft never knew any peace.

34

Dornier Do17 and Do217

In the decade 1925–35 air-minded schoolboys, and possibly even British and French intelligence experts, knew that the foreign subsidiaries set up by German aircraft companies in order to evade the terms of the 1919 Versailles Treaty (which prohibited German military aircraft) were building military aircraft. Indeed, one was openly building heavy bombers, although according to Dornier Metallbauten at the Swiss town of Alternrhein they were really civilian 'freight transports'. In 1933 the still-under-wraps Luftwaffe set up a Behelfsbomberge-schwader (auxiliary bomber group), but it was publicly called the Verkehrsinspektion der DLH, the traffic inspectorate of the national airline. Observers would also have noticed the willingness of the State Railway to run a large number of heavy Do 11C cargo aircraft on long missions by day and night without actually carrying any significant amount of cargo.

When the Luftwaffe was unmasked on 1 March 1935 the Do 11C, one of the worst bombers ever conceived, was fast being replaced by the Do 23. This was fractionally better, but still not quite the world-shattering instrument Hitler wanted. Dornier never thought it would be. It was hard at work creating the Luftwaffe's new heavy bomber, the Do 19, not furtively in Switzerland but openly in Germany. The far-sighted Generalleutnant Walther Wever, first Chief of Air Staff, repeatedly stressed the importance of strategic heavy bombers, able to reach northern Scotland or the Urals. The Do 19, dubbed the 'Ural-bomber', flew on 28 October 1936. It was an impressive four-engined machine, intended to sprout power-operated turrets armed with 20 mm cannon.

Two years earlier, in the autumn of 1934, Dornier had also flown a much smaller but faster aircraft, the Do 17 high-speed mailplane for Lufthansa's European trunk routes. Powered by two 660 hp BMW VI liquid-cooled engines, it was so slender it was called 'The Flying Pencil'. Six passengers could, with considerable difficulty, climb inside and sit down in two cramped cabins, one just behind the flight deck and the other behind the shoulder-high wing. It had all the performance Lufthansa wanted,

Potentially a great bomber, the Do 217 was less suitable when converted into the Do 217J night fighter, despite the FuG 202 Lichtenstein BC radar. Landing speed was high, while in-flight manoeuvrability and maximum speed were judged inadequate

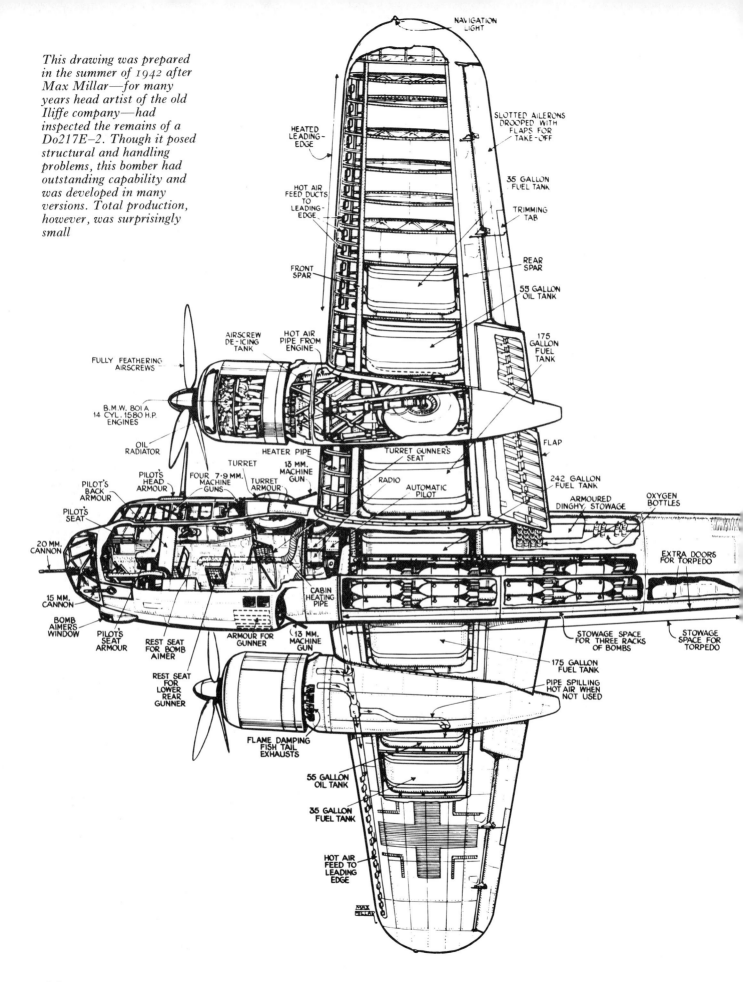

This drawing was prepared in the summer of 1942 after Max Millar—for many years head artist of the old Iliffe company—had inspected the remains of a Do217E-2. Though it posed structural and handling problems, this bomber had outstanding capability and was developed in many versions. Total production, however, was surprisingly small

NAVIGATION LIGHT

SLOTTED AILERONS DROOPED WITH FLAPS FOR TAKE-OFF

HEATED LEADING-EDGE

HOT AIR FEED DUCTS TO LEADING-EDGE

35 GALLON FUEL TANK

TRIMMING TAB

REAR SPAR

FRONT SPAR

55 GALLON OIL TANK

175 GALLON FUEL TANK

AIRSCREW DE-ICING TANK

HOT AIR PIPE FROM ENGINE

FULLY FEATHERING AIRSCREWS

FLAP

B.M.W. 801A 14 CYL. 1580 H.P. ENGINES

242 GALLON FUEL TANK

OIL RADIATOR

HEATER PIPE

TURRET GUNNER'S SEAT

ARMOURED DINGHY STOWAGE

OXYGEN BOTTLES

TURRET

13 MM. MACHINE GUN

RADIO

AUTOMATIC PILOT

PILOT'S HEAD ARMOUR

FOUR 7.9 MM. MACHINE GUNS

PILOT'S BACK ARMOUR

TURRET ARMOUR

PILOT'S SEAT

EXTRA DOORS FOR TORPEDO

20 MM. CANNON

15 MM. CANNON

CABIN HEATING PIPE

BOMB AIMERS WINDOW

PILOT'S SEAT ARMOUR

REST SEAT FOR BOMB AIMER

ARMOUR FOR GUNNER

13 MM. MACHINE GUN

STOWAGE SPACE FOR THREE RACKS OF BOMBS

STOWAGE SPACE FOR TORPEDO

REST SEAT FOR LOWER REAR GUNNER

175 GALLON FUEL TANK

PIPE SPILLING HOT AIR WHEN NOT USED

FLAME DAMPING FISH TAIL EXHAUSTS

55 GALLON OIL TANK

35 GALLON FUEL TANK

HOT AIR FEED TO LEADING EDGE

MAX MILLAR

SPECIFICATIONS

Types Do 17E, F, K and P
Engines: two 750 hp BMW VI 7·3 12-cylinder vee liquid-cooled; 17P, two 1000 hp BMW 132N nine-cylinder radials.
Dimensions: span 59 ft 0½ in (18 m); length (17E,F) 53 ft 3¾ in (16·25 m); (17P) 52 ft 9¾ in (16·1 m); height (17E, F) 14 ft 2 in (4·3 m); (17P) 14 ft 11 in (4·57 m).
Weights: empty (17E,F) 9921 lb (4500 kg); (17P) 10140 lb (4600 kg); loaded (17E) 15520 lb (7050 kg); (17F) 15430 lb (7000 kg); (17P) 16887 lb (7660 kg).
Performance: maximum speed (17E, F) 220 mph (355 km/h); (17P) 249 mph (400 km/h); service ceiling (17E) 16,730 ft (5100 m); (17F) 19685 ft (6000 m), (17P) 20340 ft (6 200 m); typical range (17E) 620 miles (1000 km); (17F) 994 miles (1600 km); (17P) 745 miles (1200 km).

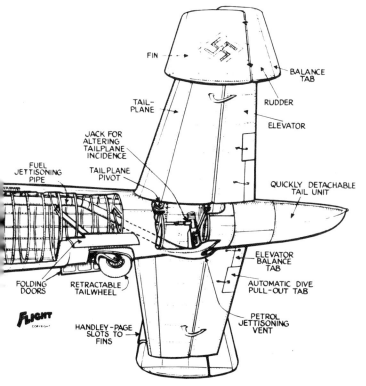

FIN

BALANCE TAB

TAIL-PLANE

RUDDER

ELEVATOR

JACK FOR ALTERING TAILPLANE INCIDENCE

FUEL JETTISONING PIPE

TAILPLANE PIVOT

QUICKLY DETACHABLE TAIL UNIT

ELEVATOR BALANCE TAB

FOLDING DOORS

RETRACTABLE TAILWHEEL

AUTOMATIC DIVE PULL-OUT TAB

PETROL JETTISONING VENT

HANDLEY-PAGE SLOTS TO FINS

FLIGHT

Types Do 217E–2, K–2, M–1, J–2/N–2, P–1
Engines: (E–2, J–2) two 1580 hp BMW 801A or 801M 18-cylinder two-row radials, (K–2) two 1700 hp BMW 801D; (M–1, N–2) two 1750 hp Daimler-Benz DB 603A 12-cylinder inverted-vee liquid-cooled; (P–1) two 1860 hp DB 603B super-charged by DB 605T in the fuselage.
Dimensions: span 62 ft 4 in (19 m); (K–2) 81 ft 4½ in (24·8 m); (P–1) 80 ft 4 in (24·4 m); length 56 ft 9¼ in (17·3 m); (E–2 with early dive brakes) 60 ft 10½ in (18·5 m); (K–2 and M–1) 55 ft 9 in (17 m); (J and N) 58 ft 9 in (17·9 m); (P) 58 ft 11 in (17·95 m); height 16 ft 5 in (5 m) (all versions same within 2 in).
Weights: empty (E–2) 19522 lb (8850 kg); (M–1) 19985 (9000 kg); (K–2, J and N) all about 21000 lb (9450 kg); (P) about 23000 lb (10350 kg); loaded (E–2) 33070 lb (15000 kg); (K–2 M–1) 36817 lb (16570 kg); (J and N) 30203 lb (13590 kg); (P) 35200 lb (15840 kg).
Performance: maximum speed (E–2) 320 mph (515 km/h); (K–2) 333 mph (533 km/h); (M–1) 348 mph (557 km/h); (J and N) about 311 mph (498 km/h); (P) 488 mph (781 km/h); service ceiling (E–2) 24610 ft (7500 m); (K–2) 29530 ft (9000 m); (M–1) 24140 ft (7358 m); (J and N) 27560 ft (8400 m); (P) 53000 ft (16154 m); range with full bomb load, about 1300 miles (2100 km) for all versions.

but the passenger accomodation was simply unacceptable, so in 1935 the three prototype Do 17s were returned to Dornier's factory at Löwenthal and pushed into a hangar. What nobody then expected was that the great Ural-bomber would be scrapped, while the unsuccessful mailplane would be the precursor of a long family of bombers that would bring terror from the sky over all Europe and rain down not only bombs but torpedoes, cannon shells and the world's first guided missiles in aerial warfare.

There was nothing much wrong with the Do 19, but Wever was killed on 3 June 1936, and his successor, Albert Kesselring, decided after deep study that money would be better spent on faster short-ranged tactical bombers to work with the Wehrmacht in its Blitzkrieg campaigns across Europe. And the Do 17 came

These Do 217E-2 (possibly E-4) bombers have the yellow band of the Eastern Front theatre round the fuselage and wings. The engines carry the 'staffel colour', yellow or white

into the picture when Lufthansa's chief test pilot, Robert Untucht, who was also the airline's Reichsluftfahrtministerium liaison officer, went to Löwenthal on a casual visit. He got one of the slim Dorniers out and flew it. He was impressed, and made a suggestion so obvious that it is strange it had not occurred to anyone at Dornier: why not a Do 17 bomber? So the V4 (fourth prototype) appeared in August 1935 as a high-speed bomber, with twin fins to increase directional stability and thus improve bombing accuracy. It was still a long way from being an operational type, but its potential was considerable.

There followed a succession of development aircraft with different engines. Curiously, none had anything like the speed of the Bristol 142, predecessor of the Blenheim, despite having a slimmer fuselage and often considerably greater horsepower. The fastest of the Do 17 prototypes could not exceed 264 mph, though it had 1 000 hp DB 600 engines which were new, semi-secret and in very short supply. It was this machine,

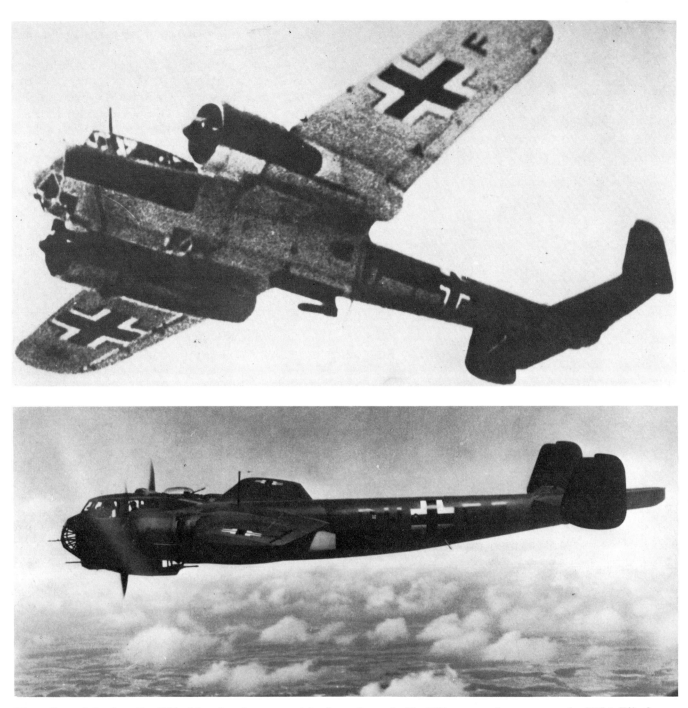

Top: *One of the first Do 17Z–2 bombers lets go a stick of 110 lb bombs. The Fafnir 323P engine, more powerful than earlier models, allowed 20 of these bombs to be carried*

An early Do 217 on test. It appears to be RH+EJ, the 12th Do 217E–0 but modified to E–2 standard with the troublesome dive-brake behind the tail

the V8 prototype, that startled the aviation world at the 1937 International Military Aircraft Competition at Zurich. The first Do 17 to be publicly displayed, it easily outperformed all non-German fighters at the competition, and unlike the speedy Bristol prototype had a wing mounted high enough for the slim body to contain a useful internal bomb bay beneath the spars. (Prof-Dr Claudius Dornier always maintained that the shoulder-high wing had been chosen for minimum drag, and not with any thought of eventual use of the Do 17 as a bomber).

By the time the DB 600-powered prototype performed at Zurich, lower-powered production Dorniers were already in service with the Luftwaffe and in action with the German Legion Kondor in the Spanish civil war. The first service versions were the Do 17E–1 bomber and F–1 reconnaissance aircraft, both with short rounded noses and 750 hp BMW VI engines giving a speed of about 220 mph. Although becoming unimpressive in 1937, this speed was nevertheless high enough in actual warfare in Spanish skies for the Republican fighters never to catch the new Dorniers, which could dive at 400 mph. In thus seeming to confirm previous conclusions reached by the Oberkommando der Luftwaffe it led to a gigantic air force being built up with KG (Kampfgeschwader, i.e. bomber wings) equipped with twin-engined tactical machines in which speed was thought to compensate for inadequate defensive armament. The early Do 17s had just two machine guns, one above at the rear and the other below, aimed by hand over a restricted arc. Another basic feature was that the crew of three were crowded together in a confined space. Although this helped communication, in that the crew could touch each other and shout without using the intercom, and was also believed to maintain morale in adverse circumstances when a solitary man might panic, it was so restrictive and inefficient that Dornier, along with other manufacturers, soon produced new versions of bombers with enlarged crew compartments.

Although several hundred of the original extra-slim Do 17 were built, including the 17M with 900 hp Bramo Fafnir radial engines, the 17P with 865 hp BMW 132N radials and the 17K exported to Yugoslavia with 986 hp French GR14N radials, most were of the later Do 17Z family with an enlarged cabin providing accommodation for four. By far the most important Dornier in the first year of the Second World War was the Do 17Z-2, with 1000 hp Fafnir radials. Capable of 255 mph, and carrying a bomb load doubled to 2205 lb internally, and with six defensive machine guns, it was a vast improvement on the original 'Flying Pencil'. It was reliable, popular, completely devoid of any flight restrictions and highly manoeuvrable. Yet in the Battle of Britain it was hacked down with ease by the Hurricanes and Spitfires. In August 1940 most aircraft still had only four guns, two at the front and single guns above and below at the rear. By the end of the month two more were in the radio operator's side windows, and many aircraft had two further guns to make a total of eight. The same thing was done with the He 111 and Ju 88, yet hasty botches are seldom effective. By late 1941 virtually all the Dornier 17 bombers were on the Eastern front, and those assigned to combat duties were increasingly being passed to the Croat units.

Small numbers were used of the Do 17Z-6 Kauz (Screech-Owl) and Z-10 Kauz II night fighters, with heavy cannon armament in a 'solid' nose. The Do 215, a bomber and reconnaissance machine with 1100 hp DB 601 liquid-cooled engines, was used in small numbers by the Luftwaffe and Hungary. The first radar-fighter kills of the Luftwaffe were gained by Ludwig Becker in a Do 215B-5 with early Lichtenstein BC radar in 1941.

In August 1938 Dornier flew the first of a much larger bomber, the Do 217. Representing a vast increase in potential, this nevertheless suffered from poor handling and lack of sufficiently powerful engines, but at the end of 1940 the first Do 217E bombers were coming off the production line. Powered by two of the new 1580 hp BMW 801 radial engines (then also selected for the new Fw 190 fighter), the 217E-1 entered service with a speed of 320 mph, internal bomb load of 4410 lb and armament of one or two forward-firing cannon and up to eight machine guns. Although far more useful than the smaller bombers, the 217 still had an ill-conceived defensive armament (in early versions the radio operator had to manage five manually aimed guns). During 1941 defensive armament improved with an electric dorsal turret with the excellent 13 mm MG 131, a similar gun in the lower rear position, and various paired groups of the small, fast-firing MG 81. The 14 ft 10 in bomb bay was given a 5 ft 8 in extension for an internal torpedo, and soon loads up to 6615 lb were being carried. Sub-types and field modifications gradually resulted in a profuse array of Do 217E variants, most of which proved highly effective on the Eastern front from June 1941.

A few were deployed against Britain and the Mediterranean. In addition to the 'solid nose' 217J night fighter, various late E-models were used by KG 2 (the only 217 bomber geschwader to remain in the West) against Britain, losing 65 of its original 88 crews in the period May to September 1942. But at Graz various gruppen of KG 100 re-equipped with the 217E-5, which could carry two Henschel 293 radio-controlled rocket stand-off missiles, and the 217K-2 which could carry the FX 1400 radio-controlled glide bomb. The K-2 also had a new bulbous crew compartment and wing span increased from 62 ft 4 in to 81 ft 4½ in. The Hs 293 went into action with II/KG 100 from Cognac on 25 August 1943, and two days later one of the 2304 lb missiles sank the corvette HMS *Egret*. In the Mediterranean Major Bernhard Jope's III/KG 100 used the 3454 lb FX to smashing effect when, on 9 September 1943, the Italian fleet sailed from La Spezia to join the Allies. Six Do 217K-2s took off from Marseilles and hit both the capital ships, *Roma* taking 1255 men to the bottom and *Italia* just managing to limp to Malta in a crippled state. Later Jope himself put a missle into HMS *Warspite* and his team hit many other Allied ships at Salerno.

The last Do 217 versions to be built were the M, P and R. The M-series were similar to the

K, with short or long wings, but powered by the 1850 hp DB 603A liquid-cooled engine as an insurance against shortage of the radial. On the night of 23 February 1944 a II/KG 2 crew bailed out of an M hit by AA fire over north Middlesex, although the damage was minor; the empty bomber glided on and made a beautiful belly landing near Cambridge, and within a few weeks was flying in RAF markings. A few Ms were converted into 217N night fighters. The P was a high-altitude reconnaissance-bomber with a pressure cabin and complex HZ-Anlage propulsion system comprising two DB 603Bs supercharged by a DB 605T in the rear fuselage. Although the 217P looked lumpy and had enormous intercooler radiators under the inner wing and a DB 605 radiator under the fuselage, the fact that each DB 603B could deliver 1440 hp at 45000 feet resulted in remarkable performance, with a speed of 363 mph at this height and a ceiling of well over 50000 feet. With the re-designed Do 317, Dornier had hoped to go even further, with greatly increased weights and 2560 hp DB 610 double engines. After troublesome development it was decided the new 317 was not much of an advance over the 217P, and five of the six prototypes were stripped of their pressurization and used as '217R' missile carriers armed with the Hs 293. Meanwhile the three 217P prototypes were exhaustively tested, but by mid-1944 all the Luftwaffe needed was fighters.

Altogether Dornier built the surprisingly modest total of 1905 Do 217s (not 1730 as often reported), of which 1541 were bombers and missile carriers. Largely electric internally, they were the company's only design to play a major role in the Second World War.

Left, above: *One of the first Do 217E–0 or E–1 bombers seen during pre-delivery testing at the maker's airfield near Friedrichshafen in 1940*
Left, below: *The long-span Do 217K–2, which also had the new crew compartment of the K–1 and M, was the first aircraft to use guided missiles in war*
Below: *The Do 217M combined the new nose with the original wing and DB 603 engines, reaching 348 mph*

Heinkel He 111

No aircraft more completely mirrored the fortunes of Hitler's Luftwaffe than the Heinkel 111. Conceived in enthusiasm in 1934 as both a high-speed airliner for Lufthansa and a formidable bomber for the still-clandestine Luftwaffe, it went into production in 1936 and by early 1937 was proving the best bomber in the Spanish civil war, with the heaviest bomb load, excellent manoeuvrability and speed high enough for fighter escort not to be needed. Lindbergh said it could conquer all Europe. Until the Battle of Britain it spearheaded the Blitzkrieg, and in 1941 continued through the Balkans and Crete to North Africa and on the Eastern Front deep into the Soviet Union. Far outnumbering all other Luftwaffe bombers except the Ju 88, it soldiered on through 1942, 1943 and even 1944, into a more hostile sky where, instead of outrunning the opposition, it had become the easiest of meat. Yet the abject failure of all the replacement programmes kept the old-stager in production right to the bitter end in 1945, years after it should have been accorded a complete retirement from front-line service. The vast Heinkel organization did what it could to keep the old bomber—called Die Späten (the Spade) by the Luftwaffe—as competitive as possible, but the task was hopeless. Skill and courage by

aircrew could not rectify the situation.

Like the single-engined He 70 of 1932 the He 111 was designed by the gifted Günter twins, Walter (a brilliant mathematician) and Siegfried (whose flair for beautiful curving shapes was to become a hallmark of Heinkel designs). The 111a prototype could have flown in 1933, but in fact the joint civil/military specification did not emerge until early 1934 and so Gerhard Nitschke could not fly the new machine until 24 February 1935. Powered by 660 hp BMW VI water-cooled vee-12 engines, the 111a reached 217 mph despite weighing up to 16755 lb, and—unlike the equally beautifully streamlined He 70—showed almost perfect handling qualities. This first machine was an empty shell but constructed as a bomber with a glazed nose and open dorsal gun position. The wing, of almost pure elliptical form, was mounted low on the fuselage. It was planned to carry the bomb load of 2200 lb in vertical cells, four along each side of the fuselage between the wing spars, with a narrow gangway between. Upon release, each bomb simply pushed open the sprung flap beneath it. Lower rear armament was to be provided by a retractable dustbin housing a gunner with a manually aimed MG 15.

Only 16 days later the second machine was

rolled out as a Lufthansa transport, named *Rostock*, and although this operated on the South Atlantic route as far as Bathurst it was later passed to the Kommando Rowehl for clandestine photo-reconnaissance in the guise of airline route-proving (it crashed whilst thus engaged, but kept its secret). The civil He 111C-series were in full service by 1936, and operated many of the most important routes up to the Second World War, later augmented by two L-series with much more powerful BMW radial engines. But the military He 111A was rejected outright because with the old BMW VI engine the performance was poor, despite the fitting of variable-pitch propellers. By this time the nose had been lengthened, the wing twice revised in shape and reduced in span, and full armament fitted. Salvation lay in the 1000hp DB 600 inverted-vee engine, first flown in the V5 prototype in early 1936. With this engine all the crisp handling and good performance returned, and the resulting production bomber, the He 111B-series, was thought by the Luftwaffe to be the best tactical bomber in the world. Despite

weighing 20536lb and having engines derated to 880 hp, the first B-1 could reach over 220 mph and the B-2 with fully supercharged engines of 950 hp attained 230 mph. In this form the new Heinkel began to equip I/KG 154 at Hanover-Langenhagen in November 1936, and after many gruppen had been equipped it went to Spain with the Legion Kondor. As long as it kept its dustbin retracted it proved almost impossible to intercept, and with a bomb load for short ranges increased to 3307lb the slim Heinkel proved extremely effective and popular.

With the D-series of 1937, the first model planned for mass-production in the gigantic 'showpiece' factory built at Oranienburg, speed jumped to 255 mph, largely because engine installation was cleaned up. But shortage of engines, caused by Daimler-Benz being swamped with orders for engines for Bf 109 fighters (which enjoyed priority), led to the E-series bomber of 1938, one of the most important pre-war bombers of the Luftwaffe. Simple substitution of the 1000hp Junkers Jumo 211A–1 allowed bomb load to be increased to 4410lb, made up of eight

Below: *One of the first three He IIIZ tugs, using fuselages of the H–6 (above) with a new centre section and a fifth engine. In the winter of 1942–43, the Z and the Me 321 failed to make a contribution to supplying the beleaguered 6th Army at Stalingrad*

43

551 lb bombs hung by their noses, the gross weight reaching 23370 lb. But the vast expanse of wing and excellent engines kept the E-series in the forefront of contemporary performance, and in Spain it not only enhanced the Heinkel's great reputation but stayed in service with the Spanish Air Force until at least 1957.

In 1937 the Luftwaffe began to receive the He 111F, with a wing which, although having the same primary box, had different secondary leading and trailing structures giving straight edges that were easier and cheaper to make. Area and efficiency were hardly affected, but the straight-tapered wing had been flying for months on nine civil G-series (basically similar to the C) before the RLM accepted the new shape for the bomber, thus leading to the F and the DB-powered J. But neither was in production long, because in January 1938 Heinkel had flown the V8, a rebuilt B–2 bomber, with an entirely different nose which changed the appearance as dramatically as the straight wing. Almost perfectly streamlined, it was completely glazed and terminated in a gun cupola on the front, offset to the right to give the pilot an unobstructed view ahead. The only drawback to this then-revolutionary front end was that the pilot had to look through Plexiglas panels that sloped acutely at a distance of

Below: *This apparently genuine photograph of an early He 111H over Warsaw in September 1939 shows the way the eight 551 lb bombs tumbled tail-first from their vertical cells. After dropping through the spring-loaded doors they fell end-over-end and oscillated for several seconds, which Allied critics said impaired accuracy. It is doubtful if actual results were affected at all, but in a war one siezes on any seemingly faulty aspect of enemy equipment*

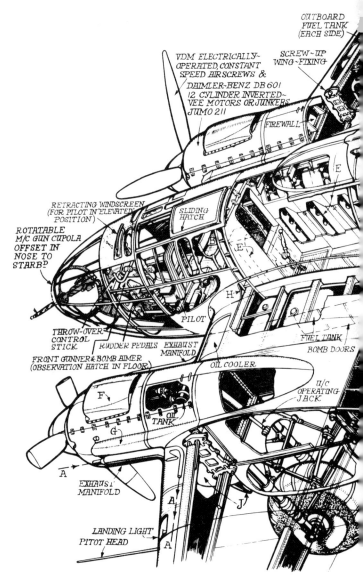

This cutaway was drawn by J. H. Clark in 1940, and shows a Jumo-powered He 111H (despite the uncertainty of the engine-type). The 'control' exercised over the tail gun was merely a trigger. The drawing was, of course, prepared from study of crashed specimens

44

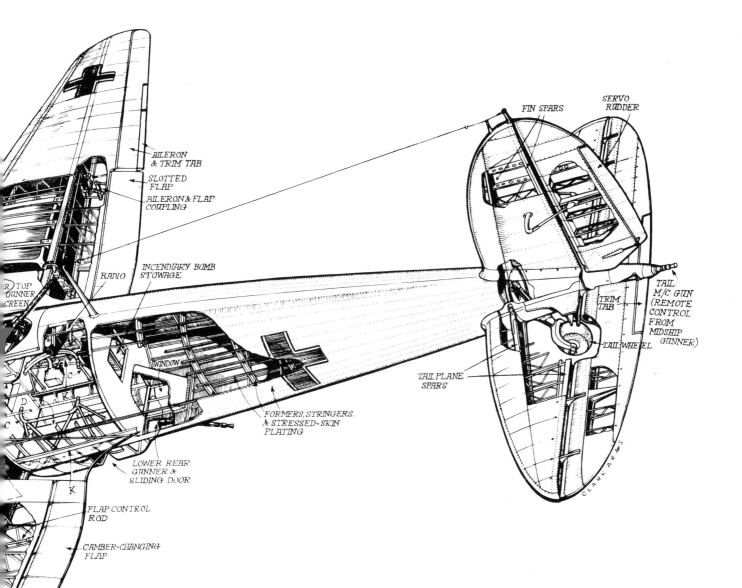

FIN SPARS

SERVO RUDDER

AILERON & TRIM TAB

SLOTTED FLAP

AILERON & FLAP COUPLING

TOP GUNNER SCREEN

RADIO

INCENDIARY BOMB STOWAGE

WINDOW

FORMERS, STRINGERS, & STRESSED-SKIN PLATING

LOWER REAR GUNNER & SLIDING DOOR

FLAP CONTROL ROD

CAMBER-CHANGING FLAP

TAIL PLANE SPARS

TAIL M/C GUN (REMOTE CONTROL FROM MIDSHIP GUNNER)

TRIM TAB

TAIL WHEEL

CLARK ARMS

HOUSING OR (S)

THE AEROPLANE Copyright

SPECIFICATIONS

He 111 B series, E series, H series and P series
Engines: (He 111H–3) two 1 200 hp Junkers Jumo 211D–2 12-cylinder inverted-vee liquid-cooled: (He 111P–2) two 1 100 hp Daimler-Benz DB 601A–1 12-cylinder inverted-vee liquid-cooled.
Dimensions: span 74 ft 1¾ in (22·6 m); length 53 ft 9½ in (16·4 m); height 13 ft 1½ in (4 m).
Weights: empty (H–3) 17 000 lb (7 720 kg); (P–2) 17 640 lb (8 000 kg); maximum loaded (H–3) 30 865 lb (14 000 kg); (P–2) 29 762 lb (13 500 kg).
Performance: maximum speed (H–3) 258 mph (415 km/h); (P–2) 242 mph (390 km/h) at 16 400 ft (5 000 m) (at maximum weight, neither version could exceed 205 mph (330 km/h); climb to 14 765 ft (4 500 m) 30–35 min at normal gross weight, 50 min at maximum; service ceiling (both) around 25 590 ft (7 800 m) at normal gross weight, under 16 400 ft (5 000 m) at maximum; range with maximum bomb load (both) about 745 miles (1 200 km).

Top: *Inspection of KG 27 'Boelcke' (He 111H–2), one of the main units used against Warsaw*
Above: *Pilot's view on a day mission (He 111P or H, 1939)*

almost two metres in front of his eyes. At night there were problems with internal reflection, and in adverse conditions the pilot had to elevate his seat, slide back the roof hatch and stick his head out, behind a small hinged windshield.

Apart from this the new nose was popular, and flying the first model to adopt it, the He 111P of autumn 1938, was in general extremely pleasant. The view in most directions was exceptional, the 1100 hp DB 601A–1 engines amply powerful enough and most reliable, and handling out-standingly good and by no means tiring. The He 111 was endowed with an immense wing, much greater in area than that of a Wellington and not far short of that of a B–24, and this kept the aircraft sedate and safe in its later years when its gross weight had been doubled and its aerodynamics destroyed by large external loads. Unlike the Do 217 it was mainly a hydraulic aircraft, and in the early war years it is doubtful if any other bomber so fully met all the needs of such aircraft in carrying heavy bomb loads, delivering them accurately, remaining service-able and meeting all the often finicky demands of its crews. On the score of cost/effectiveness the He 111P in 1938 was unrivalled.

Apart from the offset glazed nose the P also replaced the dustbin by a ventral 'bathtub' in which the gunner lay facing down and to the rear,

with a 90 degree cone of fire and less drag than the original scheme. The bombsight was on the right side of the nose, the bomb-aimer likewise having a foam-rubber pad on which he could lie when on the bombing run. On top the dorsal gunner was protected by a large Plexiglas fairing. Large numbers of P-series bombers were built, and maximum speed varied from 249 mph (typical without bomb load) to a mere 199 mph with maximum bomb load. Manufacture of the P-series ceased in early 1940 with the P–6 with 1175 hp DB 601N engines.

By this time nearly all the first-line Heinkels were fast being replaced by the definitive model in which all previous improvements were com-bined with the Jumo 211 engine. The He 111H was late arriving, for the original prototype (V19) did not fly until January 1939; but then production opened the floodgates at the rate of about 100 per month. Thus, on 1 September 1939, of 808 He 111 bombers in KG service, 400 were of the new H-series (there were 349 P-series, the rest being various earlier models). Despite increases in weight up to 27000 lb before the end of 1940, performance was maintained by the Jumo engines, which began in 1939 at 1010 hp, reached 1200 hp in the H–2 and H–3 of the early war period and levelled off at 1400 hp in the H–4 delivered in the early months of 1940. The H–4's power was destined never to be exceeded by any normal He 111 until the H–23 right at the end of the war. This power was at once put to use by adding an external plate under the left bomb flaps on which could be hung two 2205 lb bombs or one monster of 3968 lb. With this short-range load, gross weight was 30865 lb, again a figure seldom surpassed by regular production Heinkels.

So far the story of Die Späten has been one of rapid, sustained and successful development. But, possibly to Hitler's surprise, Britain and France honoured their pledge to Poland and declared war on 3 September 1939, and this was to place a burden on the Luftwaffe's chief bomber that before long proved far too onerous. Even in Poland the scattered PZL P.11c fighters, designed in 1931 and operating with little support from blitzed airbases, succeeded to an unexpect-ed extent in shooting down the stately bombers. Immediately armament was increased, typically from three machine guns to six by adding two beam-window guns and one in the nose roof, while 8 mm armour was added behind the flight deck and the two rear gunners. The H–3 of November 1939 also added a 20 mm MG FF cannon at the front of the gondola for ship strafing. Many Heinkels were to mount cannon either in this position in the front of the gondola or in the nose, for offensive purposes.

The H–3 was followed by numerous special versions, and by two further 'standard' sub-types, the H–6 (the most numerous He 111 of all) and H–16. Among the interesting variants were the H–8 with a vast balloon-cable fender for use over Britain (later replaced by leading-edge cable cutters), the H–12 for launching various types of Hs 293 stand-off missile, the H–22 for launching Fi 103 (V–1) pilotless bombs, and the final 1944–45 variant, the H–23 special saboteur transport with 1776 hp Jumo 213 engines. In between there were dozens of special versions and *Rüstsätze* standard kits for field modification. Some of the latter were extensive, the largest being the R1 kit which replaced the dorsal position (fully enclosed from the H–11 onwards) with an EDL 131 13 mm electric turret having 360° traverse. Other *Rüstsätze* kits included glider tow installations, special armour protection and various packs of the neat MG 81 guns. Previously some aircraft in the H–6 series had been fitted with a single remote-control MG 17 in the extreme tail, firing aft. A smaller number carried a grenade ejector to discourage attacks from astern.

The truth of the matter was that modern fighters could shoot down any He 111 with consummate ease, and by mid-1942 even the Eastern Front was perilous for the lumbering Heinkel in daylight. Increasingly the obsolescent bomber served in transport and towing roles, yet in the absence of replacements it also still had to equip the front-line Kampfgeschwadern. Some went in for torpedo dropping, and by 1945 the Heinkel had successfully dropped not only the L 10 Friedensengel winged torpedoes but also the Bv 246 controlled glider missile which had slender wings like a sailplane yet was made of reinforced concrete.

One version of the He 111 was not a bomber but one of the oddest aircraft in the sky. The He 111Z (Zwilling, or twin) was a five-engined tug for the Me 321 Gigant glider, produced by joining two He 111H–6 or H–16 bombers to a common centre section with a fifth engine on the centreline. Although safer than the exceedingly tricky 'Troika Schlepp' of three Bf 110 twin-engined fighters pulling one glider, the He 111Z was built only in small numbers, and the planned Z–2 bomber version never left the drawing board. Ironically, as in the case of its lifelong partner the Bf 109 fighter, the last examples of the He 111 to remain operational had British Rolls-Royce Merlin engines, with the Spanish Air Force in the 1950s. After the retirement of these licence-built CASA 2.111 aircraft the survivors were painted in Luftwaffe markings for the epic film *Battle of Britain*—but the sound of Merlins hardly fitted.

Front end of a typical He 111H (H–6 or later with separate exhaust stacks) showing the bomb-aimer/front gunner with pilot behind

Boeing B-17 Fortress

Until the early 1950s the United States was far beyond bombing range of any credible enemy, and its own bombers were equally out of range of likely targets. The only valid reason for the US Army bombing force was the repulsion of a hostile invasion fleet—although that did not seem a very likely eventuality either—which did not necessarily call for long range. It was to sink warships and troopships that the biplane Huff-Dalands and Keystones, and the trim Martin monoplane, were ordered; and their crews spent much time aiming on target vessels or ship outlines traced with tar on the bombing range at Muroc in the California desert which Hap Arnold succeeded in setting up by 1939. It is therefore remarkable that, in an environment of isolationism, financial parsimony, concentration on what the Air Corps Adjutant-General called 'that class of aviation designed for the close-in support of ground troops' and a complete absence of any strategic objective, the greatest bomber in the world should have been created in 1935.

Indeed, an even greater bomber had actually been started by the same company slightly earlier. In April 1934 the Division of Material at Wright Field had issued a far-sighted specification for a long-range bomber able to fly non-stop from the United States to Alaska, Hawaii or Panama. The Boeing Airplane Company accordingly built their Type 294, originally to have been called XBLR-1 but, in 1936, when the 'bomber long-range' category was scrapped, redesignated XB-15. The XB-15 flew on 15 October 1937. It was a real giant, with span of 149 feet and range of 5130 miles with 8000 lb of bombs. But there were no 2000 hp engines in 1937, and performance on four of 1000 hp was so poor the giant XB-15 was dropped. (On reflection, this is odd, as the 2000 hp Wright Duplex Cyclone was already running, and Pratt & Whitney were in advanced development with the Double Wasp.) The lone XB-15 subsequently served as a cargo transport, carrying loads of up to ten short tons, with the designation XC-105.

In August 1934 the Army Air Corps issued a general requirement for a new multi-engined bomber to replace the Martin, and announced a prototype competition to be held in 1935. This was taken for granted to mean a twin-engined bomber, and in fact the immediate winner of the 1935 competition was the B-18, based on the Douglas DC-2. But Boeing, encouraged by their experience with the Model 294, designed the 299 as a much larger bomber than the expected twin-engined aircraft, and built the prototype around four of the most powerful engines then available, the 750 hp Pratt & Whitney R-1690 Hornet S1EG. The aircraft flew at Seattle on 28 July 1935, and on 20 August was flown non-stop to Wright Field for the evaluation and competitive trials.

It is important to note that Boeing chose four engines in order to fly higher and faster and not to carry more bombs. The 299's design bomb load was the same as that of its rivals, eight 600 lb bombs, but it carried a larger crew of eight, five of whom could each man a defensive machine gun of 0.30 or 0.50-in calibre in the nose, dorsal, ventral and left and right waist blisters. Its performance was revealed by the average speed of 232 mph—faster than the maximum speed of its rivals—on its 2100-mile trip to Wright Field. Even the prototype could reach 250 mph at 25000 feet, and with engines fitted with GE (General Electric) turbosuperchargers considerably greater speed and height was certain. Tests had begun to show the new Boeing's potential when a 'first official flight' was scheduled for 30 October 1935, before the eyes of the Air Corps officials who were about to make their choice. Leslie Tower, the company test pilot who had done all the early flying, and the finest test pilot in the Air Corps, Maj P. P. Hill, climbed aboard and taxied out. On the takeoff run the impressive bomber kept its tail on the ground, reared up and crashed in flames, killing both pilots. Someone had forgotten to remove the elevator lock.

This disqualified the big Boeing, but its obvious potential enabled the 299 to survive the resulting criticism—and the storm of political fire from the Navy, ever-jealous of its strategic role and intensely adverse to so large a bomber—and on 17 January 1936 an order was placed for 13 service-test bombers designated Y1B–17. (The original 299 had no military designation.) These had different landing gear and armament, and 930 hp Wright R–1820–39 Cyclone engines; one had R–1820–51 engines with turbochargers and became a Y1B–17A. From March to December 1937 the 12 delivered to the Air Corps were sent to Langley Field and to the 2nd Bombardment Group of GHQ (General Headquarters) Air Force, a revolutionary new formation which at last gave the United States a basis for strategic air power—although there were still to be bitter battles with the Navy.

GHQ 2nd BG had to start virtually from scratch in proving the great new bomber and in formulating operational techniques for using it.

The experienced crews made a remarkable one-stop 5000-mile flight to Buenos Aires in February 1938 and set a succession of new records for the US coast-to-coast flight in both directions. From the start the new Boeing had impressed with its size, and when someone said 'It looks like a fort that can fly' the name Flying Fortress not only stuck but was registered by Boeing as a trade mark. Despite this, it was feather-light on the controls, and although it could not tangle with a small pursuit ship it was much less tiring to fly than many other large bombers, such as the later B–24. It was new to have a flight deck with pilot and co-pilot side-by-side, although this was common in civil transports. The reason was simply the long flight endurance, although later it was to allow for great teamwork between each pair of pilots just as is universal today on all large flight decks.

In fact the aircraft fitted with turbocharged

This was the first released photograph of B–17 production after the United States entered the war. Probably taken in January 1942, it shows the B–17E fuselage shop, with output running (the company said) at '70 per cent above the accelerated delivery schedule'

Seen here on a test flight from the Seattle factory, the first B–17E looked quite startling to people used to the earlier Fortress versions. The fin, in particular, was novel and enormous (though today long dorsal fins are common). This development aircraft was one of a handful of E-models painted in pre-war national markings; later came olive-drab finish and a succession of changed markings, followed in 1944 by a return to natural metal finish

engines had been intended as a static-test specimen, but the tough treatment meted out by 2nd BG and the 'Fort's' willing acceptance of it (once one survived an unpremeditated spin of at least nine turns) caused this aircraft to be assigned as a flying testbed and in turn led to the first true production version, the B–17B, having similar Dash–51 engines giving a speed of 311 mph at up to 30000 feet. In the 39 aircraft of this model, delivered in 1939–40, the GE turbos were on the underside of the nacelles, each spinning at some 25000 rpm in white-hot exhaust gas controlled by a 'waste gate' valve which automatically regulated the gas flow to give optimum engine power at all altitudes. Although several countries had worked on turbos, it was Dr Sanford N. Moss of GE who, researching from 1909 onwards, finally gave the Army Air Corps dramatically greater power at height, and it was used to the full for the first time in the early B– B.

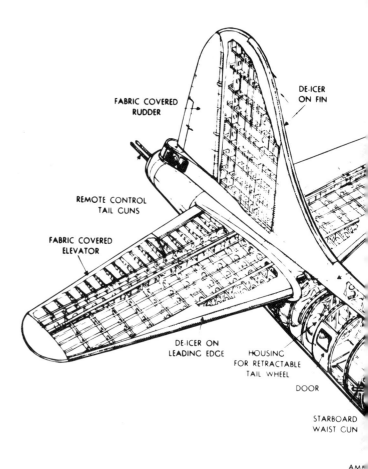

Left:
The final, and most numerous, of all B–17 models was the G, with chin turret and many other changes. Almost all were delivered in natural metal finish; this one belongs to the 385th BG

A further 38 aircraft ordered in 1939 were called B–17C, the fastest of all at 323 mph achieved with 1200 hp R–1820–65 engines despite a considerable increase in weight to 49650 lb (from 43000 lb) resulting from armour, self-sealing tanks and extra equipment. The armament, viewed against the threatening scene in Europe, appeared inadequate and twin 0·5 in guns were fitted in the dorsal and ventral positions, both totally redesigned, and there were single or twin 0·3-calibre weapons in side nose windows and new flush waist windows. In 1940 a further 42 B–17D were ordered with many minor revisions including cooling gills and a different electrical system. This kept production rolling at what seemed a good rate, and the Army Air Corps had 90 B–17s at the time of Pearl Harbour in December 1941. Significantly, the B–17 remained in the very front line to the end of the war, but almost every other type in Air Corps service at the start of the war was soon to fade from combat duty.

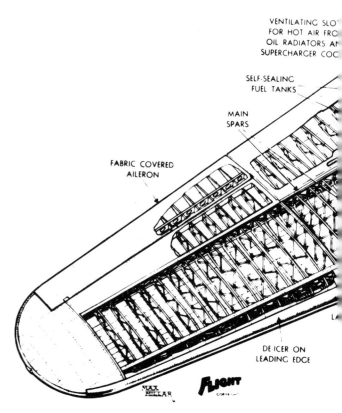

This cutaway was drawn in 1944 with the co-operation of the 8th Air Force in England. Apart from the fact that nobody at the time noticed a mis-spelt word, the drawing is instructive for the items it does not show, or explain. The actual structure of the main spar, the turbochargers, landing gears, flaps and jam-packed nacelle equipment are ignored, as are such questions as how the de-icers worked (they were of the pneumatic pulsating-rubber type). Yet such illustrations were pioneering a new art-form

SPECIFICATIONS

Types 299, Y1B–17 and B–17 to B–17G (basic data for G)
Engines: four 1 200 hp Wright R–1820–97 (B–17C to E, R–1820–65) Cyclone nine-cylinder radials with exhaust-driven turbochargers.
Dimensions: span 103 ft 9 in (31·6 m); length 74 ft 9 in (22·8 m); (B–17B, C, D) 67 ft 11 in; (B–17E) 73 ft 10 in; height 19 ft 1 in (5·8 m); (B–17B, C, D) 15 ft 5 in.
Weights: empty 32 720–35 800 lb (14 855–16 200 kg); (B–17B, C, D) typically 31 150 lb; maximum loaded 65 600 lb (29 700 kg) (B–17B, C, D) 44 200–46 650 lb; (B–17E) 53 000 lb.
Performance: maximum speed 287 mph (462 km/h); (B–17C, D) 323 mph; (B–17E) 317 mph; cruising speed 182 mph (293 km/h); (B–17C, D) 250 mph; (B–17E) 210 mph; service ceiling 35 000 ft (10 670 m); range 1 100 miles (1 760 km) with maximum bomb load (other versions up to 3 160 miles with reduced weapon load).

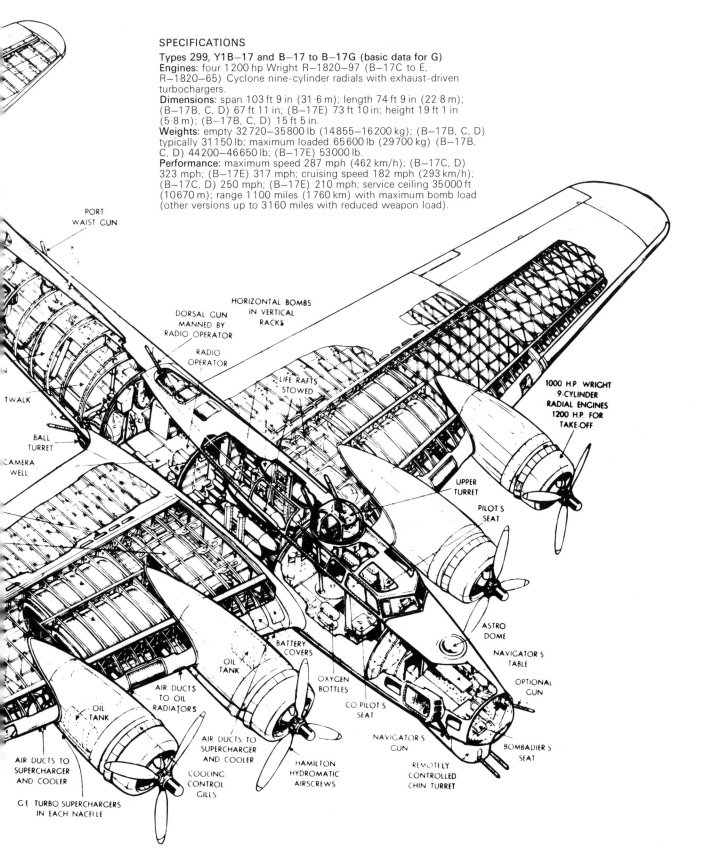

PORT WAIST GUN

DORSAL GUN MANNED BY RADIO OPERATOR

HORIZONTAL BOMBS IN VERTICAL RACKS

RADIO OPERATOR

LIFE RAFTS STOWED

1000 H.P. WRIGHT 9-CYLINDER RADIAL ENGINES 1200 H.P. FOR TAKE-OFF

TWALK

BALL TURRET

CAMERA WELL

UPPER TURRET

PILOT'S SEAT

ASTRO DOME

NAVIGATOR'S TABLE

BATTERY COVERS

OIL TANK

OXYGEN BOTTLES

OPTIONAL GUN

OIL TANK

AIR DUCTS TO OIL RADIATORS

CO-PILOT'S SEAT

AIR DUCTS TO SUPERCHARGER AND COOLER

NAVIGATOR'S GUN

BOMBADIER'S SEAT

AIR DUCTS TO SUPERCHARGER AND COOLER

COOLING CONTROL GILLS

HAMILTON HYDROMATIC AIRSCREWS

REMOTELY CONTROLLED CHIN TURRET

GE TURBO SUPERCHARGERS IN EACH NACELLE

53

Above: *The 457th Bombardment Group of the US Army 8th Air Force arrived in Britain in January 1944 and used only one type of aircraft (B–17G) and one airfield (Glatton) until after the end of the war in Europe. This Fort wears the 457th livery of a U in a triangle, supplemented later by a diagonal blue band across the tail. It is, in fact, civil N 5111N, of the Bradley Air Museum in Connecticut*

Right: *Probably taken in early 1942, this picture shows newly built B–24D Liberators on the apron at a USAAF base, with a Cessna UC–78 (T–50) for a foreign customer in the background. The nearest Lib has the special nose reserved for aircraft built on RAF account for conversion in Britain to Coastal Command GR.V standard, with chin radar and rocket launchers*

These shiny new B–17C Fortresses were the fastest of the whole family, with maximum speed at about 28 000 feet of 320 mph. This excellent colour photograph was taken at the Boeing plant at the height of the Battle of Britain, around August 1940

In 1940 the British, through the purchasing commission in Washington, made repeated requests for B–17s and in March of that year it was agreed to release 20 in exchange for full information on their combat performance (this was before Roosevelt's Lend-Lease Act). The RAF Fortress I was basically a B–17C, but after receipt they were put through a modification centre and did not become operational with 90 Squadron at Polebrook and West Raynham until 8 July 1941. The results were pathetic, and reflected little credit on the RAF which used the aircraft in ones and twos, had most of them shot down or written off within eight weeks, and merely confirmed the strength of the airframe as being able to limp back after being reduced to a heap of scrap while still at 31000 feet. Subsequently, the survivors served with Coastal Command and in the Middle East.

This disastrous experience did not destroy the Army Air Corps' belief in the massed armada of heavily-armed bombers operating by day, holding a formation close enough for each bomber's firepower to defend those near it; but it caused an almighty problem. In the words of Hap Arnold, Commanding General of the Air Corps, 'It was to hound us in our bombardment relations with the RAF for a long time . . . It was not until Casablanca, in January 1943, that I was able to convince the President and the Prime Minister of the effectiveness of the Flying Fortress when employed as we employed it . . . Despite all British arguments, our programme of precision bombing by daylight was able to continue as a first priority.' But the lesson was certainly not ignored. Boeing did not quite go back to a clean sheet of paper, but when the first 299O, or B–17E, flew on 5 September 1941 it was a totally different aircraft.

The greatest change was in armament, which now comprised a Bendix electrically-driven dorsal turret with two 0·5 in guns, an electric ventral turret sighted by a periscope in the rear fuselage, again with two 0·5 in, a further single or twin 0·5 in manually aimed from the roof of the radio compartment behind the dorsal turret, a further two 0·5 in manually aimed from new waist positions, two 0·5 in in a completely new manually-operated turret in the extreme tail, and two or three 0·30 in in the nose ball-socket mounts. To improve stability for high-altitude bombing the fin and horizontal tail were made

Top: *Test flying a new B–17G before delivery in 1943. The ocean is the Pacific but not near Seattle, for this Fort was built by Douglas at Long Beach*
Right: *One of the first F-models to reach the 8th Air Force, photographed by* Flight *in 1942 at Bassingbourn, where it was serving with the 401st BS, 91st BG*

larger, and with ten men on board the gross weight leaped to 54000 lb. The new E-model was ordered in unprecedented quantities by what on 20 June 1941 had become the Army Air Force (AAF), a first batch of 512 being followed by larger numbers for which Boeing, Vega (Lockheed) and Douglas combined resources to speed output from three large plants. Subsequently the BVD pool made nearly 13000, of which Vega and Douglas delivered 5745, the combine suffering little from the fact that to every American BVD is a make of underwear.

Almost at once the periscope and ventral turret proved unsatisfactory in use and gave way to a radically new spherical turret made by Sperry. Only small men could be ball-turret gunners, and if the turret doors were jammed by combat damage and the B–17 made a belly landing they had even less room than usual.* The stage was now set for a build-up of daylight airpower capable of fighting its way through the strongest fighter opposition and making accurate attacks on individual factories. Admittedly the navigation problem is easier by day than by night, but that is incidental. Bombing accuracy was due to the radical Norden bombsight, which in early B–17s in 1940 was kept always under guard and installed in the aircraft only just before takeoff and removed after landing. Reputedly able to 'put a bomb in a pickle barrel from 30000 feet', it was significantly more accurate than the contemporary RAF Mk XIV sight, and roughly twelve times as costly.

When Pearl Harbor was hit early on Sunday, 7 December 1941, a radar operator ignored the warning 'blips' on his newly installed set because he was told they must come from the new B–17Es of the 7th BG then on their way to Hawaii. Most of the earlier D-models at Hickam Field were destroyed in the attack. An urgent warning was signalled to the AAF commander in the Philippines to disperse his aircraft. One of the many puzzles of the war is that the following day, when the Japanese hit the Philippines, the thirty-six Fortresses at Clark Field were still on parade in a tight group and 18 were destroyed by bombs in five minutes. Subsequently the remainder were in hectic action in near impossible circumstances, moving up to 500 miles each day with negligible ground equipment and support, until in January 1942 a single battered veteran, 40–3097 *Swoose*, was flown back to the USA. In the same month the B–17E went into action in

* Belly landing procedure required the ball-turret gunner to climb out and special tools to be used to drop the turret off. The Executive Officer of an 8th AF station in England once spent several hours trying to pass the tools to a B–17 which had flown a mission without them. He succeeded.

It was normal practice for the whole crew to fly their Lanc on its air test on the afternoon before an op. There was seldom a conference—still less a parade —at the aircraft; the chaps usually walked from the crew bus, or from where they left their bikes, to the door on the right of the rear fuselage
Bombing-up a Lancaster (above), probably before 1943. Later the mix of one cookie and cases of incendiaries became almost universal, and propellers had broad paddle blades

This B–17G was not on strength of an operational unit and may have been used at a training school in the United States. At contrail height a persistent stream of ice crystals formed some 30 feet astern of each turbocharger waste-gate, making serried ranks of Fortresses visible from as far away as 50 miles

Java, with the most encouraging results.

By this time the Allied leaders had decided to put maximum effort into defeating Germany first, and on 1 July 1942 a B–17E of the 97th BG of the newly formed Bomber Command of the 8th Air Force arrived at Prestwick and flew on to its base at Grafton Underwood. On 17 August the first 8th AF mission by 'heavies' was flown against Rouen marshalling yards, the commanding general, Ira C. Eaker, flying in *Yankee Doodle* and the 97th group commander, Col Frank Armstrong, leading in *Butcher Shop*. Thus began one of the epic stories in both aviation and warfare. It began in a small way, with 12 aircraft. They did not carry a heavy load; indeed, we in the RAF used to sing a song, to the tune of *John Brown's Body*, the first verse of which began 'Fifty Flying Fortresses at 50000 feet' (repeated twice), and ending, 'but they've only got a teeny weeny bomb'. This was good-natured fun, a natural wish to keep up with the new competition and, to a small degree, based on the pre-war image of Americans as big talkers. Such feelings were soon forgotten, because the 8th Air Force went through hell and back daily, suffered

grievous losses and yet gradually gained complete supremacy in the daylight sky over the heart of Germany. They became utter professionals.

Three times the author was privileged to ride with them, once on an operational mission, and he cannot recall the names of those Fortresses without a lump in the throat. The public possibly thought they all had scantily-clad female nose art, but this was the exception. Nose art was prodigious in quantity and quality, and as the bomb groups built up in strength and multiplied in number one soon lost count until by 1944, despite enormous losses, more than 1500 B–17s were equipping 19 Bomb Groups of the 'Mighty Eighth' on missions that had incredible ups and downs but never wavered in the single-minded desire to defeat the enemy. Probably the greatest 'down' was the second Schweinfurt (ball-bearing plant) mission on 14 October 1943, when 60 of 291 B–17s were shot down and 101 suffered combat damage. This was the last deep-penetration mission without fighter escort. Thereafter the P–47, P–38 and P–51 fighters flew top cover and weaved alongside during most

This B–17G, A Bit O'Lace, *was one of the veterans of the 8th Bomber Command; in this Charles E. Brown photograph one can count the bomb symbols. The 447th BG insignia of a K in a black circle is backed up by yellow wing-tips and tail control surfaces, twin green bands on rear fuselage and blue chevron on upper right and lower left wings*

of the outbound and inward legs. By early 1944 the fantastic P-51 with drop tanks was able to accompany the heavies all the way to Berlin or Czechoslovakia and back. This was the beginning of the end for Nazi Germany; when Goering saw that the Luftwaffe no longer had command of its own airspace he said 'I knew the war was lost'.

After building the 512 E-models Boeing switched to the B-17F, with a longer nosecap of blown Plexiglas and nearly 400 less-obvious changes including paddle-blade propellers. The number of Fs was 3405, followed by no fewer than 8680 of the B-17G, the final basic model, with twin-0·5 in chin turret, enclosed waist positions and other changes. Other variants included the F-9 reconnaissance version, YC-108 VIP transport, CB-17 utility transport, BQ-7 'Aphrodite' radio-controlled missile conversion with 20000 lb of Torpex explosive, YB-40 and TB-40 escort fighters with extra guns and 7300 lb of ammunition, the Allison-engined XB-38 and the Navy's PB-1W early-warning aircraft which, after the war, were rebuilt with APS-20 radar as the first aerial

surveillance aircraft apart from an Avenger testbed. Some 50 aircraft were converted as B-17H search/rescue machines carrying life-boats, and there were several trainer versions.

In 1943 the B-17G entered service with the RAF and 85 were used by Coastal Command and, more importantly, as primary carriers of two secret RAF electronic countermeasures, Jostle and Piperack, operating with 100 Group. Equally exciting was the Luftwaffe's use of captured B-17s—with the cover-designation Dornier 200—for numerous clandestine operations from Norway to Jordan, chiefly by I/KG 200 to land agents and material behind Allied lines. No bomber was ever more liked and respected than this big, gentle and tough machine which, more than any other in history, took its courageous crews through an inferno of flak and fighters to hit an enemy where it hurt most—not only on the ground but in the sky too. So the English-speaking nations can be grateful for the far-off 1934 Air Corps men who asked for a bomber to fend off a mythical invasion fleet, and grateful to Boeing for taking a mighty commercial risk.

Above: *Crews checking things over before a night op. Usually, when the target was a strategic one planned in advance, there was nothing more to be said; the crew arrived at dispersal, possibly several miles from the briefing hut and sometimes on a different (satellite) airfield, knowing all they could be told about the mission. After spring 1944 targets were often tactical ones linked with the Allied invasion and here last-minute changes were common*

Left: *Over the target, especially later in the war—say from late 1942 until late 1944—was almost indescribable activity. The Pathfinders, led by the Master Bomber, would put down various colour-coded markers (green in this instance) which the enemy could not duplicate without foreknowledge. The cascades of cookies and incendiaries (in this case ordinary GP bombs, which was unusual) would then rain down for anything from two minutes to an hour, depending on the force committed and the density of the bomber stream. Automatic weapons (the intermittent golden spurt) seldom reached to Lancaster levels*

Junkers Ju 87

No weapon has ever aroused greater controversy than the dive-bomber, and the Ju 87 'Stuka' in particular. In favourable circumstances it proved the perfect partner to the Panzer division in rolling forward the baleful hegemony of the Swastika across a land area larger than the Romans conquered. In unfavourable circumstances it was reduced to furtive scurrying at treetop height, mainly by night, in missions that did not involve dive-bombing at all. There are, in fact, two separate arguments: the technique of dive-bombing, and the worth of the Ju 87. Dive-bombing was shown in a few isolated trials in the First World War to be a potentially accurate way of putting one or more bombs on a target. It was avidly practised by the US Navy in 1928–45, but faded in favour of either shallower dive attacks or the introduction of proper weapon-aiming systems. But in its heyday in the 1930–43 period it so influenced the Luftwaffe that steep dive-bombing capability was demanded of every bomber including the large He 177, with troublesome consequences for

the new German bomber programmes.

It is often thought that German fixation on the dive-bomber stemmed from the enthusiasm of Ernst Udet, the ace of the First World War who in 1932 watched the technique in the United States and arranged for the import into Germany the following year of two Curtiss Hawk IIs (similar to the US Navy BFC–2) with secret funding by the Reischsluftfahrtministerium. In fact dive-bombing had played a central role in German air force studies throughout the 1920s, and was the prime mission of the Junkers K 47 series built in some numbers at Dessau and in Sweden in 1928–30. Udet, who was Hitler's director of aircraft procurement until he committed suicide in 1941, had flown the K 47 and a US Navy Helldiver, and when plans for the Luftwaffe became faster-moving and more overt he worked with Goering and Milch to produce dive bombers better than the Americans. Trials with Fw 56 Stösser fighter-trainers showed accuracy of 40 per cent, allegedly twice the percentage within the target circle achieved by

Almost certainly of the 29th production Ju 87B–1, this photograph was taken in late 1938 and shows the authorized markings. Previously the swastika had been on a white disc on a scarlet tail band. There were various changes in 1939, most notably in the adoption of a different Balkenkreuz (national marking) on wing undersurface and fuselage

Above left: *Propaganda picture showing aircrew with a B-series prototype (probably the V7) in early-1938 markings*
Above right: *A B-0 pre-production aircraft on the company stand at the 1939 Brussels airshow*
Above: *This Ju 87A-2, a full production example of the early A-series, is seen at the Stuka-Vorschule in early 1941*

conventional bombers. But when these trials took place the die was already cast. The Henschel Hs 123 biplane had been selected as the *Sofort* (immediate, or stop-gap) dive-bomber, and Udet's office had issued its January 1935 specification for the definitive article. Moreover, the specification had been drawn up around the design of an aircraft already fast taking shape as a company private venture: the Ju 87.

Like several important German prototypes of the period the Ju 87 V1 (first prototype) was fitted with an imported Rolls-Royce Kestrel engine, of up to 640 hp (at full-throttle height of 14000 feet), driving a traditional wooden fixed-pitch propeller. Unlike most previous Junkers aircraft it had a smooth stressed skin, instead of corrugated sheet, but it retained an odd tail with rectangular fins on the tips of the tailplane, as in the K 47, and the trousered landing gears were attached at the lowest points of a sharply cranked wing (fitted with the company's patented 'double wing' trailing-edge surfaces), which gave better clearance under the belly for loading a large bomb. About two months after its first flight in April/May 1935 (the date is unrecorded) this aircraft crashed due to tail failure, but by June 1936 the single-finned Ju 87

V2 was ready to compete in trials at Rechlin against the Ar 81 (psychologically ruled out from the start because it was a biplane), the Ha 137 (a single-seater, thus not meeting requirements) and Heinkel's He 118. In fact it had been taken almost for granted that the Ju 87, started by Dipl-Ing Hermann Pohlmann as the basis of the whole programme, would be chosen for the Luftwaffe. The He 118 cast a spanner into the works because it was much faster than the Ju 87, more manoeuvrable and clearly more advanced in design. If it had won there is no doubt it would have proved more formidable, but Udet —untypically—entered a near-vertical dive with the He 118's propeller in fine pitch, blew up the engine reduction gears, pulled the tail off and took to his parachute. Exit Heinkel.

Following a pre-series batch of the Ju 87A-0 in 1936, delivery began of the production 87A-1 in January 1937, with 640 hp Junkers Jumo 210Ca inverted-vee-12 and, later, a VDM constant-speed propeller. About 200 A-1 and A-2 were built, equipping StG (Stuka-geschwader) 162 and 165. The term 'Stuka' is derived from the German for dive-bomber, Sturzkampfflugzeug, but has historically come to be synonymous with the Ju 87. The 87A-1

65

was colloquially called Stuka as early as 1937 when several saw extensive combat service in Spain. Results there were little short of fantastic, which did little for the careers of the opponents of dive-bombing, notably Oberst Wolfram von Richthofen, chief of technical development, who just before the Rechlin trials had issued a directive discontinuing the whole programme. (For his pains, he was soon appointed to command a Stuka wing.)

In 1938 the A-series was succeeded by the Ju 87B–1, with spatted wheels, a completely new fuselage and the best engine in Germany, the Jumo 211Da rated at 1200 hp and with direct fuel injection instead of a carburettor. This dramatic increase in power enabled the Stuka to carry a bomb of 1102 lb, or one of 551 lb and four on underwing racks of 110 lb. Production increased until in 1939 output reached 557. This was planned as the phase-out of the Ju 87, which was thought to be vulnerable and obsolescent. But at 04.34 on 1 September 1939 Oberleutnant Bruno Dilley winged over into a vertical dive above a Polish demolition crew at the Dirschau bridge and blew them to smithereens, 11 minutes before the official time for the start of the Second World War. From then until the collapse of mighty France on 25 June 1940 the Stukagruppen proved time and again the key element in the successful realization of the Blitzkrieg concept of lightning warfare.

The central feature of Blitzkrieg was the application of overwhelming force at specific points, to keep the front constantly advancing and avoid the slightest risk of the land battle degenerating into static trench warfare. On countless occasions the Ju 87 was the instrument for the delivery of this overwhelming force. The detailed history of the Polish campaign is at once impressive and horrifying. Impressive because it became routine to place 1102 lb bombs exactly on pockets of resistance within 100

This meticulous drawing by John Weal is one of the best modern cutaways of any Second World War aircraft, and it is far better than any similar drawing would have been when the aircraft was new (because standards and techniques have improved out of all recognition). The subject is the Ju 87D–3, a ground-attack model of the important and numerous D-series family which entered combat service in early 1942

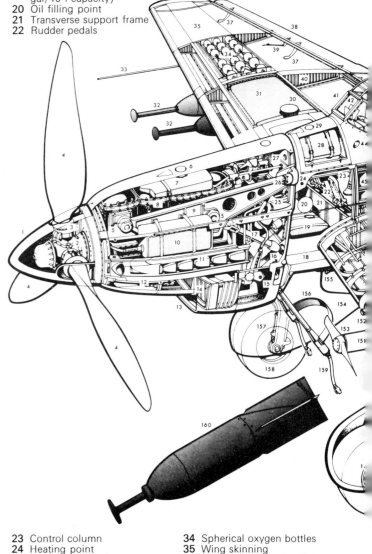

1 Spinner
2 Pitch-change mechanism housing
3 Blade hub
4 Junkers VS 11 constant-speed airscrew
5 Anti-vibration engine mounting attachments
6 Oil filler point and marker
7 Auxiliary oil tank (5·9 Imp gal/26,8-l capacity)
8 Junkers Jumo 211J–1 12-cylinder inverted-vee liquid cooled engine
9 Magnesium alloy forged engine mount
10 Coolant (Glysantin-water) header tank
11 Ejector exhaust stubs
12 Fuel injection unit housing
13 Induction air cooler
14 Armoured radiator
15 Inertia starter cranking point
16 Ball joint bulkhead fixing (lower)
17 Tubular steel mount support strut
18 Ventral armour (8 mm)
19 Main oil tank (9·9 Imp gal/45 l capacity)
20 Oil filling point
21 Transverse support frame
22 Rudder pedals
23 Control column
24 Heating point
25 Auxiliary air intake
26 Ball joint bulkhead fixing (upper)
27 Bulkhead
28 Oil tank (6·8 Imp gal/31 l capacity)
29 Oil filler point and marker (Intava 100)
30 Fuel filler cap
31 Self-sealing starboard outer fuel tank (33 Imp gal/150 l capacity)
32 Underwing bombs with *Dienartstab* percussion rods
33 Pitot head
34 Spherical oxygen bottles
35 Wing skinning
36 Starboard navigation light
37 Aileron mass balance
38 'Double wing' aileron and flap (starboard outer)
39 Aileron hinge
40 Corrugated wing rib station
41 Reinforced armoured windscreen

SPECIFICATIONS

Ju 87A, B and D series
Engine: (Ju 87B–1) one 1100 hp Junkers Jumo 211Da 12-cylinder inverted-vee liquid-cooled; (Ju 87D–1, D–5) 1300 hp Jumo 211J.
Dimensions: span (Ju 87B–1, D–1) 45 ft 3¼ in (13·8 m); (D–5) 50 ft 0½ in (15·25 m); length 36 ft 5 in (11·1 m); height 12 ft 9 in (3·9 m).
Weights: empty (B–1, D–1) about 6080 lb (2750 kg), loaded (B–1) 9371 lb (4250 kg); (D–1) 12600 lb (5720 kg); (D–5) 14500 lb (6585 kg).
Performance: maximum speed (B–1) 242 mph (390 km/h); (D–1) 255 mph (408 km/h); (D–5) 250 mph (402 km/h); service ceiling (B–1) 26250 ft (8000 m); (D–1, D–5) 24000 ft (7320 m); range with maximum bomb load (B–1) 373 miles (600 km), (D–1, D–5) 620 miles (1000 km).

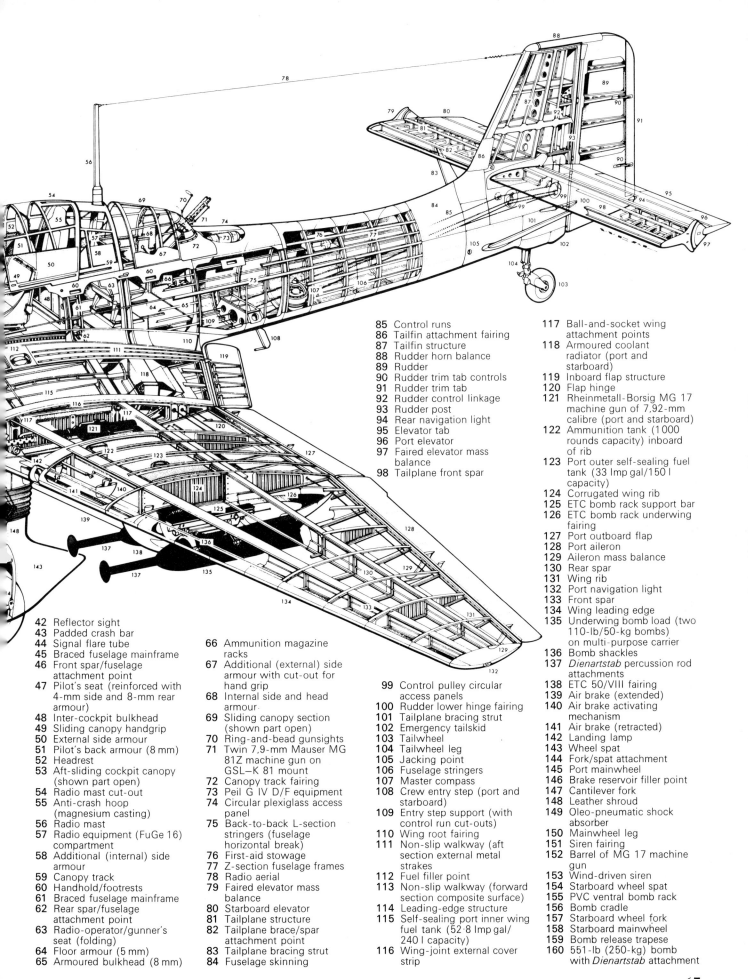

85 Control runs
86 Tailfin attachment fairing
87 Tailfin structure
88 Rudder horn balance
89 Rudder
90 Rudder trim tab controls
91 Rudder trim tab
92 Rudder control linkage
93 Rudder post
94 Rear navigation light
95 Elevator tab
96 Port elevator
97 Faired elevator mass balance
98 Tailplane front spar

117 Ball-and-socket wing attachment points
118 Armoured coolant radiator (port and starboard)
119 Inboard flap structure
120 Flap hinge
121 Rheinmetall-Borsig MG 17 machine gun of 7,92-mm calibre (port and starboard)
122 Ammunition tank (1000 rounds capacity) inboard of rib
123 Port outer self-sealing fuel tank (33 Imp gal/150 l capacity)
124 Corrugated wing rib
125 ETC bomb rack support bar
126 ETC bomb rack underwing fairing
127 Port outboard flap
128 Port aileron
129 Aileron mass balance
130 Rear spar
131 Wing rib
132 Port navigation light
133 Front spar
134 Wing leading edge
135 Underwing bomb load (two 110-lb/50-kg bombs) on multi-purpose carrier
136 Bomb shackles
137 *Dienartstab* percussion rod attachments
138 ETC 50/VIII fairing
139 Air brake (extended)
140 Air brake activating mechanism
141 Air brake (retracted)
142 Landing lamp
143 Wheel spat
144 Fork/spat attachment
145 Port mainwheel
146 Brake reservoir filler point
147 Cantilever fork
148 Leather shroud
149 Oleo-pneumatic shock absorber
150 Mainwheel leg
151 Siren fairing
152 Barrel of MG 17 machine gun
153 Wind-driven siren
154 Starboard wheel spat
155 PVC ventral bomb rack
156 Bomb cradle
157 Starboard wheel fork
158 Starboard mainwheel
159 Bomb release trapese
160 551-lb (250-kg) bomb with *Dienartstab* attachment

42 Reflector sight
43 Padded crash bar
44 Signal flare tube
45 Braced fuselage mainframe
46 Front spar/fuselage attachment point
47 Pilot's seat (reinforced with 4-mm side and 8-mm rear armour)
48 Inter-cockpit bulkhead
49 Sliding canopy handgrip
50 External side armour
51 Pilot's back armour (8 mm)
52 Headrest
53 Aft-sliding cockpit canopy (shown part open)
54 Radio mast cut-out
55 Anti-crash hoop (magnesium casting)
56 Radio mast
57 Radio equipment (FuGe 16) compartment
58 Additional (internal) side armour
59 Canopy track
60 Handhold/footrests
61 Braced fuselage mainframe
62 Rear spar/fuselage attachment point
63 Radio-operator/gunner's seat (folding)
64 Floor armour (5 mm)
65 Armoured bulkhead (8 mm)

66 Ammunition magazine racks
67 Additional (external) side armour with cut-out for hand grip
68 Internal side and head armour
69 Sliding canopy section (shown part open)
70 Ring-and-bead gunsights
71 Twin 7,9-mm Mauser MG 81Z machine gun on GSL–K 81 mount
72 Canopy track fairing
73 Peil G IV D/F equipment
74 Circular plexiglass access panel
75 Back-to-back L-section stringers (fuselage horizontal break)
76 First-aid stowage
77 Z-section fuselage frames
78 Radio aerial
79 Faired elevator mass balance
80 Starboard elevator
81 Tailplane structure
82 Tailplane brace/spar attachment point
83 Tailplane bracing strut
84 Fuselage skinning

99 Control pulley circular access panels
100 Rudder lower hinge fairing
101 Tailplane bracing strut
102 Emergency tailskid
103 Tailwheel
104 Tailwheel leg
105 Jacking point
106 Fuselage stringers
107 Master compass
108 Crew entry step (port and starboard)
109 Entry step support (with control run cut-outs)
110 Wing root fairing
111 Non-slip walkway (aft section external metal strakes
112 Fuel filler point
113 Non-slip walkway (forward section composite surface)
114 Leading-edge structure
115 Self-sealing port inner wing fuel tank (52·8 Imp gal/ 240 l capacity)
116 Wing-joint external cover strip

metres of the leading German troops. Horrifying because one can imagine the scene, for example, at Piotrkow railway station where 40 Stukas caught an entire infantry division de-training. At Hela, German warships caught the two most formidable units of the Polish Navy, *Gryf* and *Wycher*; the Germans were driven off by the stubborn Poles, but when the Stukas were called in they reduced both warships to sunken hulks in a matter of minutes. One Allied navy after another was to learn the hard way that without opposition a Stuka was lethal to almost any ship. Quite apart from the very real effect of a Ju 87 attack, the psychological effect—especially as the aircraft increasingly carried sirens on the landing gear—often caused utter panic not only among thousands of refugees but even among seasoned troops. So Ju 87B production actually increased in 1940 instead of coming to an end.

It was the Stuka that drove the Allied warships from Norway, leaving almost a dozen on the bottom, and then beat a path from Germany to the Channel in little over ten days. But in the Battle of Britain things were different. For the first time the command of the air was so bitterly disputed as to be in doubt, and in these circumstances the Ju 87 became extremely vulnerable. For example on 17 August I/StG 77 sent 28 aircraft to destroy the radar station at Poling, near Littlehampton. They hit Poling, but were caught by RAF fighters and lost 12 aircraft in a few minutes. The Stukas soon pulled out, but in November again tried strikes against shipping. On the 14th III/StG1 was intercepted without its planned fighter cover and lost one-quarter of its strength. But what could replace the Stuka? It appeared in newer versions, notably the Ju 87D with 1410 hp Jumo 211J and a bomb load of up to 3968 lb, and production, which was tapering to a close in late 1941, was increased sharply in 1942.

It was indisputable that the Stuka, vulnerable as it was to fighters or flak, was ideal for destroying ships, land strongpoints and many other targets that hardly any other aircraft could reliably hit at all. In the Balkans, Crete, North Africa, Malta and, above all, on the Eastern Front, the ageing Stuka dropped heavy bombs with pinpoint precision, and did many other jobs with all the Axis air forces. The D–3 at last broke away from dive-bombing to serve as a Schlachtflugzeug (close-support aircraft). Incidental duties included glider towing, training, carriage of casualties or saboteurs in overwing pods, torpedo dropping and, in the stillborn 87C, carrier-based attack. The most important of the late versions was the Ju 87G, a D–5 converted

A Ju 87B–2 serving with Italy's Regia Aeronautica. Appearance in Italian markings led to an Allied belief that the type was built in Italy, and the fictitious designation 'Breda 201 Pichiatelli' was circulated in Allied magazines

to carry two 37 mm BK 3·7 guns under the wings, with clips of six armour-piercing rounds. Although the big guns made the aircraft even more unwieldy than before, they were highly effective against Soviet tanks. Beyond dispute the greatest tank-killer in history was Oberleutnant Hans-Ulrich Rudel of I/StG 2 who was credited with a final total of 519 Soviet armoured vehicles, nearly all of them main battle tanks.

During 1943 each Stukageschwader progressively became a Schlachtgeschwader, and progressively the Ju 87 was replaced by the Fw 190. By mid-1944 all but a single proud Gruppe (Rudel's) had become a Nachtschlacht (night assault) unit, skulking over the wrecks of the German armies trying to do what harm they could to the hordes of well-equipped enemies. Those who had previously been on the receiving end were delighted.

Like most of Hitler's great warplanes the Ju 87 was built in ever-greater quantities simply because there was nothing planned to replace it. Stukas poured off the lines in 1943–44, when they really were obsolete, and the accepted figure for total deliveries is 5709, by September 1944, when all aircraft production was stopped except for fighters.

Above left: *Almost certainly taken at Berlin-Tempelhof, where the Ju 87B was built by Weser-Flugzeugbau, this 1940 photograph shows hand-pump refuelling. The double-wing flaps are down*
Above right: *A Ju 87G-1, with tail on a trestle, tries out its tank-killing BK 3.7 guns at the test butts. Though a sitting duck for fighters, the G-model was effective against armour*
Below: *This formation winging its way across the Western Desert is almost certainly a Staffel from St.G 3, which was the first Stukageschwader to reach North Africa in early 1941*

Vickers-Armstrongs Wellington

Everyone who knows anything about the Wellington knows that it was the supreme example of 'geodetic' construction. Instead of a normal structure its airframe took the form of a metal basketwork. This made it unusual in many ways, but the structure was a side issue. The central fact was that, of all the RAF bombers of the Second World War or any other era, the Wellington was built in greater numbers than any other, in more versions, for more purposes. Odd it may have been, but it was thoroughly well liked and did a wonderful job in all its varied roles.

British industry had adopted metal instead of wood for aircraft structures, but had yet to realize the superiority of the all-metal stressed-skin kind of airframe becoming common in the United States. It seemed to Wallis that the ideal way to built an aeroplane was to make it of thousands of small but simple bits, many of them identical. When these numerous strips of metal, each a few inches long, had all been riveted together—or, more strictly, to even smaller cross-shaped links—the result was a hollow light-alloy basket the shape of the fuselage or wing. One or two strong spars or

L4280 was the 69th aircraft in the original production batch built at Weybridge in 1938. It has the early Vickers 'roll-top desk' turrets, each intended to mount twin Brownings. The turret never worked properly, though the gunner's Perspex moulding gave an unobstructed view

The man responsible for geodetic construction was B.N. (now Sir Barnes) Wallis, one of the best-known engineers of this century. From the First World War he had been designing airships, and it was his evolution of an efficient geodetic structure for the Vickers R.100—the privately built airship which behaved perfectly but which was scrapped when the faulty State-designed R.101 crashed—that made him study whether the technique could be used in aeroplanes. In the early 1930s the

longerons were then added to give the structure some rigidity.

Despite this, a Wellington flexed and stretched in a way that amazed those not used to it. The pilot's control wheel did not stay still, and in rough air moved bodily to and fro as the elevator cables became loose or taut. It was said that one could never state the span or length, except qualifying it by also giving the time to which the measurement referred. There were many other odd characteristics, but Wallis's purpose had

Top: *though the print was marked SECRET, the wartime censor has nevertheless dutifully airbrushed-out the background to this picture of one of the many oddball Wellingtons. L4250, an early Mk I, became the first Mk II (Merlin X engines), then tested the Vickers 40 mm turret intended for the Boulton Paul P.92, and finally received twin fins. Picture taken in October 1941*
Above: *X3763 was a refreshingly normal Wellington III, built at Squire's Gate. Whereas the original Mk I had long Perspex windows along the fuselage the Mk IC had intermittent windows and the III had none, but it did have rear windows for new beam guns*

not been to confuse. He had reasoned that a geodetic aircraft should be light and efficient, easy to make, tough and robust, and easy to repair. Beyond dispute, the Wellington could 'take it', and after returning to base with large chunks shot away it was easier to repair than any other aircraft.

Vickers flew the original prototype, the B.9/32 or Type 271, on 15 June 1936. It was a good-looking but rather bulbous machine, its fabric covering doped silver and with no visible armament. With two Bristol Pegasus engines of 850 hp each it demonstrated excellent performance, and the production machine promised exceptional range with a bomb load of up to 4500 lb carried internally. By 1937 the design was being greatly modified, and on 23 December 1937 the first production Wellington I showed most of the changes externally. There was now a simple Vickers gun turret at each end, the tail was totally redesigned, the tailwheel (previously spatted) was retractable, the main landing gears were quite different, and the shape of the fuselage had been changed. By the outbreak of

the Second World War the standard model was the IA, with much better power-driven turrets and 1000 hp Pegasus engines. By this time orders had reached enormous totals, and soon Wellingtons poured from the old Vickers factory inside Brooklands racetrack and from two specially built 'shadow factories' at Chester and Blackpool.

Until May 1940 the RAF was forbidden to bomb Germany, but was allowed to try to bomb the German fleet. Squadrons of the new Wellingtons were thus in action on the second day of the war, valiantly dropping bombs (that often failed to explode) on armoured decks from low level in daylight. On 18 December 1939 an exceptionally large force of 24 Wellingtons searched for naval targets in the Schillig Roads and off Wilhelmshaven. Unknown to the RAF the Luftwaffe had Freya early-warning radar, and the RAF formation was detected and tracked while a large force of Bf 109 and 110 fighters was scrambled to intercept it. The Messerschmitts were flown by skilled and experienced pilots, eager to demonstrate their superiority. Nine months later they were to find the going

Though there were several wartime Wellington cutaways, none even approached this modern John Weal drawing of a Wellington III, with an 'exploded' view of the flotation bags stowed above the bombs. Of course, the three-cell bay could not carry Light-Case 'blockbuster' bombs, but Wellingtons were important in Bomber Command to VE-day

SPECIFICATIONS

Type 415 and 440, Wellington I to T.19

Engines: variously two Bristol Pegasus nine-cylinder radials, two Rolls-Royce Merlin vee-12 liquid-cooled, two Pratt & Whitney Twin Wasp 14-cylinder two-row radials or two Bristol Hercules 14-cylinder two-row sleeve-valve radials; for details see text.
Dimensions: span 86 ft 2 in (26·26 m); (V, VI) 98 ft 2 in, length (most) 64 ft 7 in (19·68 m), (some, 60 ft 10 in or, with Leigh light, 66 ft); height 17 ft 6 in (5·33 m), (some 17 ft).
Weights: empty (IC) 18 556 lb (8417 kg); (X) 26 325 lb (11 940 kg); maximum loaded (IC) 25 800 lb (11 703 kg); (III) 29 500 lb (13 381 kg); (X) 36 500 lb (16 556 kg).
Performance: maximum speed (IC) 235 mph (379 km/h); (most other marks) 247–256 mph (410 km/h); (V,VI) 300 mph (483 km/h); initial climb (all, typical) 1050 ft (320 m)/min; service ceiling (bomber versions, typical) 22 000 ft (6710 m); (V, VI) 38 000 ft (11 600 m); range with weapon load of 1 500 lb (680 kg), typically 2 200 miles (3 540 km).

1 Forward navigation light
2 Two 0·303-in Browning machine guns
3 Frazer-Nash power-operated nose turret
4 Turret fairing
5 Parachute stowage
6 Bomb-aimer's control panel
7 Nose turret external rotation valve
8 Bomb-aimer's window
9 Bomb-aimer's cushion (hinged entry hatch)
10 Parachute stowage
11 Rudder control lever
12 Fuselage forward frame
13 Camera
14 Elevator and aileron control levers
15 Bomb-bay forward bulkhead (canted)
16 Cockpit bulkhead frame
17 Pilot's seat
18 Control column
19 Nose compartment/cabin step
20 Instrument panel
21 Co-pilot's folding seat
22 Windscreen
23 Hinged cockpit canopy section (ditching)
24 Electrical distributor panel
25 Aerial mast
26 R.3003 controls mounting
27 Tail unit de-icing control unit
28 Armour-plate bulkhead
29 Wireless-operator's seat
30 Wireless-operator's desk
31 Motor generator (wireless installation) and H.T. battery stowage
32 Bomb-bay doors
33 T.R.9F wireless unit crate
34 Aldis signal lamp stowage
35 Navigator's desk
36 Navigational instrument and map stowage
37 Navigator's seat
38 Folding doors (sound-proof bulkhead)
39 Fire extinguisher (on leading-edge fuselage frame)
40 Flying-controls locking bar ('nuisance bar') stowage
41 Wing inboard geodetic structure
42 Cooling duct exit louvre
43 Flame-damper exhaust tailpipe extension
44 Engine cooling controllable gills
45 Bristol Hercules XI radial engine
46 Exhaust collector ring
47 Three-blade Rotol electric propeller
48 Three-piece engine wrapper cowl
49 Carburettor air intake scoop
50 Engine mounting bearers
51 Starboard oil tank
52 Starboard nacelle fuel tank (58 Imp gal)
53 Wing forward fuel tank train (52 Imp gal, 263-l inboard, 55 Imp gal, 250-l centre, 43 Imp gal, 195-l outboard)
54 Twin-boom inboard wing spar
55 Wing aft fuel tank train (60 Imp gal, 272-l inboard, 57 Imp gal, 259-l centre, 50 Imp gal, 227-l outboard)
56 Fuel filler caps
57 Spar twin/single boom transition, 227-l
58 Pitot head piping
59 Cable cutters
60 Pitot head
61 Spar construction
62 Starboard navigation light
63 Starboard formation light
64 Aileron control rod stop bracket
65 Ball-bearing brackets
66 Starboard aileron
67 Aileron control rod
68 Aileron control articulated lever
69 Aileron trim tab control cable linkage
70 Aileron trim tab
71 Trim cables
72 Aileron control rod joint
73 Fuel jettison pipe

tougher, but the fat-bellied bombers were sitting ducks—especially when attacked with cannon beyond the range of their little 0·303 in Brownings, or attacked from abeam where the Wellington turrets could not aim. Before long ten bombers had been shot into the sea; nearly all the others were badly damaged. Never again did the RAF send 'heavies' in formation in daylight; indeed Bomber Command thereafter tried to operate mainly by night.

In 1940 deliveries began of the Wellington II with Merlins and the Mk III with the powerful sleeve-valve Hercules, followed by a modest 220 Wellington IVs with American Twin Wasps. The Mks V and VI were of intense technical interest because they had pressure cabins and very special high-blown engines (Hercules and Merlin, respectively) for operation at 40000 feet. These were among the first high-altitude pressurized aircraft, and RAF personnel learned in the hardest possible way how to solve the problems. Shirtsleeved crews today at that height would be amazed to discover the intensity of the difficulties. It took ten minutes to get in or out, and at the end of a mission everything inside would be frozen solid with thick ice from

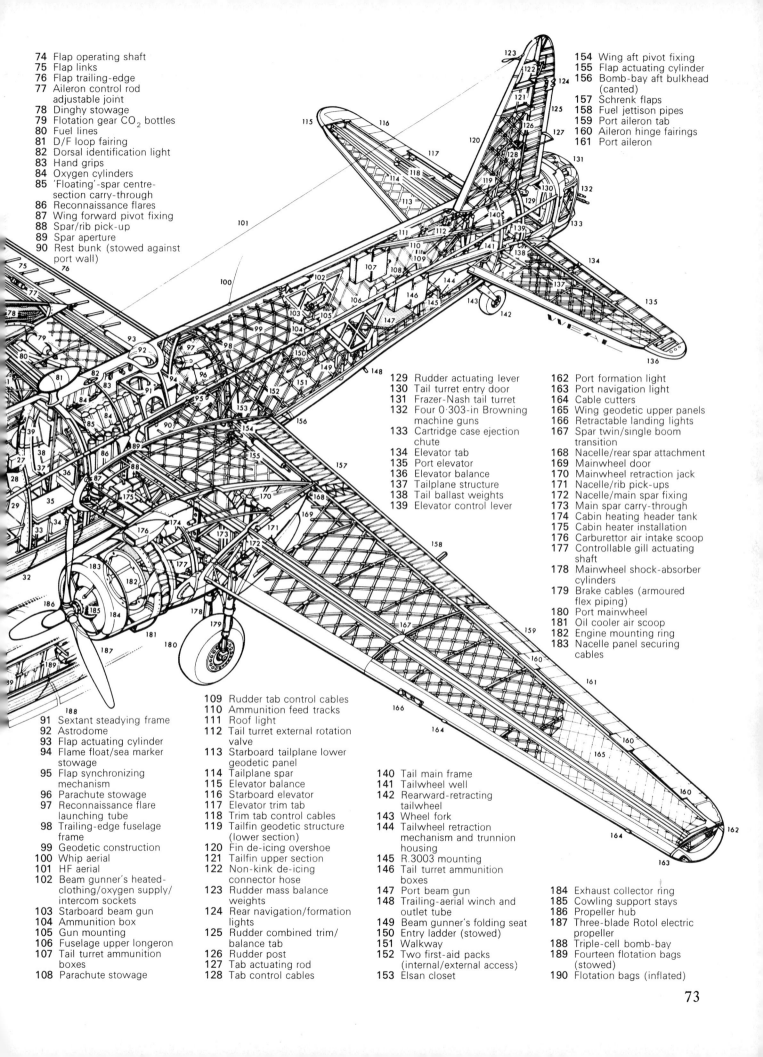

74 Flap operating shaft
75 Flap links
76 Flap trailing-edge
77 Aileron control rod adjustable joint
78 Dinghy stowage
79 Flotation gear CO_2 bottles
80 Fuel lines
81 D/F loop fairing
82 Dorsal identification light
83 Hand grips
84 Oxygen cylinders
85 'Floating'-spar centre-section carry-through
86 Reconnaissance flares
87 Wing forward pivot fixing
88 Spar/rib pick-up
89 Spar aperture
90 Rest bunk (stowed against port wall)

91 Sextant steadying frame
92 Astrodome
93 Flap actuating cylinder
94 Flame float/sea marker stowage
95 Flap synchronizing mechanism
96 Parachute stowage
97 Reconnaissance flare launching tube
98 Trailing-edge fuselage frame
99 Geodetic construction
100 Whip aerial
101 HF aerial
102 Beam gunner's heated-clothing/oxygen supply/intercom sockets
103 Starboard beam gun
104 Ammunition box
105 Gun mounting
106 Fuselage upper longeron
107 Tail turret ammunition boxes
108 Parachute stowage

109 Rudder tab control cables
110 Ammunition feed tracks
111 Roof light
112 Tail turret external rotation valve
113 Starboard tailplane lower geodetic panel
114 Tailplane spar
115 Elevator balance
116 Starboard elevator
117 Elevator trim tab
118 Trim tab control cables
119 Tailfin geodetic structure (lower section)
120 Fin de-icing overshoe
121 Tailfin upper section
122 Non-kink de-icing connector hose
123 Rudder mass balance weights
124 Rear navigation/formation lights
125 Rudder combined trim/balance tab
126 Rudder post
127 Tab actuating rod
128 Tab control cables

129 Rudder actuating lever
130 Tail turret entry door
131 Frazer-Nash tail turret
132 Four 0·303-in Browning machine guns
133 Cartridge case ejection chute
134 Elevator tab
135 Port elevator
136 Elevator balance
137 Tailplane structure
138 Tail ballast weights
139 Elevator control lever
140 Tail main frame
141 Tailwheel well
142 Rearward-retracting tailwheel
143 Wheel fork
144 Tailwheel retraction mechanism and trunnion housing
145 R.3003 mounting
146 Tail turret ammunition boxes
147 Port beam gun
148 Trailing-aerial winch and outlet tube
149 Beam gunner's folding seat
150 Entry ladder (stowed)
151 Walkway
152 Two first-aid packs (internal/external access)
153 Elsan closet

154 Wing aft pivot fixing
155 Flap actuating cylinder
156 Bomb-bay aft bulkhead (canted)
157 Schrenk flaps
158 Fuel jettison pipes
159 Port aileron tab
160 Aileron hinge fairings
161 Port aileron
162 Port formation light
163 Port navigation light
164 Cable cutters
165 Wing geodetic upper panels
166 Retractable landing lights
167 Spar twin/single boom transition
168 Nacelle/rear spar attachment
169 Mainwheel door
170 Mainwheel retraction jack
171 Nacelle/rib pick-ups
172 Nacelle/main spar fixing
173 Main spar carry-through
174 Cabin heating header tank
175 Cabin heater installation
176 Carburettor air intake scoop
177 Controllable gill actuating shaft
178 Mainwheel shock-absorber cylinders
179 Brake cables (armoured flex piping)
180 Port mainwheel
181 Oil cooler air scoop
182 Engine mounting ring
183 Nacelle panel securing cables
184 Exhaust collector ring
185 Cowling support stays
186 Propeller hub
187 Three-blade Rotol electric propeller
188 Triple-cell bomb-bay
189 Fourteen flotation bags (stowed)
190 Flotation bags (inflated)

73

No prizes are offered for guessing the location of these Wellington GR.XIV ocean patrol aircraft in 1943. The XIV, with Hercules XVII engines, was the ultimate Coastal Command version with ASV.III radar, retractable Leigh light and (not yet on these examples) eight underwing rockets. In the background are a gaggle of Martinet tugs and a Stringbag

the interior atmosphere. Any attempt to dry the air gave the crews rasping sore throats so that they could not speak. Flying controls froze solid, and oil leaking from a propeller hub froze on the blades and riddled the fuselage like bullets. Despite immense efforts these whale-like machines never became operational.

By this time the basic bomber was the Mk X, very similar to the III but fitted with Hercules giving 1675 hp. No fewer than 3804 of this mark were delivered, at a rate of approximately 200 per month. Hundreds served in regular Bomber Command squadrons on night missions over Germany, and on minelaying and many other missions. Meanwhile the less-powerful Mk I variants were rebuilt with grotesque radar installations, huge rings for detonating magnetic mines, strange torpedo or gun installations, bulged radomes, or multi-million candlepower Leigh lights, and used by Coastal Command to destroy U-boats and hit German shipping by day and night. Such aircraft received the mark numbers VIII, XI, XII, XIII and XIV, while

some of the in-between models were transports for airborne forces. Most of Coastal Command's machines were at first imperfect conversions, but the later models, especially the XIV, were first-class purpose-built aircraft with the powerful Hercules engine, advanced radar and much new search and attack equipment including four rocket projectiles under each outer wing.

Even as late as 1944 the Wellington X was almost as numerous in Bomber Command as the Lancaster or Halifax. It had only marginally lower performance, had the same four-gun turret, was easy to fly and maintain, and carried the 4000 lb light-case 'blockbuster' bomb which some of the four-engined machines could not. In theory at least Bomber Command machines also had beam guns aimed through side windows, while most four-engined heavies after the Halifax I had only the mid-upper turret, with poor vision underneath where a Luftwaffe night fighter was most likely to attack. Crews called the Wellington the Wimpey, after Popeye's friend J. Wellington Wimpey. Wimpeys set a remarkable record in flying more than 180000 operational missions against the enemy. Countless individual exploits of aircraft and crew-members deserve to be recorded, but none could surpass that of one Wellington that deliberately 'trailed its coat' in front of the Luftwaffe's new night fighters.

The RAF was desperately eager to find out about these hostile interceptors, and knew only that they carried a device called 'Emil-Emil' which helped them track down RAF bombers. Tests with special receivers in England showed that Luftwaffe aircraft were using a radio device operating on a frequency of 490 megahertz (490 million cycles), but the RAF needed to know if this was definitely Emil-Emil. So a Wellington IC went out on 3 December 1942 to try to find German night fighters. Alone, it cruised over Germany, tracked by the Freya radars on the ground and then by the Würzburg dishes that could give ground guidance to the night fighters. The six men in the Wellington knew that at any moment they might be riddled with cannon shells—and that is precisely what happened. As the Wimpey was shot through and through, the radio operator was transmitting back to England the details of the attack, and even the identity of the night fighter, a Ju 88. Remarkably, they managed to limp back to crash-land in the sea off Ramsgate, and all the crew lived although four were seriously wounded.

Another pioneer mission that called for great courage and skill was flown by a Wellington of the RAF Fighter Interception Unit (FIU) at Ford, Sussex, in 1944. What was a Wimpey doing at FIU, especially as late as 1944? Simply that the Wellington was an ideal aircraft in which to fit special equipment, such as new radars, either for research and operational trials or for training aircrew. It could carry almost anything, and was docile and nice to fly, especially if one was accustomed to its strange but endearing quirks. In August 1944 a white-painted radar-packed Wellington XI at FIU suddenly found itself engaged in tricky operations against the enemy. The Heinkels of III/KG3 were crossing the North Sea only just above the tops of the waves, burdened by 'V–1' flying bombs hung below the inboard left wing. The original missile sites in France had been overrun, and the lashup on the old Heinkel was a crude but effective substitute. In the dark the missile launchers were hard to find, and even harder to shoot down.

So FIU sent a Wellington out as a flying radar station in company with radar-equipped Mosquitoes. The Wimpey was able to use modified ASV (air to surface vessel) radar to spot the bombers as they came in hugging the sea. It was the first use of an AWACS (Airborne Warning and Control System). The Wellington crew were able to close with the target and give accurate guidance to the Mosquitoes in the pioneer example of airborne GCI (ground control of interception)—which is self-contradictory! The method had many successes, and a target in pitch darkness just above the sea travelling at not much above the stalling speed of a banking Mosquito suddenly ceased to be safe from interception.

After the Second World War many Wellington Xs were converted as unarmed crew trainers and designated Wellington T.10. The last of 11461 Wimpeys was retired in 1953. It was also the last Geodetic aircraft because Vickers had only limited success with the larger Warwick and none with the very advanced Windsor. Fabric covering was not right for later, faster machines; but it was fine for the reliable Wimpey.

N2887 was a Weybridge-built Mk IA, with Pegasus engines. It survived operations and is seen here with the Central Gunnery School in early 1943. A few months later it started yet another career rebuilt as an unarmed Mk XV transport. Some transport Wimpeys had turrets painted on; it just might have made all the difference

W5795 was the prototype Wellington VI, one of the strange whale-like high-altitude models which never went into service. The pilot's Perspex pimple, projecting above the pressurized crew-capsule, can just be seen between the propeller blades. Engines were two-stage Merlin 60s

Bristol Blenheim

It was partly due to curiously motivated British editors but mainly to a most reactionary outlook by both the RAF and Imperial Airways that Britain, the first country ever to build an aircraft entirely of stressed-skin construction (in 1920), should in 1934 have no such aircraft in use or even contemplated. Virtually every machine in the RAF or Imperial Airways had fabric covering, and except for a handful of research or long-range experimental aircraft, all the military types were biplanes. How long this state of affairs might have continued is interesting to contemplate, and even the Hurricane began life with a fabric covering. But in March 1934 the newspaper magnate Lord Rothermere asked the Bristol Aeroplane Company to build him a comfortable executive machine faster than any other civil aircraft in Europe (what he really meant was 'faster than any in America'). The resulting Bristol 142 reached 307 mph in 1935, compared with the 255 mph of the Gladiator, the RAF's next-generation fighter which did

not begin to reach the squadrons until two years later.

The Bristol directors had been reluctant to build the Type 142, because—believe it or not —they were afraid a modern aircraft might offend the Air Ministry, their best customer. This could well have happened, but in fact the Air Staff and Air Ministry were, in 1934, just beginning to notice that the world was not standing still around them, and that in Europe there were aircraft being built as fast and almost as advanced in design as in the far-off United States. (And they did not even know about the bombers in the Soviet Union, which included the SB–2, the best of the lot.) So instead of being offended Bristol's best customer showed great interest. The Air Ministry actually bought a Northrop monoplane from the Americans to learn about the British-invented stressed-skin construction, and was delighted when Lord Rothermere, having got more press coverage for his newspapers than at any other time since 1918,

K7033, apparently seen here at Martlesham Heath, was the Blenheim prototype. In fact the first Blenheim was merely the first off the production line, because the Bristol 142 had explored most of the problems. Some of the initial batch had dual control yet, as related in the text, pupils found difficulty in accepting such a 'modern' aircraft

As there were no deliberate gaps in pre-war numbering, this Mk I can safely be described as No 27 off the Filton production line. It was photographed by John Yoxall of Flight *on a visit to 90 Sqn at Bicester in 1937. The dorsal turret is in the fully raised position*

presented the 142 to the Air Council after naming it *Britain First*.

It is almost beyond belief that the Air Ministry should have been unaware of the existence of the 142 in 1934, but nothing was done about a military version until the aircraft had flown a year later. Then Bristol were asked to prepare a study for a bomber version, and in July 1935 Capt Frank Barnwell, chief designer, showed how he would turn the 142 into the 142M, with pilot and nav/bomb-aimer in the short glazed nose, with a Browning machine gun

fixed to fire ahead, a bomb bay under a wing raised to the mid-position, and a retractable machine-gun turret on the rear fuselage. The result was Specification B.28/35 and an order for 150 aircraft, with the name Blenheim. By this time-wasting and circuitous method did Britain get its first modern military aircraft of the 1930s, and comparison with the Hawker Hind light bomber is interesting. The Hind, first flown in September 1934 and delivered to the RAF from December 1935 until September 1938, carried a 500 lb bomb load at a maximum speed of 163 mph (186 mph clean) for a range of 430 miles. The Blenheim I carried a 1000 lb load at up to 285 mph for 1125 miles. This performance seemed so good that the fact that the armament, one fixed and one movable machine gun, was no better than the Hind's seemed immaterial.

A major factor in the advance of British aviation technology at this time was Roy Fedden, the forceful chief designer of Bristol engines. He had almost singlehandedly forced through the licence-manufacture of American variable-pitch propellers, which had made a difference of almost 30 mph to *Britain First*. His insistence on 100-octane fuel had added almost 50 per cent to the power of the Mercury engines used in the Blenheim, from 640 to 905 hp, and his recognition that the RAF could not fight a war on vegetable oil bulldozed through type-tests of all the new engines on mineral oil. By no means least, when he had needled and prodded until the Government at last had to pull its head right out of the sand and undertake a crash programme of expansion, the Air Staff turned to Fedden. He masterminded the entire Shadow Programme under which the Air Ministry created new factories that were 'shadows' of the Bristol plant, right down to the finest details of tooling and manufacturing techniques. The first choice for Shadowing was the 840 hp Mercury VIII used in the Blenheim I, and six Shadow Factories were built at Bristol and in the Midlands, to be operated by the established car companies. The Blenheim I was also ordered from A. V. Roe Ltd

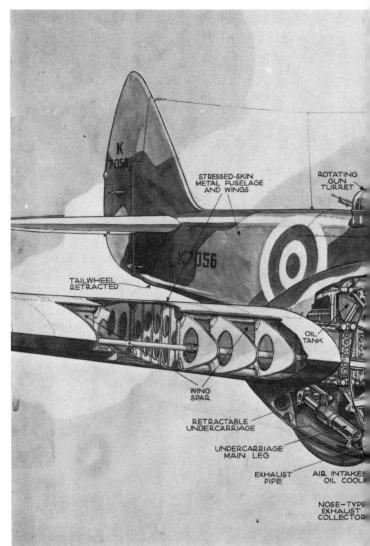

STRESSED-SKIN METAL FUSELAGE AND WINGS

ROTATING GUN TURRET

TAILWHEEL RETRACTED

OIL TANK

WING SPAR

RETRACTABLE UNDERCARRIAGE

UNDERCARRIAGE MAIN LEG

EXHAUST PIPE

AIR INTAKES OIL COOLER

NOSE-TYPE EXHAUST COLLECTOR

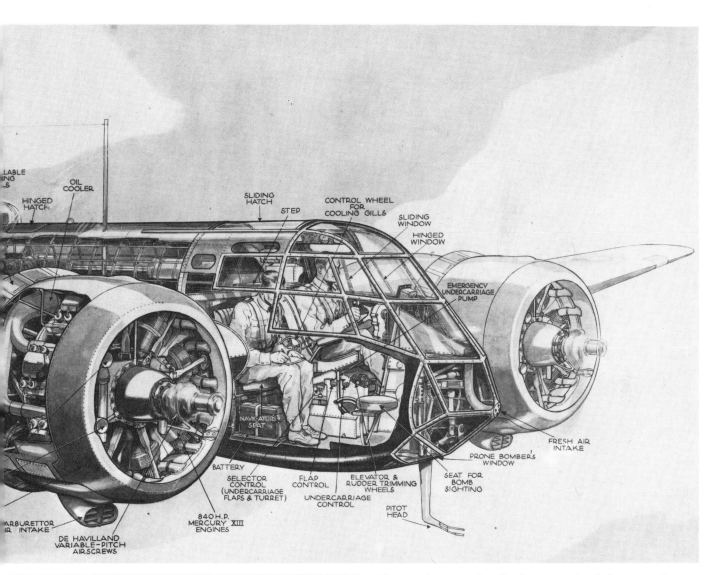

Labels visible on cutaway illustration:

LABLE ING S · HINGED HATCH · OIL COOLER · SLIDING HATCH · STEP · CONTROL WHEEL FOR COOLING GILLS · SLIDING WINDOW · HINGED WINDOW · EMERGENCY UNDERCARRIAGE PUMP · FRESH AIR INTAKE · PRONE BOMBERS WINDOW · SEAT FOR BOMB SIGHTING · PITOT HEAD · ELEVATOR & RUDDER TRIMMING WHEELS · UNDERCARRIAGE CONTROL · FLAP CONTROL · SELECTOR CONTROL (UNDERCARRIAGE FLAPS & TURRET) · BATTERY · NAVIGATORS SEAT · 840 H.P. MERCURY XIII ENGINES · DE HAVILLAND VARIABLE-PITCH AIRSCREWS · ARBURETTOR IR INTAKE

Above: *An exceptionally fine example of the pen and watercolour wash style of cutaway that was popular between the wars. Obviously Max Millar was not allowed even to hint at the bomb load, nor the fuel tankage or the fixed gun in the left wing. Incidentally, how strange that these bombers should have had variable-pitch propellers three years before any were supplied for RAF fighters!*

V6083 was one of a batch of 800 Blenheim IVL bombers delivered in 1941 from the Roots Securities shadow plant at Blythe Bridge. Fractionally more chance of survival was afforded by the twin-gun dorsal and chin turrets

SPECIFICATIONS

Types 142 M, 149 and 160 Blenheim/Bisley/Bolingbroke (data for Blenheim IVL)
Engines: two 920 hp Bristol Mercury XV (I, Bolingbroke I, II, 840 hp Mercury VIII; Bolingbroke IV series, 750–920 hp Twin Wasp Junior, Cyclone or Mercury XX; Blenheim V, 950 hp Mercury XXX)
Dimensions: span 56 ft 4 in (17·17 m) (V, 56 ft 1 in); length 42 ft 9 in (13 m) (I, 39 ft 9 in; Bolingbroke III, 46 ft 3 in; V, 43 ft 11 in); height 12 ft 10 in (3·91 m) (Bolingbroke III, 18 ft).
Weights: empty 9790 lb (4441 kg) (I, Bolingbroke III, 8700 lb; V, 11000 lb); loaded 14400 lb (6531 kg) (I, 12250 lb; Bolingbroke 13400 lb; V, 17000 lb).
Performance: maximum speed 266 mph (428 km/h); (I) 285 mph; (early IV) 295 mph; (Bolingbrokes and V) 245–260 mph; initial climb 1500 ft (457 m)/min (others similar); service ceiling 31500 ft (9600 m) (others similar except Bolingbroke III, 26000 ft); range 1950 miles (3138 km); (I) 1125 miles; (Bolingbrokes) 1800 miles; (V) 1600 miles.

at Chadderton, and Rootes Securities was formed to set up a gigantic Shadow Factory at Speke, Liverpool, where output eventually passed the one-a-day of Bristol's Filton factory. After the outbreak of war Rootes built a further Shadow plant at Blythe Bridge, Staffs, and pushed output to three a day.

The Bristol 142M Blenheim prototype (L7033) flew on 25 June 1936. At this small beginning, the Blenheim was still a company private venture, never asked for in any Air Ministry forward planning but pushed under the RAF's nose. The Air Ministry agreed that, once the

with short grass airfields, but its supposed complexity, fast takeoff and landing, and absolute newness posed terrible psychological difficulties for an RAF brought up on technology absolutely unchanged since 1918. The first aircraft to reach the service, delivered to 114 Sqn at Wyton in March 1937, cartwheeled and was destroyed on landing. Before the outbreak of war more than 100 Blenheims had been written off in accidents, almost all due to a difficulty in accepting it as an ordinary and safe aircraft (much the same happened in 1941–43 in the United States when numerous B–26

Apart from a bleached specimen at Kufra Oasis (probably long ago melted down and turned into tourist souvenirs) the only Blenheim in the world is BL–200, the last of 55 built in Finland, and preserved at Luonetjärvi. The right wing is hardly the original shape

immediate RAF need (supposed then to be 150 aircraft) had been met, Bristol could sell the Blenheim abroad. The result was a series of major export contracts, and Finland and Jugoslavia also built the Blenheim under licence. Canada adopted a later model as the Bolingbroke for coastal reconnaissance with the RCAF, with licence production by Fairchild. One of the strangest of all Britain's aircraft exports took place in November 1939 when the British Government ordered British ferry pilots to deliver 13 Avro-built Blenheims to Romania, to keep that country on the Allied side. The Romanians took the Blenheims and soon afterwards joined the Axis.

In the 1930s the Blenheim was what in today's Americanized idiom would be called 'a hot ship' It could, in fact, have been wholly compatible

Marauder crews perished because they had heard that the type was dangerous and called the Widow-maker—so they crashed).

In 1936 Air Ministry issued a specification, 11/36, for an interim coastal reconnaissance aircraft. Bristol built a long-nosed Blenheim called Bolingbroke, but chief test pilot Uwins did not like the windscreen so far ahead. The result was a machine with a curious asymmetric nose with a proper nav/bomb-aimer compartment on the right side but the original pilot windscreen, and this was renamed Blenheim IV. Later batches had greater fuel capacity, so more power was needed and 920 hp Mercury XV engines were fitted. By 1939 production had switched entirely to this much better and slightly faster version, which soon became more sluggish with the addition of a twin-gun dorsal turret, twin-gun under-nose turret (firing aft, sighted by the nav/bomb-aimer), armour, self-sealing tanks, short-wave radio including IFF, and other much-needed items that had been overlooked previously.

At the start of the Second World War the RAF still had 1007 Blenheim Is, making it just second to the Battle in numerical importance. Like the single-engined Fairey aircraft it still seemed a formidable modern bomber, and on the very day the war began one gallant crew of 139 Sqn went out from Wyton and photographed the German Fleet. Bombing German land was

airborne radar, fitted from July 1939. But bitter experience demonstrated that the Blenheim could not operate against the Luftwaffe without suffering unacceptable losses. Dozens of squadrons flew out to North Africa, India, the Far East, Iraq, Greece and many other hot spots. In the weeks following the German invasion of the Soviet Union, in the summer of 1941, up to six squadrons of Blenheims made gallant day-light bombing raids as far as Cologne (and most got back!) to keep up pressure from the West and try to prevent Luftwaffe units leaving for the Russian Front. Elsewhere Blenheims were

Another pleasant view of V6083 (Mk IVL) showing the square shape of the aft-facing chin turret.
This particular aircraft is seen with the code-letters of No 18 Sqn, which had Blenheims for five busy years and saw its effectiveness decline annually

not allowed, and the next day ten Blenheims and eight Wellingtons bombed the pocket battleship *Admiral von Scheer* from mast height. Four Blenheims were shot down. At least this showed that, unlike the fumbling and frustrating attempts at early night bombing, they found the target; but German records showed that only eight bombs hit the warship and six failed to explode.

In the Phoney War of 1939–40 the Blenheim IV was the busiest aircraft in the RAF, for six squadrons (18, 53, 57, 59, 114 and 139) were in France, flying long reconnaissance missions over Germany and back to Britain, while other units tried to put dents in the German Fleet. Although outside the scope of this book, the Blenheim had also become the RAF's first long-range fighter, with four fixed Brownings and the world's first

flown by pilots of many nationalities—those of Finland and Romania, of course, being on 'the wrong side'—their longest and toughest campaign being in India and Burma.

The final variants were a close-support version with a ton of armour and fixed guns, called Bisley I, which did not go into production, and the tropicalized Blenheim V, which did. Powered like the Bisley by 950 hp Mercury XXX engines, the Mk V made at Blythe Bridge had much better protection than earlier models, but was slower in consequence, and one of the last daylight missions in the European theatre was by ten Mk Vs in December 1942, over Tunisia, from which only one, shot to pieces, returned. Of course, 60 Bf 109Gs against ten Blenheims was a bit unfair, and something not anticipated in 1936.

Top: *Outwardly indistinguishable from the B–29 built by the other three plants, the B–29A had a much greater fuel capacity and gross weight raised from 124000 to 141000 lb. All the 1119 Superforts built at Renton were A-models*
Bottom: *A Renton armourer checking a B–29A rear ventral barbette, surely the neatest possible package with such accurately aimed firepower. Drag of these installations was one-eighth that of the B–17 ball turret*
Top right: *Final flight-line check on 42–93844, another Renton-built B–29A. In its day this was an exceptionally large, powerful and heavy aircraft, yet it is far outstripped in all respects by today's 737, the baby of Boeing's present range*
Below right: *The 35th B–29A to be built at Wichita, this was one of the first production batch which were painted; all subsequent Superforts were natural metal*

Junkers Ju88

At the outbreak of the Second World War the Ju 88 was just coming into service with the Luftwaffe. A year later 88s were lying all over southern England, and when Sir Peter Masefield found one with four quite separate machine guns all intended to be aimed by one man—and even the Master Race had only two hands—he wrote, 'structurally the Ju 88 is good, but militarily it is just a hotch-potch of ideas, not all of them good ideas'. Today a lot of water has gone under the bridge, and I myself had a shock when, in 1946, I was fortunate enough to fly a captured 88 for myself. A considered judgement today must be that it was one of the great warplanes of history. Unlike every other German bomber of the 1930s, it did not swiftly become obsolescent but went from strength to strength. This was partly through sheer force of circumstance; in 1945 the new 88 versions were as formidable in several roles as anything in the sky.

The aircraft had its genesis in the 1935 *Schnellbomber* (fast bomber) specification which concentrated solely on high-speed level and dive-bombing. It was a challenging specification, calling for 'the speed of a fighter', 500 kmh (311 mph), and exactly like the thinking of de Havilland that led to the development of the Mosquito, although the Germans did ask for a single, defensive machine gun. The rival Focke-Wulf company, having scored a zero with the earlier Fw 57, declined to submit a design, and the Henschel Hs 127 and Messerschmitt Bf 162 soon fell by the wayside. The Ju 85 with twin fins progressed to the Ju 88 in March 1936 and the Ju 88 V1 eventually emerged from the expanding Dessau plant in a remarkably short time on 8 December 1936, flying on the 21st of that month.

A key factor from the start was that Heinrich Koppenberg, who took over the vast Junkers empire when its great anti-Nazi founder was removed in 1934, was insistent that Junkers designs should abandon corrugated sheet metal in favour of stressed-skin airframes. He hired two Americans, W. H. Evers and Alfred Gassner, to prod his stressmen day and night

Top: *A 1941-style Ju 88 of the series between A–4 (which it probably is) and A–17. It has factory/second-line code GB/OE and has yet to reach a combat unit, or be painted with a coloured theatre band*
Above: *In contrast, this Ju 88, probably an A–6, is highly operational, and wears one of the tropical colour schemes and the white band denoting the Mediterranean theatre. It is probably in Tunisia with KG54*

into building a truly advanced airframe, and that of the first prototype was recognizably similar to that of the 15000th Ju 88 eight years later. This production total was more than double that of any other German bomber, and was exceeded by only two other bombers in history, the B–17 and B–24. But perhaps the Ju 88 cheated because 40 per cent were fighter versions.

Powered by 1000 hp DB 600Aa engines, the first Ju 88 crashed, but the third introduced the company's own Jumo 211 engine, the fourth had the definitive front end with seats for a crew of four in close proximity (where they were supposed to improve each other's morale), and the fifth took on the shape of a record-breaker and in March 1939 flew a 1000 km (621·4-mile) circuit at 321·25 mph with a useful load of

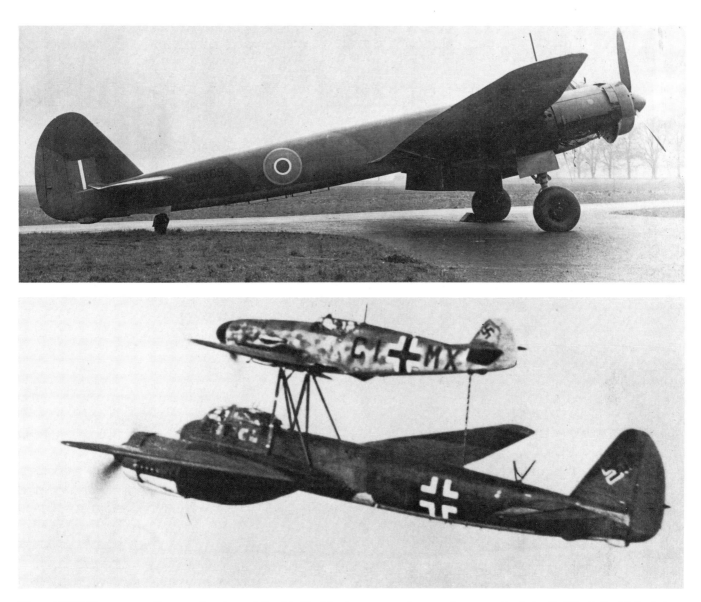

Top: *HM509 was one of a growing fleet of flyable Ju 88s that were taken on the strength of the RAF. A Ju 88A–5, it landed by mistake at Chivenor, Devon, in perfect condition*
Immediately above: *One of the very few air-to-air photographs of a Mistel combination. That shown is the original prototype, tested at the DFS in early 1943, comprising a Bf 109F–4 on a Ju 88A–4*

2000 kg (4409 lb). This was beyond the capability of any non-Soviet bomber at that time, and also beyond that of the standard 88, which at less than gross weight could not exceed 280 mph and thus did not even meet the original specification. Various small delays held back delivery of the Ju 88A–0 pre-production batch until just before the invasion of Poland, and the first Ju 88 unit, I/KG 30, did not become operational until 26 September 1939.

Walking round the A–1, the first production version, one was struck by the length of the single legs of the landing gears, which put the nose 15 feet off the ground. These legs contained unique shock absorbers in the form of a stack of steel ring-springs which used mutual friction to damp the rebound. The generous tyres, which when retracted rotated 90° on the legs to lie flat under the unbroken lower wing skins, enabled the 88 to operate throughout the war from fields that on the Eastern Front were often quagmires, despite gross aircraft weights that rose eventually to over 34000 lb. The cockpit was not as cramped as that of the Blenheim but the general feeling was matey, with the pilot high on the left, navigator close on the right or prone when bomb-aiming, the flight engineer just behind the pilot and manning the upper rear gun, and the radio operator on the right, from where he could squeeze down to man the lower rear gun at the back of the bomb-sight gondola. By far the most impressive feature was the bomb load: up to 5284 lb, mostly carried internally though each of the four large racks under the inner wings could carry up to 1102 lb.

Early 88s were far from perfect. With maximum

85

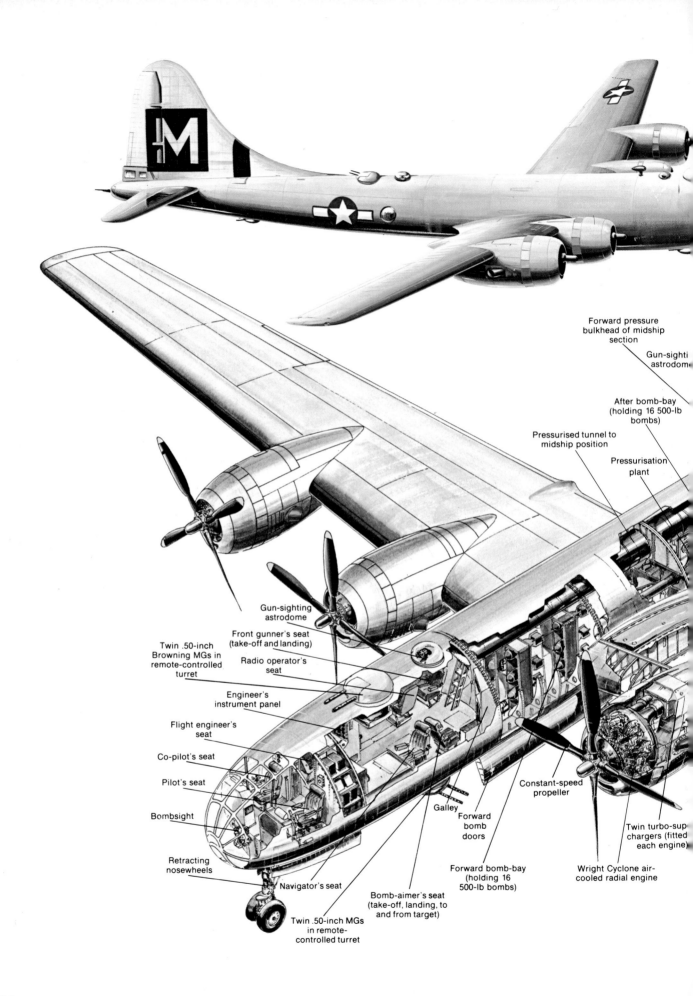

Forward pressure
bulkhead of midship
section

Gun-sighti
astrodom

After bomb-bay
(holding 16 500-lb
bombs)

Pressurised tunnel to
midship position

Pressurisation
plant

Gun-sighting
astrodome

Front gunner's seat
(take-off and landing)

Radio operator's
seat

Twin .50-inch
Browning MGs in
remote-controlled
turret

Engineer's
instrument panel

Flight engineer's
seat

Co-pilot's seat

Pilot's seat

Bombsight

Retracting
nosewheels

Navigator's seat

Galley

Forward
bomb
doors

Constant-speed
propeller

Twin turbo-sup
chargers (fitted
each engine)

Wright Cyclone air-
cooled radial engine

Forward bomb-bay
(holding 16
500-lb bombs)

Bomb-aimer's seat
(take-off, landing, to
and from target)

Twin .50-inch MGs
in remote-
controlled turret

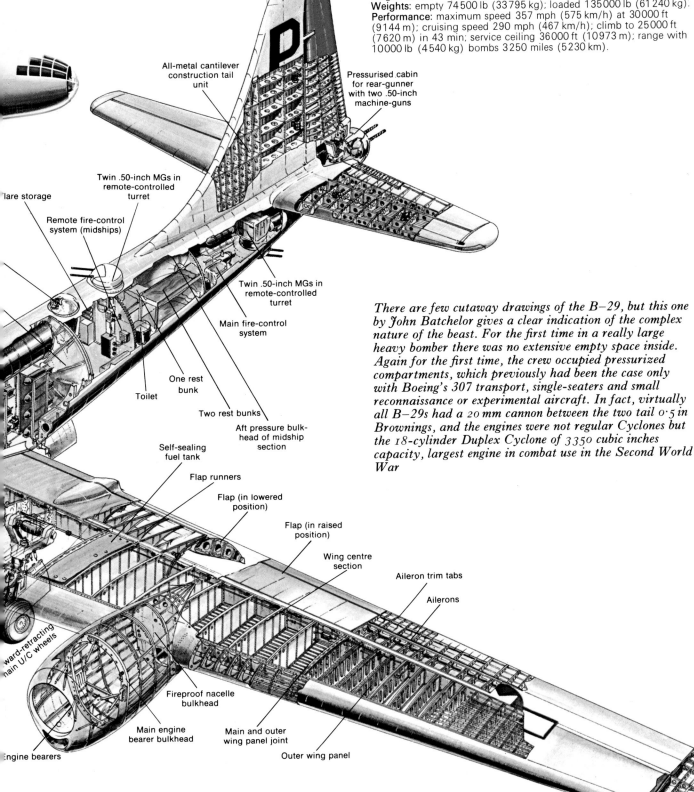

SPECIFICATIONS

Types 345, B–29 to –29C

Engines: four 2200 hp Wright R–3350–23 Duplex Cyclone 18-cylinder radials each with two exhaust-driven turbochargers.
Dimensions: span 141 ft 3 in (43·05 m); length 99 ft (30·2 m); height 27 ft 9 in (8·46 m).
Weights: empty 74 500 lb (33 795 kg); loaded 135 000 lb (61 240 kg).
Performance: maximum speed 357 mph (575 km/h) at 30 000 ft (9144 m); cruising speed 290 mph (467 km/h); climb to 25 000 ft (7620 m) in 43 min; service ceiling 36 000 ft (10 973 m); range with 10 000 lb (4540 kg) bombs 3250 miles (5230 km).

All-metal cantilever construction tail unit

Pressurised cabin for rear-gunner with two .50-inch machine-guns

Twin .50-inch MGs in remote-controlled turret

lare storage

Remote fire-control system (midships)

Twin .50-inch MGs in remote-controlled turret

Main fire-control system

One rest bunk

Toilet

Two rest bunks

Aft pressure bulk-head of midship section

Self-sealing fuel tank

Flap runners

Flap (in lowered position)

Flap (in raised position)

Wing centre section

Aileron trim tabs

Ailerons

ward-retracting ain U/C wheels

Fireproof nacelle bulkhead

Main engine bearer bulkhead

Main and outer wing panel joint

Outer wing panel

ngine bearers

There are few cutaway drawings of the B–29, but this one by John Batchelor gives a clear indication of the complex nature of the beast. For the first time in a really large heavy bomber there was no extensive empty space inside. Again for the first time, the crew occupied pressurized compartments, which previously had been the case only with Boeing's 307 transport, single-seaters and small reconnaissance or experimental aircraft. In fact, virtually all B–29s had a 20 mm cannon between the two tail 0·5 in Brownings, and the engines were not regular Cyclones but the 18-cylinder Duplex Cyclone of 3350 cubic inches capacity, largest engine in combat use in the Second World War

bomb load, take-off was fraught and protracted, and the A–2 had assisted-take-off rocket attachments. Out-of-the-ordinary manoeuvres were forbidden, and there were structural failures both in the air and on landing. With full bomb load it was difficult to exceed 248 mph, and not only was the standard 60° dive attack dangerous, but the large, slatted dive brakes tended to fail. In a society with a 'free' press the 88 would have been the subject of damning articles such as today are written about aircraft suffering no more than routine development problems. What such 'instant' experts might not have wished to understand was that the 88 was at the start of its career, a career possibly more complex in terms of technical development than any other aircraft in history. At least 102 separate prototypes were built, and some of these eventually became quite different aircraft with such numbers as 188 or 388, or test-beds for the 288 which had little in common with the others, other than the last two digits of its number.

This development process began with the A–4 of early 1940 (discounting the A–3, an A–1 with side-by-side dual controls for training), which introduced a new structure with greater strength, a longer-span wing, 1350 hp Jumo 211J engines, metal-skinned ailerons inset from the tips, and a maximum bomb load of no less than 7280 lb, though this was seldom carried. Delays with the new engine caused production first to switch to the interim A–5, which was an A–1 with the new wing. The Battle of Britain saw the real blooding of the 88, the A–1 and A–5 being present in numbers, and production by an extensive network of subcontractors and assembly plants had already reached the level of 300 per month. The A–5, no longer subject to flight restrictions, proved by far the most durable of all the Luftwaffe bombers. Its manoeuvrability was in a class by itself, and in a steep dive it often outdistanced Spitfires. The highly restricted A–1, however, suffered substantial losses, and it was in an attempt to find an answer to this that the poor flight engineer was

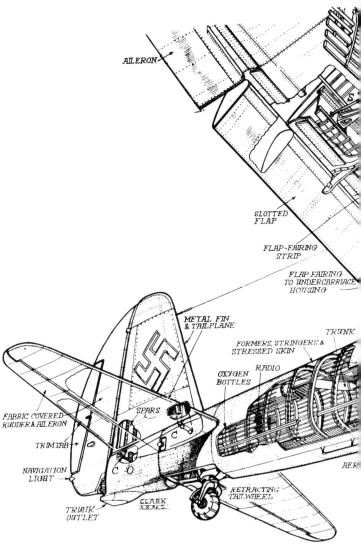

Considering the circumstances under which it was drawn, this cutaway by J. H. Clark is outstanding, and it has a style that—except for the use of seriffed capitals for the keyed items—still looks modern. The subject is the original short-span A–1 model, and the illustration was prepared from inspection of a single wreck

SPECIFICATIONS

Types Ju 88A–4, C–6, G–7, S–1
Engines: (A–4) two 1340 hp Junkers Jumo 211J 12-cylinder inverted-vee liquid-cooled; (C–6) same as A–4; (G–7) two 1880 hp Junkers Jumo 213E 12-cylinder inverted-vee liquid-cooled; (S–1) two 1700 hp BMW 801G 18-cylinder two-row radials.
Dimensions: span 65 ft 10½ in (20·13 m) (early versions 59 ft 10¾ in); length 47 ft 2¼ in (14·4 m); (G–7, 54 ft 1½ in); height 15 ft 11 in (4·85 m); (C–6) 16 ft 7½ in (5 m).
Weights: empty (A–4) 17637 lb (8000 kg); (C–6b) 19090 lb (8660 kg), (G–7b) 20062 lb (9100 kg); (S–1) 18300 lb (8300 kg); maximum loaded (A–4) 30865 lb (14000 kg); (C–6b) 27500 lb (12485 kg); (G–7b) 32350 lb (14690 kg); (S–1) 23100 lb (10490 kg).
Performance: maximum speed (A–4) 269 mph (433 km/h); (C–6b) 300 mph (480 km/h); (G–7b) (no drop tank or flame-dampers) 402 mph (643 km/h); (S–1) 373 mph (600 km/h); initial climb (A–4) 1312 ft (400 m)/min; (C–6b) about 985 ft (300 m)/min; (G–7b) 1640 ft (500 m)/min; (S–1) 1804 ft (550 m)/min; service ceiling (A–4) 26900 ft (8200 m); (C–6b) 32480 ft (9900 m); (G–7b) 28870 ft (8800 m); (S–1) 36090 ft (11000 m); range (A–4) 1112 miles (1790 km); (C–6b) 1243 miles (2000 km); (G–7b) 1430 miles (2300 km); (S–1) 1243 miles (2000 km).

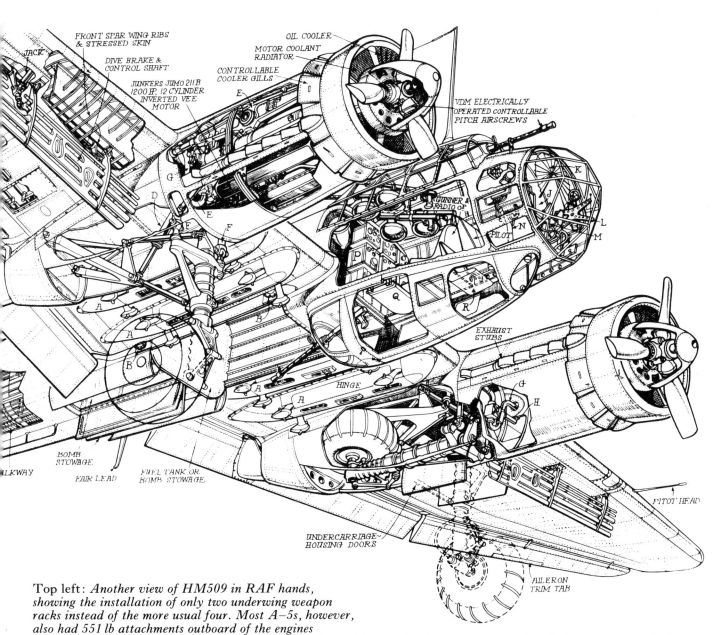

FRONT SPAR WING RIBS
& STRESSED SKIN

OIL COOLER

MOTOR COOLANT
RADIATOR

JACK

DIVE BRAKE &
CONTROL SHAFT

CONTROLLABLE
COOLER GILLS

JUNKERS JUMO 211 B
1200 H.P., 12 CYLINDER
INVERTED VEE
MOTOR

E

VDM ELECTRICALLY
OPERATED CONTROLLABLE
PITCH AIRSCREWS

G

D

E

F

K

J

GUNNER &
RADIO OP

PILOT

N

L

M

P

Q

R

EXHAUST
STUBS

A

HINGE

A

G

H

BOMB
STOWAGE

LKWAY

FAIR LEAD

FUEL TANK OR
BOMB STOWAGE

B

A

PITOT HEAD

UNDERCARRIAGE
HOUSING DOORS

AILERON
TRIM TAB

Top left: *Another view of HM509 in RAF hands,
showing the installation of only two underwing weapon
racks instead of the more usual four. Most A—5s, however,
also had 551 lb attachments outboard of the engines*
Below: *Forming the greatest possible contrast with the Ju 88A—1, this Jumo-powered Ju 188A—2 was photographed at
Farnborough in 1945 in the company of an even later Ju 88 descendant, the BMW-engined Ju 388L—1 with wooden
ventral pannier. These were mainly fine aircraft, and had Junkers not wasted so much effort on the Ju 288 they could
have been in service in 1942*

WE142 was one of a batch of 27 Canberra PR.3 photo-reconnaissance aircraft built by English Electric in 1953. Colour schemes went through several metamorphoses. The prototype Canberra was all-turquoise. Early production machines had green/grey camouflage above and black sides and undersurfaces, with white serial numbers. In 1952 the black changed to grey-blue (as seen on this aircraft), and in 1954—to fall into line with the Buzz-numbers of the USAF—the number was painted much larger, to be legible from a distance. WE139 of the same batch won the 1953 UK–New Zealand air race, averaging 495 mph for almost 12000 miles sometimes given four hand-held MG 15 guns to shoot with.

Learning the hard way, the A–4 had far superior defensive armament, typically comprising two 13 mm MG 131s and up to seven of the neat fast-firing MG 81 machine guns—all, however, aimed by hand. Some versions, such as the A–14, had a 20 mm MG FF cannon firing below and ahead for use against shipping, while the A–13 was converted from the A–4 for close-support duties with up to 16 machine guns firing ahead, plus 1102 lb of fragmentation bombs carried internally. The A–15 had a much-enlarged bomb bay, faired by a wooden structure, capable of carrying 6614 lb internally, while the A–17 carried two torpedoes plus special aiming equipment. A few standard A–4s were supplied to the Italian Regia Aeronautica and to Finland, while larger numbers served with Romania and Hungary on the Eastern Front.

The 88B had a much better front of the fuselage with lower drag and more room, but though acclaimed by crews in 1940 it was decided not to disrupt production by changing to this. Later, via the 88E with BMW radials and dorsal turret, this design led to the Ju 188. The Ju 88C was the first of many fighter versions, of which the most important were the various sub-types of C–6, some of which carried night-fighter radar. One model, the C–4, could have the awe-inspiring forward-firing armament of four 20 mm MG FF cannon, two MG 15s and 12 MG 81s, the latter in two six-gun pods on the wing racks. A common device with C-series fighters on the Russian front was to paint the glazed nose of the original bomber around the gun barrels, but whether this deceived Soviet pilots more than once is not known.

The D was a long-range reconnaissance model, and the first 88 to fly in the United States was a D–1/Trop, flown to Cyprus on 22 July 1943 by a defector from the Romanian Air Force; it was tested by the RAF, which by then had a whole squadron of 88s, and then shipped to Wright Field with the US number FE 1598. The G was an aircraft designed as a fighter from the start, and an outstanding aircraft in every respect. A deadly foe of RAF night 'heavies', it eliminated nearly all the shortcomings of earlier fighter versions and, instead of being a tricky and frightening machine, was pleasant to fly despite carrying SN–2 Lichtenstein (or later) radar, the Naxos which homed on bombers' H_2S radars, Flensburg which homed on Monica tail-warning radar, and many other devices including Bernadine ground guidance receivers intended to defeat British prowess with electronic counter-measures which were in use at the time.

The Ju 88H was a reconnaissance version with range considerably greater than that of the D, the fuselage being lengthened by almost 11 feet. The P was a diverse family of big-gun aircraft intended to deal with Soviet tanks, and though some showed promise the numbers in action were not large. For armament the basic P–1 had a monster 75 mm PaK 40, but the weight and length of this gun, combined with extensive armour, made this the slowest of all 88s (244 mph) and easy meat for fighters. The P–2 with two 37 mm BK 3·7s was often tested against USAAF bomber formations, while the P–4 with 50 mm BK 5 was used, though with little success, as a night fighter.

One of the faster 88s, outpaced only by the best of the G-series fighters which could reach 400 mph, was the S-series bomber in which bomb load, armament and armour were sacrificed to speed. Powered by the excellent 1730 hp BMW 801G–2 radial, with GM–1 (nitrous oxide) power boost, the S–1 could reach 379 mph in full combat trim, but carried only 14 SD 65 bombs of 143 lb each or, with consequent reduction in speed, two 2205 lb bombs on new external racks. Features included a smooth round nose and elimination of the ventral gondola, the armament being a single dorsal MG 131. The S–2 boldly added the cavernous wooden-faired bomb bay of the A–15, with 6614 lb capacity, and with 1810 hp BMW 801TJ turbo-charged engines the speed at high altitude nudged 400 mph. These were among the last bomber versions built, in mid-1944. A corresponding photo-reconnaissance type was the T-series which, without drop tanks, could reach 410 mph with the Jumo 213A engine which was used by some of the late-model G-series fighters.

This completes the list of basic variants, which were in the forefront of battle throughout the European theatre, fulfilled almost every conceivable military function (including that of transport, for there were several VIP or special-purpose communications variants) and probably achieved more in trying to defeat Hitler's enemies than any other single weapon including the Bf 109 and the Type VIIC U-boat. It was the most important Axis aircraft in the Mediterranean theatre to the end of the war, the most important offensive aircraft on the Eastern Front, the most important anti-shipping aircraft (KG 30 alone sank almost half of the ill-fated convoy PQ 17), and the most important night fighter, destroying more RAF bombers than all other NJG aircraft combined. It was also one of the very few types of Luftwaffe bomber that

dared raid Britain after the Battle of Britain, though it did so at its peril. In January 1944 the unfortunate *Angriffsführer England*, General-major Pelz, launched his entire force, mostly still equipped with the old 88A–4, against London. Two days later he struck again. Hardly any bombs fell on London and 57 aircraft were shot down. The kind of deadly opposition they met can be judged from the fact that in these attacks the RAF pilot, John Cunningham, and his navigator Rawnsley managed to shoot down a nimble Fw 190 at night with 20 rounds.

Increasingly in such a sky there was less and less place even for the tough, fast and courage-ously flown '*Acht und Achtzig*', which for recognition purposes was always called *die drei-finger 88* (three finger) because of its long, jutting engines. In 1943 the stage was set for the final act, and it was one of the strangest in air warfare. After successful trials with various aircraft mounted above DFS 230 gliders, to see if tugs were necessary, the Mistel (mistletoe) programme was launched in which a fighter was mounted on a pylon above a Ju 88. At first the 88s, mostly old and battle-worn A–4s, were used in training programmes without much modification. The first three S (*Schulung* i.e. training) versions were the S1, with a Bf 109F above an 88A–4, the S2, with an Fw 190A–8 above an 88G–1, and the S3, with an Fw 190A–6 above an 88A–6. The S3 had a disadvantage be-cause the Fw 190A–6 used 95-octane fuel and could draw none from the lower component as could other combinations. All were problematical,

for on take-off the design weight of the 88 was often exceeded and tyres burst, with disastrous results.

What was the point of the Misteln? Basically, it was a primitive form of air-to-surface missile, no cruder than the BQ–7 radio-controlled B–17 Fortress and, unlike the US scheme, there was no need for a human crew in the 88, even for take-off. The pilot of the fighter had complete control of both components, with buttons on his control column operating either the 88's rudder, ailerons or elevators, though in cruising flight he could disengage and let the combina-tion be steered by the bomber's two compasses and autopilot. Casting off, the fighter pilot could head for home or, in a few cases, retained radio control of the bomber. Normally the lower component was just left on autopilot in an engines-on shallow dive, pointing at the target. The operational version, code-named Beethoven, was a rebuilt Ju 88 with a monster 8380 lb hollow-charge warhead and long contact fuse in place of the crew compartment. There were actually three main operational versions, all with Fw 190s above either a G–1 or long-fuselage G–10 missile. A special unit, which became II/KG 200, was built up in strength in the autumn of 1944 awaiting Operation *Eisenhammer* (iron hammer) that was to demolish the Führer's enemies in one cataclysmic blow. In the event, the Misteln were frittered away in a succession of last-ditch attacks on tactical objec-tives, ships or bridges. And they could not have influenced the outcome of the war anyway.

Above: *Getting aboard a Canberra PR.7 of No 13 Sqn RAF, which was one of the last RAF units to be based in Malta. There is not one RAF pilot who would not love another chance to climb through that low door and spend an hour in the most effortless and forgiving of all jet bombers*
Top right: *This Day-Glo striped B.2 is a veteran Canberra doing a stint as a Silent Target at RAF West Raynham. Silent means emitting no electromagnetic signature by not using radio or radar. The operator is 85 Sqn, now a Bloodhound air-defence missile unit ; Silent Targets are now flown by 100 Sqn*
Right: *This colourful Canberra is a Venezuelan B(I).88, a B(I).8 completely refurbished and re-equipped. Venezuela uses four types of Canberra, including regular bomber, PR and training versions*

Handley Page Halifax

Right up to his death in 1962 Sir Frederick Handley Page was a caricature of the tycoon planemaker. Large, mean and generous, kindly and scathing by turns, he was one of the nearest things in modern times to a Roman emperor. It was tough working for him—especially as his own technical expertise, like his business sense, was profound—yet his chief designer from 1923 to 1945, George Volkert, outlasted him (by 15 years, to date). 'HP' is best remembered for his great early biplanes, bombers for the First World War and transports for Imperial Airways. Yet by far the most important of the company's aircraft was the Halifax, and this never gained the fame it richly merited. It was eclipsed by another bomber, the Lancaster.

Both Lancaster and Halifax were the result of P.13/36, a specification for a bomber of much less than half their capability. That Britain was able to mass-produce the two great four-engined bombers at the right time was pure luck, and the RAF could easily have found itself fighting the Second World War with aircraft of P.13/36 calibre. Indeed, when that specification was issued, on 8 September 1936, for a bomber capable of carrying an 8000 lb load at high speed (well over 200 mph was expected), and with a two-gun nose turret and four-gun tail turret, it was a dramatic advance over the fabric-covered biplanes Virginia and Heyford. Handley Page tendered to the new specification, along with Avro and, surprisingly, Hawker. All knew they had to offer all-metal stressed-skin construction; and there was only one engine in sight, the Rolls-Royce Vulture.

Though engines in the 1500–2000 hp class, were on the drawing board at Napier, Bristol, and Armstrong Siddeley, the Derby company had an edge in the assurance they could give that they could deliver on schedule. The Vulture was a liquid-cooled X-form engine with two sets of Peregrine cylinder blocks on a common crankcase. The Peregrine in turn was an advanced development of the well-proven Kestrel. All seemed set fair for whichever P.13/36 bomber was chosen; the winner would undoubtedly be by far the most advanced twin-engined warplane in the world. Unfortunately, however, the Vulture was to have so many problems that it was abandoned, as related in the chapter on the Lancaster. Handley Page had the foresight to drop it long before the problems were fully apparent.

Volkert already had a design for a new bomber: the B.1/35 specification had brought forth the H.P.55 (serial K8179) with two

The unarmed first prototype Halifax, seen in an official photograph (no background, of course) taken on 29 November 1939. Not visible in this view are the large slats, which were later judged to be unnecessary. Colour was dark green/dark earth/yellow

W7676 was the 17th of a 1941 batch of 200 Halifax IIs built by Handley Page. Though extremely impressive aircraft, they were a bit on the slow side and not very much better than the Stirling in climb and ceiling. Later the Halifax was improved out of all recognition

Hercules, Vulture or, at a pinch, developed Merlins. This was never built, the final winner in this case being the Warwick. Volkert accordingly scaled up the 55 to produce the H.P.56, choosing two Vultures. In April 1937 two prototypes were ordered (L7244 and 7245), but the ink on the order was hardly dry before Volkert and 'HP' agreed that the result was inadequate. Short Brothers were well ahead with a much bigger bomber, the Stirling, to the earlier B.12/36 specification. It had four Hercules engines, and the H.P.56 would be markedly inferior. 'HP' himself went to the Air Ministry and, like the feared debater he was, came away with the authority to switch to four Rolls-Royce Merlins. On paper there was no doubt whatever that the new four-engined machine, the H.P.57, would be superior to the 56. Gross weight could take a great leap from 26300 to 40000 lbs, and even so performance showed an all-round improvement.

On 3 September 1937 the two H.P.56 serial numbers were switched to prototypes of the new H.P.57, which was later named Halifax. Over the next two years it took shape as a warplane of formidable capability. In the view of the Air Staff the three new heavy bombers—discounting the Warwick—were to be rated: Stirling, No 1; Halifax, No 2; and Manchester, the Avro design that followed specification P.13/36, a poor No 3. In the final years of peace the Stirling increasingly came to be regarded as the bomber that would win any war against Hitler's Germany. However, though 2375 of the giant Stirlings were built, it was not a success, partly because its structure was too heavy, partly because its endless series of bomb bays could not be adapted for the monster light-case bombs of 4000 and 8000 lb size that had not been thought of before the war, and above all because to fit into existing hangars its span was limited to under 100 feet, and this crippled its performance. Thankfully, Britain did not have to rely on it.

In early 1938 an order was placed for 100 Halifax Is, to specification 32/37, closely followed by another 100 of the Mk II type, described later. Though it was not easy to appreciate it at the time, aircraft were already becoming too complex for the British industry's small companies, and though in the Second World War a half-million men and women on the shop floor were to perform prodigies of production, repair and modification, the desperate lack of engineers caused almost every design and development programme to run late. The Halifax was one of the first to experience these delays, and lateness almost became the norm in subsequent years throughout this hard-pressed industry. Incidentally, 'HP' laughed loudest of the critics of the Americans for needing so many engineers.

Eventually, on 25 October 1939, Major Cordes made a satisfactory first flight in L7244, which had no turrets and was painted Training Yellow underneath. The flight took place at Bicester, the sections having been trucked to this RAF airfield immediately on outbreak of war, because it was feared the Luftwaffe would bomb the Radlett factory. It took Handley Page ten months to get the second Halifax, with turrets fitted, flying, on 17 August 1940. But by this time the production line was really working, and the RAF No 35 Squadron was proudly taking deliveries from 23 November of the same year.

Powered by four 1280 hp Merlin X engines, driving Rotol constant-speed propellers, the Mk I Series I had as armament a two-gun Boulton Paul nose turret, a four-gun tail turret of the same make, and two hand-aimed beam guns aft of the wing. Gross weight was 55000 lb, maximum bomb load 13000 lb in cells in the fuselage and inner wing, and maximum speed 265 mph. There were many odd features. The five fuel cells in each wing could be emptied through surprisingly large jettison pipes, three under each wing, which discharged behind the slotted flaps; there were rubber joints under the flap hinge-axes. Under each Merlin were two circular coolant radiators and a central oil radiator, all inside a common duct of complex profile. Above the inboard engines were ram inlets leading via monster heat exchangers to large ducts supplying hot cabin air (most welcome on a ten-hour trip in winter). The Messier landing gears had enormous bridge structures cast from light alloy, while the big tailwheel was fixed, though it could easily have been designed to retract. Pilots remember the asymmetry of the flight-deck windows, as well as the bank of engine and propeller controls using patented Bloctube linkages. All seven crew stations had liberal provision of pale-greenish armour, and flying the big bomber was no problem at all.

98

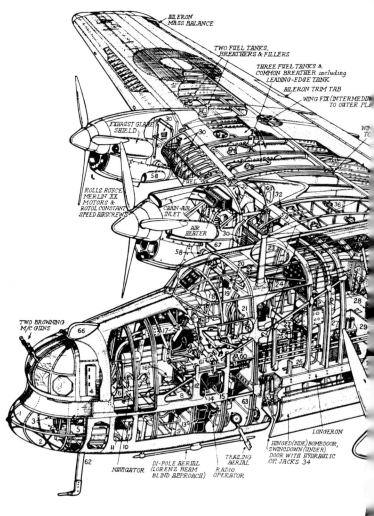

J. H. Clark drew this cutaway illustration of the Halifax II Series I in 1942. At that time the great Handley Page bomber had travelled quite a distance along the path of development, but it was to go many times further. In the structural detailing, bomb bays, fuel-jettison pipes, engine installations and many other areas it showed the philosophy of 1937, some of which persisted to the end of the programme

1 Navigation light
2 Bomb aimer's flat window
3 Bomb sight and arm rests
4 Turret balance flap
5 Bomb aimer's cushion
6 Hot-air hoses in spent cartridge tray
7 Navigator's folding seat
8 Navigator's table, lamp and chart
9 Camera stand
10 Parachute stowage
11 Gyro azimuth stand
12 Repeater compass
13 HT and LT units (radio)
14 Transmitting and receiving sets (radio)

15 Main electrical panel
16 Step-up to pilot's cockpit (parachute stowage underneath)
17 Main instrument panel, engine controls
18 Folding seats (second pilot and engineer)
19 Fuel cock controls
20 Motor starter buttons
21 Emergency flare releases
22 Sextant rest
23 Astro-dome
24 Engineer's instrument panel
25 Engineer's platform
26 Hot air to wireless operator (oxygen bottles nearby)

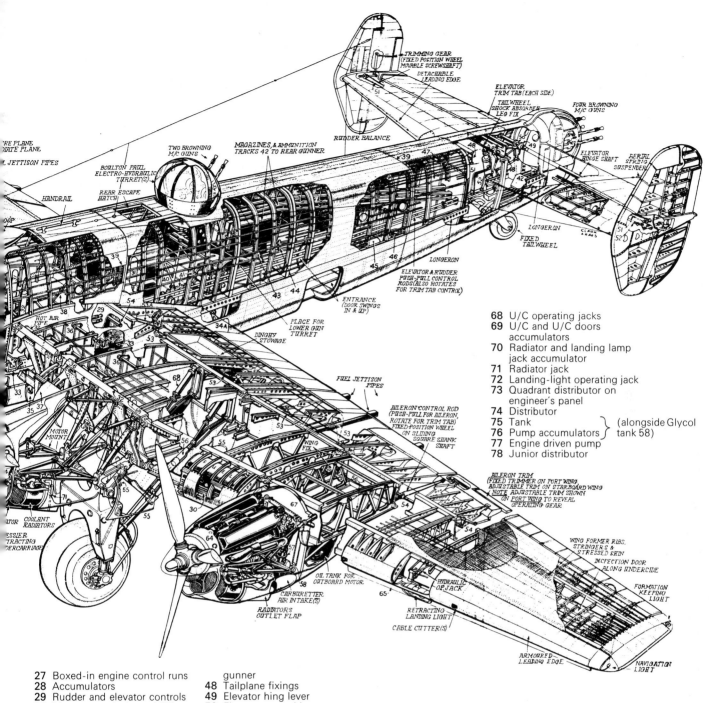

TRIMMING GEAR
(FIXED POSITION WHEEL
MOVABLE SCREWSHAFT)
DETACHABLE
LEADING EDGE

ELEVATOR
TRIM TAB (EACH SIDE)
TAILWHEEL
SHOCK ABSORBER
LEG FIX

FOUR BROWNING
M/C GUNS

ELEVATOR
HINGE SHAFT

AERIAL
SPRING
SUSPENDER

RUDDER BALANCE

TWO BROWNING
M/C GUNS

MAGAZINES, & AMMUNITION
TRACKS 42 TO REAR GUNNER

BOULTON PAUL
ELECTRO-HYDRAULIC
TURRET(S)

RE PLANE
DIATE PLANE

L JETTISON PIPES

REAR ESCAPE
HATCH

HANDRAIL

LONGERON

CLASS
AHEAD

LOOP

FIXED
TAILWHEEL

LONGERON

ELEVATOR & RUDDER
PUSH-PULL CONTROL
RODS (ALSO ROTATES
FOR TRIM TAB CONTROL)

HOT AIR
PIPE

ENTRANCE
(DOOR SWINGS
IN & UP)

PLACE FOR
LOWER GUN
TURRET

DINGHY
STOWAGE

FUEL JETTISON
PIPES

AILERON CONTROL ROD
(PUSH-PULL FOR AILERON,
ROTATE FOR TRIM TAB)
FIXED-POSITION WHEEL
ON SLIDING
SQUARE SHANK
SHAFT

WING
FIX

MOTOR
MOUNT

AILERON TRIM
(FIXED TRIMMER ON PORT WING,
ADJUSTABLE TRIM ON STARBOARD WING.
NOTE ADJUSTABLE TRIM SHOWN
ON PORT WING TO REVEAL
OPERATING GEAR)

COOLANT
RADIATORS

WING FORMER RIBS,
STRINGERS &
STRESSED SKIN

INSPECTION DOOR
ALONG UNDERCIDE

FORMATION
KEEPING
LIGHT

OIL TANK FOR
OUTBOARD MOTOR

CARBURETTER
AIR INTAKE(S)

RADIATORS
OUTLET FLAP

HYDRAULIC
OP JACK

RETRACTING
LANDING LIGHT

CABLE CUTTER(S)

ARMOURED
LEADING EDGE

NAVIGATION
LIGHT

SIER
TRACTING
DERCARRIAGE

68 U/C operating jacks
69 U/C and U/C doors
   accumulators
70 Radiator and landing lamp
   jack accumulator
71 Radiator jack
72 Landing-light operating jack
73 Quadrant distributor on
   engineer's panel
74 Distributor
75 Tank
76 Pump accumulators } (alongside Glycol tank 58)
77 Engine driven pump
78 Junior distributor

27 Boxed-in engine control runs
28 Accumulators
29 Rudder and elevator controls
30 Motor controls (out of 27)
31 Emergency hydraulic hand
   pumps and hydraulic
   accumulators
32 Hot air trunks from heater on
   inboard motors
33 Lower spar boom
34 Bomb door hinges and
   operating jacks
34a Rear hinge, no jack
35 Doors to wing bomb cells
36 Wing bomb door operating
   rods and jack
37 Leading edge section
38 Rest bunk each side
39 Jointing frames
40 Step up to turret
41 Flame floats and sea markers
42 Ammunition tracks
43 Flare chutes
44 Emergency axe stowage
45 Elsan lavatory
46 D/R compass
47 Bulkhead and door to tail

   gunner
48 Tailplane fixings
49 Elevator hing lever
50 Elevator control lever
51 Rudder trim controls
52 Rudder control rods
53 Flap controls and operating
   jack
53a Interconnecting wire (port to
   starboard flap)
54 Aileron controls
55 U/C doors and operating jack
56 Fuel tank supports
56a Undercarriage bungee device
57 Carburettor air intake
58 Glycol tank (airscrew
   de-icing)
59 Oil tank for inboard motor
60 Rudder trim
61 Aileron trim
62 Pressure head
63 Trailing aerial reel stowage
64 Glycol header tank
65 Inspecting door along wing
   leading edge
66 Cover for turret connections
67 Motor firewall

SPECIFICATIONS

Types H.P.57 Halifax I, H.P.59 Mk II Series 1A, III, H.P.61 Mk V, B.VI and VII, C.VIII and A.IX

Engines: four Rolls-Royce Merlin vee-12 liquid-cooled or Bristol Hercules 14-cylinder two-row sleeve-valve radial (see text).
Dimensions: span (I to early III) 98 ft 10 in (30·12 m); (from later III) 104 ft 2 in (31·75 m); length (I, II, II Srs 1) 70 ft 1 in (21·36 m); (II Srs 1A onwards) 71 ft 7 in (21·82 m); height 20 ft 9 in (6·32 m).
Weights: empty (I Srs 1) 33860 lb (15359 kg); (II Srs 1A) 35270 lb (16000 kg); (VI) 39000 lb (17690 kg), loaded (I) 55000 lb (24948 kg); (I Srs 1) 58000 lb (26308 kg), (I Srs 2) 60000 lb (27216 kg); (II) 60000 lb; (II Srs 1A) 63000 lb (28576 kg), (III) 65000 lb (29484 kg), (V) 60000 lb; (VI) 68000 lb (30844 kg); (VII, VIII, IX) 65000 lb.
Performance: maximum speed (I) 265 mph (426 km/h); (II) 270 mph (435 km/h); (III, VI) 312 mph (501 km/h); (V, VII, VIII, IX) 285 mph (460 km/h); initial climb (typical) 750 ft (229 m)/min; service ceiling, typically (Merlin) 22800 ft (6950 m); (Hercules) 24000 ft (7315 m); range with maximum load (I) 980 miles (1577 km); (II) 1100 miles (1770 km); (III, VI) 1260 miles (2030 km).

A study by Charles E. Brown of one of the first Halifax B.IIIs to have the increased-area fins that significantly reduced bombing errors and improved engine-out handling. It was by no means common to find the tailwheel retracted, but the Mk III was much faster than the old Merlin-powered models, and had better armament

Operations began in daylight, against the German battle-cruiser *Scharnhorst* and similar targets, but there were casualties and the RAF reluctantly learned that not even their four-engined heavies could expect to survive indefinitely in daylight. However, by 1942, when the night battle began in earnest, production was really rolling.

The Stirling dominance had faded and its crews, apprehensive at below 16000 feet, had begun to be able to buy life insurance once more as they were switched to paratrooping, glider towing and electronic countermeasures. The Halifax, however, went from strength to strength. Output was multiplied by the English Electric factory (Dick Kerr works) at Preston, Rootes shadow factory at Speke, Fairey Aviation at Stockport, and the London Aircraft Production Group which harnessed most of the workshops of London Transport, with final assembly at Aldenham. By 1943 the Halifax team numbered 51000, in 41 factories, producing new aircraft at the rate of almost one an hour.

This was despite the fact that—though one does not recall it that way—there was a vast multiplicity of types. Here is a simplified list.

Mk I Series II Stressed to gross weight of 60000 lb, but with original fuel capacity. Actual gross, 58000 lb.

Mk I Series III Additional fuel cells. Gross weight 60000 lb.

Mk II Series I 1390 hp Merlin XX engines, two-gun Boulton Paul (Hudson-type) dorsal turret instead of manual beam guns.

Mk II Series I (Special) Speed and ceiling had been adversely affected by the resistance of the dorsal turret and power-reducing flame-damping exhaust muffs added to all Halifaxes after the start of night operations. In this version the lost performance was more than restored by removing the muffs, the dorsal turret and the front turret, the nose simply being a painted metal fairing. Probably this should have been done on all RAF night bombers.

Mk II Series IA Nose replaced by more elegant streamlined cap of blown Perspex, with a single, manually aimed Browning. Merlin XXII engines with improved flame-damping exhausts and Morris block radiators in new low-drag cowlings (one aircraft had long inner nacelles extending behind the wing). Radio mast removed and aerial attached to D/F loop 'acorn'. Shallower astrodome. Retractable tailwheel. New paint finish with reduced drag. After first batch, new Boulton Paul (Defiant-type) four-gun dorsal turret. In final three batches, new rectangular fins of increased area to improve directional stability and hence bombing accuracy.

The sum of these changes was a dramatically better aircraft with cruising speed increased from 195 to 215 mph.

Mk III Bristol Hercules XVI 14-cylinder sleeve-valve radials of 1615 hp, driving DH Hydromatic propellers. Retractable tailwheel standard, together with H₂S ground-mapping radar in rear fuselage with ventral radome (H₂S was first tested in Halifax II V9977, but seldom fitted to Merlin versions). In third batch, wing span increased from 98 ft 10 in to 104 ft 2 in with rounded tips. The gross weight was 65000 lb and the change of engine and wing-span transformed the 'Halibag' and made it, in my opinion, superior in performance to the Lancaster, though perhaps not in economy and all-round efficiency. In September 1943 Halifaxes had been restricted to 'less-hazardous' targets, though I have yet to understand what this meant, because they went in force on every major Bomber Command mission. With the Mk III this restriction, such as it was, was removed.

Mk IV Research prototype for testing engine installations, including Elektron (magnesium) structures.

Mk V Series I (Special) and Series IA Similar to corresponding Mk II versions but with completely different Dowty hydraulics and landing gear, four-blade propellers and glider-tow cleat. Often 0·5 in manually aimed ventral gun—just what the basic bomber needed, but these aircraft were almost all used by Coastal Command for meteorological and anti-submarine duties!

Mk VI Self-contained power 'eggs' with 1800 hp Hercules 100 engines. Pressurized fuel system and tropical filters for use with Tiger Force in the Far East. Gross weight 68000 lb.

Mk VII Similar to VI but Hercules XVI engines because of shortage of Hercules 100s.

C.VIII Multi-role transport. Hercules XVI engines, no armament or combat equipment. Interior arranged for 11 passengers, 24 troops, ambulance duty (casevac) or freight. Detachable cargo pannier under former bomb bay with capacity of 8000 lb.

A.IX Airborne forces supply-drop transport. Hercules XVI engines. Interior arranged for 16 paratroops, with special airborne-forces equipment. Glider tow cleat. Boulton & Paul D-type tail turret with two 0·5 in guns.

Subsequently there were various special-role conversions and experimental variants, but these nine marks accounted for 6176 aircraft, two out of every five British 'heavies' produced during the Second World War. Partly because the rival 'Lanc' was the pre-eminent bomber operating

Immediately below: *Photographed in June 1945, LV838 was a rather rare bird, a C.VI. This was a cross between the high-performance B.VI bomber and the A.IX airborne-forces transport, and fitted with the freight container of the C.VIII!*

Bottom of page: *The prototype Halifax V, photographed in September 1942. This was similar to a late-series Mk II but with Dowty landing gear and hydraulics.*

Despite the long flame-damped exhausts, the B.VI was a splendid performer, markedly faster than standard Lancasters and very similar to its comrade-in-arms in most other areas.
This official portrait was taken on a dull day in October 1944

from Britain, the Halifax saw far more diverse service, in more places. Unlike the Lancaster it served extensively in the Mediterranean and Italy, in the Far East and India, and with many RAF commands other than Bomber Command. It was the standard bomber of the Canadian squadrons of 6 Group and the Free French squadrons of 4 Group. The GR.II, GR.V and GR.VI were key equipment of Coastal Command from 1942, and a GR.VI made the last RAF operational Halifax mission in March 1952.

Probably the Halifax's main career outside bombing was with airborne assault. From late 1942 hundreds of Mks III, V and VII were the chief British tugs for heavy gliders, and—after unsuccessfully trying Stirling IVs—the only tugs capable of towing the tank-carrying Hamilcar. Indeed even the old Mk II was used in this role in the first-ever long-distance glider assault, the epic mission to a heavy-water plant in south Norway on 19 November 1942. The Halifax was also by far the most important of all Allied long-range aircraft in the Special Duties role, flying clandestine missions to drop agents or other key loads all over Europe. Some of the very first batch of Mk I Halifaxes flew such hazardous missions in 1941 from Tempsford as far as Czechoslovakia. Modifications included a drop hole in the main floor, static lines for parachutes, and a fairing over the tailwheel to prevent a parachute hang-up.

After the Second World War there were yet further versions of this great aircraft, such as the Met.IX strategic weather aircraft and a whole collection of civil Halifaxes and its development, the Halton, which did tremendous work on the Berlin Airlift. But it would be misleading to suggest that the Halifax was used for so many tasks because it was inferior as a heavy bomber. It was a great bomber, and the original user, 35 Squadron, was also one of the pioneer Pathfinder units, using H_2S and Oboe to guide the main force that followed it to the target. The Halifax was also the most important aircraft of the legendary 100 Group, whose aircraft fought the secret war of electronics which helped the other bombers get through to their destinations.

Almost certainly taken at the Aeroplane & Armament Experimental Establishment at Boscombe Down, in March 1944, this picture shows HX226, the first production B.III which had flown nine months previously. The censor forgot to brush out the Stirling and Lancaster in the background

Consolidated-Vultee B-24 Liberator

The B–24 Liberator, like the Halifax, always ran second in fame to its partner in arms, in this case the B–17. But it was built in far greater numbers and in an even greater variety of versions for almost every duty one can imagine, apart from its main role as a bomber, including fighting, training and carrying heads of state in utmost luxury. To the pilot it was exciting, but a handful. Instead of being a sedate lady, as was the Fortress, it was distinctly demanding and needed flying all the time—unless, of course, one had a PhD and knew which of the myriad of switches and other controls would cut in the fabulous Minneapolis-Honeywell autopilot, that did things in 1942 that other aircraft seldom did until the 1950s!

The B–24 production programme was possibly the greatest aircraft-manufacturing effort in all history. Not in terms of money, because for the price of one modern fighter you could buy about 150 B–24s; but in technical effort, the multiplicity of parts needed and total weight of airframes, it is hard to find anything which can equal the feat of manufacturing, including spares, 19203 of these complicated machines. In fact, this total is greater than that of any other single type of American aircraft.

The B–24 was designed four years later than the B–17 Fortress, at a time of technical change even more rapid than usual, by a gifted team who lacked nothing in experience and facilities. Their prior bomber studies had been exhaustive. They knew all there was to be learned from the early B–17 and XB–15. They had already produced an extremely advanced flying boat, the Consolidated 31, that used the most efficient wing then in existence—the Davis wing—with the exceptional aspect ratio of 11·55, as long and slender as that of a championship sailplane. This wing, changed only to fit four engines instead of two, and to house landing gear instead of stabilizing floats, was the wing for the new bomber. The tail was the same, too. Everything seemed set for the greatest bomber the world had ever seen, and when, in January 1939, the newly appointed Commanding General of the US Air Corps, 'Hap' Arnold, told Consolidated to build a bomber that would 'fly the skin off any rivals' the company had little doubt that they could do just that.

Yet the odd thing is that, when the B–17 and B–24 were thundering in awe-inspiring hordes across the sky of Nazi Germany, there was hardly anything to choose between them. Perhaps the B–24 used fractionally less petrol per mile. Maybe its cruising speed tended to be a little faster—but what did this last matter when all in the huge formations were held to

While British photographs tend to have either no caption (if they are official) or an inane one such as 'German planes setting out to bomb the enemy' (if they come from an agency), American ones are invariably meticulous. This Army Air Force picture shows a B–24D of the 403rd BS, 43rd BG, parked in a revetment at Dobodura strip, New Guinea, on 11 June 1943. What more could one wish!

1 Rudder trim tab
2 Fabric-covered rudder
3 Rudder hinges (metal leading-edge)
4 Starboard tailfin
5 Leading-edge de-icing boot
6 Starboard rudder horn
7 Rudder push-pull tube
8 Rear navigation light
9 Tailplane stringers
10 Consolidated (or Motor Products) two-gun electrically-operated tail-turret (0·5-in/12,7-mm)
11 Elevator torque tube
12 Elevator trim tab
13 Elevator frame (fabric-covered)
14 Rubber trim tab
15 Tab control linkage
16 Rudder post
17 Light-alloy rudder frame
18 HF aerial
19 Tailfin construction
20 Metal-covered fixed surfaces
21 Tailplane front spar
22 Port elevator push-pull tube
23 Elevator drive quadrant
24 Elevator servo unit
25 Rudder servo unit
26 Ammunition feed track (tail turret)
27 Fuselage aft main frame
28 Walkway
29 Signal cartridges
30 Longitudinal 'Z'-section stringers
31 Control cables
32 Fuselage intermediate secondary frames
33 Ammunition box
34 Aft fuselage camera installation
35 Lower windows
36 'Waist'-gun support mounting
37 Starboard manually-operated 'waist'-gun (0·5-in/12,7-mm)
38 'Waist' position (open)
39 Wind deflector plate
40 'Waist' position hinged cover
41 Port manually-operated 'waist'-gun (0·5-in/12,7-mm)
42 Dorsal aerial
43 Ball-turret stanchion support beam
44 Ammunition box
45 Ball-turret stanchion
46 Midships window
47 Turret well
48 Cabin floor
49 Tail-bumper operating jack
50 Tail-bumper fairing
51 Briggs-Sperry two-gun electrically-operated ball-turret (0·5-in/12,7-mm)
52 Turret actuation mechanism
53 Bomb-door actuation sprocket (hydraulically-operated)
54 Bomb-door corrugated inner-skin
55 Bomb-bay catwalk (box keel)
56 Bomb-bay catwalk vertical channel support members (bomb release solenoids)
57 Bomb-door actuation track and rollers
58 Wing rear spar
59 Bomb-bay access tunnel

60 Fuselage main frame/bulkhead
61 D/F loop housing
62 Whip antenna
63 Oxygen cylinders
64 Aileron cable drum
65 Starboard flap extension cable
66 Wing rib cut-outs
67 Wing centre-section carry-through
68 Two 5-man inflatable dinghies
69 Flap hydraulic jack
70 Flap/cable attachments
71 Hydraulically-operated Fowler flap
72 Wing rear spar
73 Port mainwheel well and rear fairing
74 Engine supercharger waste-gate
75 3 auxiliary self-sealing fuel cells (port and starboard)
76 Wing outer section
77 Aileron gear boxes
78 Flush-riveted smooth metal wing skinning
79 Port statically-balanced aileron (fabric covered)
80 Port wingtip
81 Port navigation light
82 Wing leading-edge de-icing boot
83 Hopper type self-sealing oil tank (32·9 US gal/124,5 litres)
84 Engine nacelle
85 1 200 hp Pratt and Whitney Twin Wasp R—1830—65 fourteen-cylinder two-row radial engine
86 Hamilton-Standard Hydromatic constant-speed airscrew
87 Landing/taxiing light
88 Nacelle structure
89 Supercharger ducting
90 12 self-sealing inter-rib fuel cells (wing centre-section)
91 Martin two-gun electrically-operated dorsal turret (0·5-in/12,7-mm).
92 Turret mechanism
93 Fuselage main frame/bulkhead
94 Radio compartment starboard window
95 Bomb-bay catwalk access trap
96 Radio-operator's position
97 Sound-insulation wall padding
98 Emergency escape hatch
99 Pilot's seat
100 Co-pilot's seat
101 Co-pilot's rudder pedals
102 Instrument panel
103 Windscreen panels
104 Compass housing
105 Control wheel
106 Control wheel mounting
107 Control linkage chain
108 Fuselage forward main frame/bulkhead
109 Pitot heads
110 Navigator's chart table
111 Navigator's compartment starboard window
112 Chart table lighting
113 Astro-dome
114 Consolidated (or Emerson) two-gun electrically-operated nose-turret (0·5-in/12,7-mm)
115 Turret seating

116 Optically-flat bomb-aiming panel
117 Nose side-glazing
118 Bombardier's prone couch
119 Ammunition boxes
120 Navigator's swivel seat
121 Navigator's compartment entry hatch (via nosewheel well)
122 Nosewheel well
123 Nosewheel door
124 Forward-retracting free-swiveling nosewheel (self-aligning)
125 Mudguard
126 Torque links
127 Nosewheel oleo strut

128 Angled bulkhead
129 Cockpit floor support structure
130 Nosewheel retraction jack
131 Smooth-stressed Alclad fuselage skinning
132 Underfloor electrics bay
133 'Roll-top desk' type bomb-bay doors (four)
134 Supercharger nacelle 'cheek' intakes
135 Ventral aerial (beneath bomb-bay catwalk)
136 Nacelle/wing attachment cut-out
137 Wing front spar nacelle support

There were several good contemporary cutaways of the B-24, but none to surpass this modern Weal drawing of a B-24J, the most numerous of all versions. The example illustrated is unusual in retaining the pneumatic de-icer boots of earlier models. Perhaps the artist found that having four engines to play with was still not enough to show all that goes on, even to obscuring the main gear!

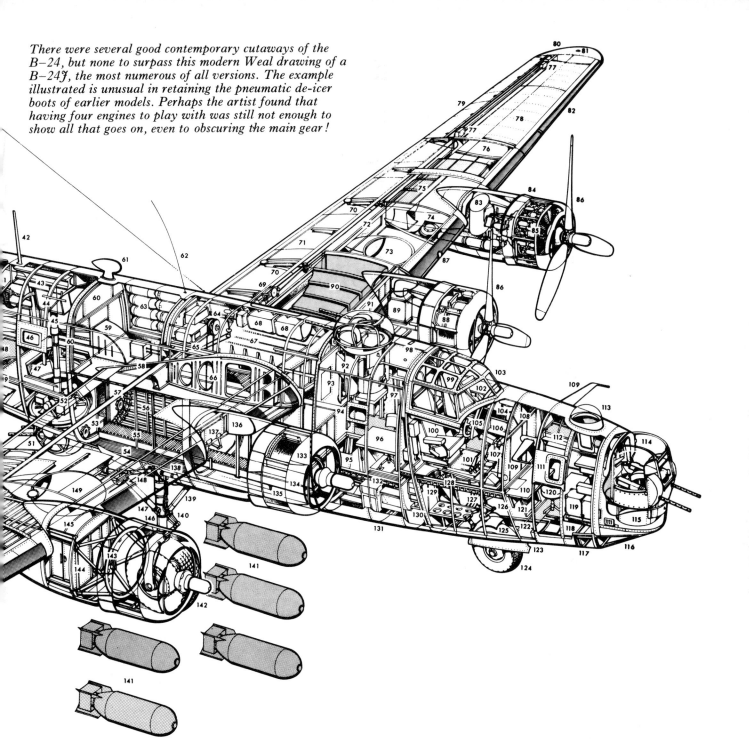

138 Undercarriage front pivoting shaft
139 Drag strut
140 Bendix scissors
141 Internal bomb load (max. 8000 lb/3632 kg)
142 Starboard mainwheel
143 Engine-mounting ring
144 Firewall
145 Monocoque oil tank
146 Mainwheel oleo (Bendix 'pneu-draulic' strut)
147 Side brace (jointed)
148 Undercarriage actuating cylinder
149 Starboard mainwheel well and rear fairing

150 Fowler flap structure
151 Wing front spar
152 Wing leading-edge de-icing boot
153 All-metal wing structure
154 Spanwise wing stringers
155 Aileron trim tab (starboard only)
156 Wing rear spar
157 Wing ribs (pressed and built-up former)
158 Statically-balanced aileron (metal frame)
159 Starboard navigation light
160 Wing-tip structure

SPECIFICATION

B-24J Liberator B.VI.
Engines: four 1200 hp Pratt & Whitney R-1830-65 Twin Wasp 14-cylinder two-row radials.
Dimensions: span 110 ft (33·5 m); length 67 ft 2 in (20·47 m); height 18 ft (5·49 m).
Weights: empty 37000 lb (16783 kg); loaded 65000 lb (29484 kg).
Performance: maximum speed 290 mph (467 km/h); initial climb 900 ft (274 m)/min; service ceiling 28000 ft (8534 m); range at 190 mph (306 km/h) with 5000 lb (2268 kg) bomb load, 2200 miles (3540 km).

This picture captures much of the atmosphere of the Pacific air war. Engineers, often the Marine Corps Seabees (from CB, construction battalion), hacked out good airstrips on the coral atolls, and put the palm trees to good use, but when the aircraft was the B–24, space was often tight and dispersal impossible

exactly the same speed, usually about 235 mph?

Back in 1939, however, the scores of talented engineers, under Ian M. 'Mac' Laddon, bent over their drawing boards in the beautiful city of San Diego to try to create the world's most advanced bomber in one year. Arnold had set them a challenge: he wanted a speed better than 300 mph, a service ceiling of 30000 feet and range of 3000 miles. When Americans have a challenge they have a habit of meeting it, and though Laddon said it took 'plenty of sweat from the collective Consolidated brow', the Model 32 prototype, with Army Air Corps designation XB–24 and serial (tail number) 39–680, flew nine months after the contract was signed, on 29 December 1939. In Britain, Halifax development took 26 months and the Manchester 35.

From stem to stern the XB–24 was unusual. The Davis wing had a reflex section which allowed the use of deep spars and a capacious space between them. This interior space was fully utilised to house 1952 Imp/gal of fuel in 12 inter-rib cells (later, augmented by six auxiliary cells, all of the self-sealing type by 1941) as well as the main undercarriage, which had very large single wheels on single legs, and was retracted sideways by a hydraulic jack to lie inside the wing between the inner and outer nacelles. At the time the 'tricycle' landing gear was novel and bold. The fuselage was equally original, with a fat, stumpy aspect resulting from a unique bomb bay occupying the whole space

under the shoulder-high wing. Front and rear section of the bay were about eight feet high, initially for carrying the largest bombs vertically, nose-up, though horizontal stowage was finally adopted. A catwalk separated the bays into further left and right-hand sections and also served as the main keel structural member holding the nose and tail together. To reduce drag on the bombing run, the bomb doors operated like a roll-top desk, the fuselage skins over them being flexible with corrugated inner stiffeners and being opened by large sprockets geared to hydraulic motors, with emergency hand cranks. Standing on the catwalk as the doors opened (not normally permitted, but thanks to the crew of *Marco Polo* I speak from experience) caused one to grip the nearest vertical stanchion with white knuckles.

Potentially the new bomber was great, but when performance tests began Consolidated were shocked at achieving a maximum speed of only 273 mph using 1200 hp Twin Wasp R–1830–33 engines, which were slightly more powerful than the Cyclones of the old B–17C, which easily did 320 mph. Laddon was as puzzled by the poor performance as, two years later, Roy Chadwick was puzzled by the good performance of the Lancaster. Already the Air Corps had ordered seven YBs and 36 B–24As and the *Armée de l'Air* had signed for 120, straight off the drawing board. Admittedly the engines did not yet have their turbo-super-

Yet another Pacific-war Liberator, an unpainted J of the 865th BS, 494th BG, heading for Arakebecan Island in the Palau Group of the Carolines, on 25th November 1944

chargers, but the San Diego team, working closely with the expanding staff at Wright Field, urgently refined the airframe and internal systems, fitted Goodrich pulsating de-icer boots bigger than ever made before, eliminated the fixed slots, achieved a gross weight increase from 41000 to 46000 lb and began to think seriously about revised armament. The six 0·30-calibre guns, all aimed by hand by six men, could be improved upon.

France collapsed, and the British took the first main batches of aircraft and then added another 164, all paid for in cash before delivery. The US Army Air Corps knew there was still a long way to go with development and held off, generously (they said) allowing the frantic British to have the first 26 machines off the line. Britain was delighted. As Hap Arnold said, we 'seemed to like the B-24 much better than the B-17', and as he gave top priority to building up his own B-17 strength, against every obstacle put in his path by Congress and the War Department, he was only too glad to let the British buy as many of the rather disappointing Consolidated bomber as they wanted. So on 17 January 1941 the first LB-30A (LB = Liberator, British requirements) made its maiden flight painted in RAF green/brown camouflage and using serial No AM258, which had previously been given in error to the former civil Consolidated 28 (pre-Catalina) *Guba* made in the same factory. The LB-30A was an unarmed

transport, yet it was vital to Britain's war effort because, unlike every other available aeroplane, it could fly for $19\frac{1}{4}$ hours at 193 mph and thus could safely cross as a matter of routine the challenging and hostile North Atlantic.

On 4 May 1941 the first LB-30A, by now named Liberator by the RAF (the Americans usually used the same name later on) but carrying civil markings and operated by a BOAC crew, took off from Prestwick, Scotland, on the new machine's first mission. Until after the end of the war it was the mainstay of the Atlantic Return Ferry Service, later operated by RAF Ferry Command, which flew ferry pilots back to North America after delivering other aircraft to Britain. This was far from a 'piece of cake'; in August 1941 alone, 53 men, nearly all experienced pilots, were killed in three Libs that flew into Scottish hills within minutes of takeoff. The following year one of these early aircraft, by now fitted with passenger windows, opened a regular service to Cairo, from Hurn. It was tough enough avoiding the Luftwaffe on such a gruelling flight, but to be shot down just south of Falmouth on the return flight as one of the Liberators was by a Polish Spitfire, was tragic. They were hard times.

By mid-1941 the newly created US Army Air Force had begun to accept the first B-24A bombers, still with R-1830-33 engines but cleared to weights up to a useful 53000 lb, and now armed with six 0·5-in and two 0·3 in guns, the latter pair in the tail, and all aimed by hand. In the RAF, the Liberator GR.1 entered service with 120 Squadron of Coastal Command, stationed at Nutt's Corner, Belfast. The first model to see combat duty, it was a remarkable transformation of an outstanding but undeveloped aircraft into one that could do a tremendous job over the grey Atlantic. The bomb bay could carry 8000 lb of depth charges and every other Coastal Command cargo. Five 0·303-in Brownings (not 0·3 or 0·5 as is often said) were mounted, two in the tail, one each in the left and right beam hatches and one in the ventral tunnel, while under the belly behind the nosewheel was a battery of four 20 mm Hispano cannon, firing ahead and aimed by the pilot's reflector sight. On the wings and rear fuselage was an incredible array of aerials of the Mk II ASV (air to surface vessel) radar, which thrilled schoolboy spotters of the time, who all knew exactly what it was. These VLR (very long range) aircraft closed the gap in mid-Atlantic where U-boats had previously worked with little hindrance, despite being limited by the RAF to an all-up weight of 44950 lb.

In 1941 the Consolidated company's growth was 'the greatest of any private enterprise in history'. Employment at San Diego zoomed from 3170 to 33000. A mile up Pacific Highway a completely new Plant 2 was built and in full production within a year. Though America was not at war, the atmosphere was charged with vital energy, as Liberators and Catalinas poured off the lines. Outside the original factory the founder, Major Reuben H. Fleet, had a sign mounted saying NOTHING SHORT OF RIGHT IS RIGHT in letters nine feet high and stretching 480 feet above the city skyline—until in December the whole plant vanished under camouflage nets. However, after Pearl Harbor, things really took off. In April 1941 ground had been broken for a completely new B–24 plant at Fort Worth, Texas. In February 1942 the bombers were in mass production on two powered assembly lines in a windowless air-conditioned building 4000 feet long and 320 feet wide. This was fantastic enough but an even bigger factory was built by Ford at Willow Run, Detroit, to feed B–24 parts to Fort Worth and also to another assembly plant run by Douglas at Tulsa, Oklahoma. Reuben Fleet pulled a wry face at so many rivals learning the Convair (Consolidated-Vultee) heat-treatment and other closely guarded secrets, but times had changed and there was nothing he could do about it. For two months two floors of the Spreckels Theater building in San Diego were filled day and night with Convair and Ford

engineers converting thousands of B–24 drawings and specifications to auto-industry practice. Then Willow Run became one of the world's wonders, almost turning out a B–24 an hour, either complete or in parts for Fort Worth and Tulsa. Other parts came from two other companies, Vultee at Los Angeles and Stinson at Nashville, while huge modification centres were set up at Elizabeth City, Louisville and at Tucson. The tide of Liberators could almost have won the war by itself.

While all this was going on, the B–24 began to mature as a bomber—and for 27 other uses. The B–24A of mid-1941 opened the USAAF Ferrying Command Atlantic route on 1 July 1941, and soon two of them carried the Harriman mission to Moscow, achieving a final non-stop leg of 3150 miles. From Moscow one came back via Cairo, central Africa and Brazil, while the other staged through Iran, India, Singapore, Port Moresby, Darwin, Wake Island, Hawaii and back to Washington. The result was masses of detailed information about the airfields on the Allied ferry routes used until after the war. The RAF Liberator II, of which 139 were delivered in mid-1941, had turrets manufactured in Britain and shipped to the USA for installation. Four-0·303 Boulton Paul turrets were fitted in the tail and above the trailing edge of the wing, three similar guns being positioned in the waist and nose positions. The nose was lengthened by 31 in, Curtiss Electric propellers were used, and an authorised all-up weight of 46250 lb allowed the bomb load to reach 10000 lb. From December 1941 the Mk II was in action with Coastal Command, painted white on the sides and under-surface, and a little later black-painted planes of 159 and 160 Squadrons dropped bombs on the Afrika Korps in the Western Desert.

Back in 1940 Pratt & Whitney had managed to get the turbocharged R–1830–41 cleared for flight in the XB–24B, and after extensive development a completely new engine installation was put into production that did more than any other to push Pratt & Whitney to a record monthly delivery of 3377 engines by March 1943. It had a flat-oval section, because on each side was an air duct serving the engine itself and the oil coolers. Engine air was piped to the underside of the nacelle, seven feet behind the firewall, where was the GE turbo that pumped in more and more air as the B–24 climbed so that full power was still being generated at over 20000 feet. This transformed the sluggish aircraft into one almost as good as Laddon's men had hoped. Speed rose from 265 to 310 mph, and ceiling jumped from 22000 feet to 32000 feet. This experimental version was also the testbed for self-sealing tanks, armour and numerous other improvements.

From it stemmed the B–24C, of which nine were built, and the first mass-production model, the B–24D. The C introduced American electrically driven turrets, each with two 0·5 in guns, one in the tail by Consolidated and a Martin turret just behind the flight deck, the manual guns being retained in nose and beam positions. The propellers reverted to Hamilton Hydromatics. The B–24D, of which 2738 were built, introduced the outer-wing fuel cells, optional long-range tanks in the bomb bay, provision for two 4000 lb bombs on underwing racks,

shot down, mostly over the heavily defended target, and the survivors were scattered all over the Middle East.

In England the B–24 joined the growing 8th Air Force in September 1942, when the B–24D formed the 44th Bomb Group, 'The Flying Eightballs', which outdid every other B–24 group in shooting down 330 confirmed enemy fighters though it lost 153 aircraft in action. The B–24D operated with the AAF throughout the Middle and Far East, soon almost totally displacing the B–17 from the latter theatre. Many also operated in the ASW (Anti-Submarine Warfare) role, with radar, and these were progressively transferred to the

One in the ETO (European Theater of Operations) : Extra Joker, *apparently of the 490th BG, holds formation after taking severe battle damage over Austria in late 1944. She was a B–24H*

R–1830–43 engines, and three extra 0·5 in guns, two in the sides of the nose and one in the ventral tunnel. At a weight of 67800 lb, with restricted manoeuvrability, it was possible to carry eight 1600 lb bombs, a total of 12800 lb.

There were 170 blocks (batches) of San Diego-built Ds, and many others from Fort Worth and ten from Tulsa. Most were AAF bombers, and their first mission, and the first of any significance by the AAF in Europe, being a token raid by 13 aircraft of a special detachment under Col H. A. Halvorsen from Fayid, Egypt, to the Ploesti refinery in Romania. This mission succeeded mainly in alerting the Axis so that a hot reception was waiting when, on 1 August 1943, 177 later B–24s went to Ploesti again, this time from Benghazi, Libya. One of the great epics of air warfare, the second raid would have been a stunning success had it not been for the first. As it was, 57 Liberators were

US Navy as PB4Y–1 Liberators, of which three squadrons were most active in Britain. Excluding aircraft transferred in the field, the RAF received 260 B–24Ds as Liberator IIIs, most of them becoming GR.III Coastal machines with such equipment as later ASV.VI radar, Leigh Light (a powerful ASW searchlight) and H_2X precision-bombing radar, the top turret usually being a four-0·303-in Boulton Paul. The RAF also received 122 GR.V Liberators with even more extensive ASW gear and increased fuel capacity, a few having stub wings on the forward fuselage carrying eight 60 lb rockets.

Modifications of the B–24D included the XF–7 strategic reconnaissance aircraft, converted by Northwest Airlines at St Paul and carrying 11 cameras, which led to the production F–7; the C–87 Liberator Express transport, usually seating 20 passengers, of which 276 were

On 1 August 1943 a small force of B–24s flew the long mission from North Africa to England, on the way bombing the previously unattacked Concordia Vega oil refinery at Ploesti, Romania. The main effect of this raid was to spur a fantastic increase in the defences, and when B–24s of the 15th Air Force attacked in strength on 31 May 1944 they found the flak intense. This dramatic photograph, taken right over the target, contains at least 220 shell-bursts

built, as well as related machines such as the RAF Liberator C.VII and US Navy RY–2; the AT–22 (later TB–24) crew trainer, principally for flight engineers for the B–29 and B–32; the XB–24F with hot-air de-icing; the CB–24 ex-operational aircraft stripped of combat gear and used as brightly painted Lead Ships for the combat Bomb Groups and Air Divisions; the C–109 tanker for carrying 2900 gallons of fuel over 'The Hump' from India to China to support B–29 missions from China; and the XB–41 fighter with seven twin-0·5 in turrets.

One of the turrets on the one-off XB–41 was a Briggs-Sperry ball turret behind the bomb bay, with two 0·5 in guns. This became standard on most future bomber versions, starting with the B–24E with Curtiss propellers and, in Ford and Convair production, R–1830–65 engines. British designation for the E was Mk IV, but none appear to have been built. In late 1942 yet another assembly line started rolling: North

American Aviation at Dallas, Texas, which began with 430 B–24Gs with a lengthened nose and fitted with a Consolidated or Emerson twin 0·5 in turret. Another 738 were built with the Emerson nose turret by Consolidated as the B–24H, while Ford (1780) and Douglas (582) had the Consolidated turret. The RAF Liberator GR.VI and B.VI, the latter equipping 14 squadrons in the Far East, had a Boulton Paul four-0·303 tail turret, so all four turrets were of different make.

Almost identical, the B–24J was built by all five manufacturers to a total of 6678, and served in every theatre of the Second World War. By September 1944 this great aircraft equipped 455 groups of the AAF overseas, and countless units with other services. The J lost the black strips along its leading edges because it usually had hot-air de-icing, and most had the Dash-65 engine, later aircraft having the new GE B–22 turbos, giving better altitude performance. But as they were cleared to operate at weights up to 71 400 lb they needed extremely careful piloting, and compared with the B-17 appeared to catch fire more readily and were certainly almost impossible to ditch safely. In the Pacific opposition was usually slight, and the B-24 bore the main burden of strategic bombing in 1942-45.

Most Navy J-models (PB4Y-1) had a near-spherical Erco nose turret and different bombardier station. The AAF's B-24L had two manually-aimed tail guns, while the M had the lightweight Motor Products tail turret. Convair built 916 Ms and Ford 1677. There was a veritable shoal of modifications and one-off variants based on these important late models. The final production model was the N, with a single fin giving a startling 11 mph higher speed. This tail had been tested in 1943 on a B-24D, which also had 1350 hp Dash-75 engines, the result being the XB-24K. So improved was it

that the new tail was chosen for all future production, though only a few Ns were delivered before production was terminated on 31 May 1945. It is odd that the single fin took so long to mature. It had previously been standardized in a taller form on the C-87C, RY-3 and Liberator C.IX transports, and even Mr Churchill's *Commando*, previously an old Mk II, had such a fin. The B-24N also had completely new nose and tail turrets, the former being similar to that of the much larger Convair B-32 Dominator.

This is still not the end of the story because late in the war the completely redesigned PB4Y-2 Privateer went into action in an ASW and ocean-patrol role with the US Navy, with vertical-oval engines, totally different (very heavy) armament and the extra-tall fin of the transports. Later these 739 extremely complex machines were redesignated P4Y and one was shot down whilst doing secret electronic reconnaissance round the Soviet Union.

One of the most horrific of all air war photographs, this shows a B-24H of the 15th Air Force hit by flak over northern Italy right at the very end of the European war in April 1945. In about 50 per cent of occasions a B-24 abandoned by its pilot gyrated so violently that nobody could get out, but with a wing missing its fall might have been a little steadier. Even the sedate B-17, much easier to fly, could be lethal in imprisoning its crew under high g forces

Avro Lancaster

By far the most famous British bomber, and ranking with the Spitfire fighter and a few other warplanes in popular appeal, the Lancaster was absolutely first-rate from the very beginning. So it never changed much, and apart from saying what it achieved—which was plenty—this chapter can be quite brief. But the Lancaster did not just happen; it was derived from the Manchester which, like the Halifax, was designed to specification P.13/36 calling for a powerful twin-engined bomber. Seldom in history was an aircraft at once so good and bad as the Manchester.

Previously A. V. Roe, Ltd., at Chadderton, in north-east Manchester, had built a remarkable number of aircraft, and the Manchester was Type 679 (numbers began at 500), but they had little experience of modern stressed-skin construction. Great credit is therefore due to chief designer Roy Chadwick for creating a marvellously clean and simple design, structurally elegant and incomparably easier to produce than the rival Stirling. The oval-section fuselage was divided into five sections to help in rapid subcontract manufacture, and almost the whole of its lower half consisted of a bomb bay, not the

plurality of small bays of the Stirling and Halifax, but one cavernous space enclosed by two monster doors. Design bomb load was 10350 lb, but Chadwick deliberately made the bay over-large in the hope that engine power might be able to be increased. The wing design was also neat, with a rectangular centre section carrying the engines and main landing gear and straight-tapered outer panels. These outer panels were amazingly short, and when the prototype (L7246) first appeared in the summer of 1939 it looked more like a fast mailplane or racing plane than a bomber. It had no turrets, and the Rolls-Royce Vulture engines were little larger than installations of half their promised 1760 hp.

One reason for the long delay there was in producing a prototype was the extreme disparity in complexity between the 679 and its predecessors, whereas American engineering teams had in general progressed in more logical steps. Another was the fact that, in parallel with design and prototype construction, a gigantic mass-production complex of subcontractors and Shadow Factories had to be set up, though this had begun in 1937–38 merely as an insurance against a major emergency but with only token

R5689 was the most-photographed of all Lancasters; Flight took this photograph on 28 August 1942 when S/L Everitt's N-Nan of 50 Sqn at Swinderby was displayed for the world's press. The row of small windows betray her Manchester ancestry. By sheer bad luck she was written off only a month later, in the hands of another crew, due to engine failure on the approach

orders for actual aircraft. It had been intended to buy a large and ever-growing number of Manchesters from this strong industrial team, but from late 1937 Rolls-Royce encountered extremely severe problems with the Vulture. Some, such as those with the connecting rods, were fundamental; others were more readily curable, but the engine company's dynamic works director—'Hs' in Rolls-Royce shorthand but later to become Lord Hives—argued that further work was not worth the manpower. But in August 1939, two weeks after the Manchester's first flight, the Vulture unfortunately passed its Type Test at 1800 hp, and 'Hs' was overruled.

There are advantages in having two engines instead of four separate engines of lesser power, and the Germans tried for years to prove this with the He 177. Britain could have done so with the Manchester if only Rolls-Royce had made the Vulture out of two Merlins.

However, Chadwick had his ear to the ground, and put forward projects for the Manchester IIB (two Bristol Centaurus), IIN (two Napier Sabres) and III (four Merlins). But production to original Specification 19/37 was already building up. Trials with catapult takeoffs and arrested landings called for by this specification

DS771 was a Hercules-engined Mk II. Built by Armstrong Whitworth, this variant had a deepened bomb bay and usually an FN.64 ventral turret—and the Manchester-inherited windows

were fortunately soon abandoned, but the Manchester grew an odd little central fin to improve poor directional stability. Later the production Manchester I had a much larger central fin, and outer wing panels of more reasonable size added, the span increasing from 80 ft 2 in to 90 ft 1 in. Armament took the form of a two-gun nose turret, four-gun tail turret and Frazer-Nash FN.21A two-gun ventral turret, aimed periscopically. Gross weight was 50000 lb. Production built up at Avro, with Metropolitan-Vickers, Fairey and Armstrong Whitworth fast coming on stream. Deliveries began to 207 Sqd in November 1940 and the Manchester went into action on 24 February 1941.

Before the end of 1940 all new deliveries were

of the Manchester IA, with two larger tail fins and no central fin, a tailplane increased in span from 22 feet to 33 feet, and Vulture IIs rated at 1845 hp, allowing gross weight to reach 56000 lb, compared with the 26000 lb of the original P.13/36 aircraft. In March 1941 another Vulture passed a Type Test at 2010 hp, but this could not save it from extinction. Though the Manchester served with ten squadrons of Bomber Command and a few reached Coastal Command, to complete a flight without a big-end failure seemed almost the exception. No 97 Squadron, continually grounded like the others, got tired of being known as 'The 97th Foot'.

Fortunately salvation was at hand. In July 1940 'Hs' had at last persuaded the Air Ministry to sanction a four-Merlin conversion. Avro, desperately eager to get on with this, did not have the design manpower to do both the new wing and the engine installation. Again 'Hs' found the answer. Like Roy Fedden at Bristol, Col. L. F. R. Fell of Rolls-Royce had turned the company's basic engines into standardised powerplants that could almost be bolted without modification on to any suitable airframe and 'Hs' chose these. The Merlin had been created for the Beaufighter II, and it was all ready for the new Avro bomber. Before long it was in large-scale production at the new Scottish factories, backed up by others such as Morris Motors, Standard Cars, Alvis and Sunbeam-Talbot, with little difference between 'inners' and 'outers' for four-engined installations.

This left Chadwick free to get on with the new outer wing design, and while he was about it, at the height of the Battle of Britain, he also designed a completely new transport with the same wing, but mounted high on a capacious fuselage. The bomber was given the type number 683, and was later named Lancaster; the transport became the Avro 685 York. But Chadwick had no authority to devote effort to a transport, and when in 1942 he could spare drawing-office capacity and get ahead with it, he was thwarted by the fact that there was a vague understanding—since widely misreported as a firm agreement—that all transports should be made in the United States. Thus the York was worked on more or less furtively by the proverbial two men and a boy and did not reach the RAF until 1945.

In December Metrovick's works were bombed, destroying their first batch of 13 Manchesters, but they went on to deliver 52 to bring total deliveries up to 209. Fairey and Armstrong Whitworth had their contracts cancelled, but the latter was well ahead with production and, together with Avro and Metrovick, planned to

114

Left, above: *Test launch of an AGM–86A ALCM (air-launched cruise missile) from an NB–52G trials aircraft over White Sands missile range in New Mexico. Painted all-white, this special B–52 is packed with instrumentation to gather as much information as possible on the behaviour of the missile. When President Carter cancelled the B–1 he said cruise missiles would do instead—a belief most experts consider unjustified*
Left, below: *Taken before the fitting of the EVS (Electro-optical Viewing System), this photograph shows the final variant, the turbofan-engined B–52H, carrying four Skybolts, the air-launched ballistic missile cancelled by President Kennedy in 1962*
Above: *Another missile formerly carried by the B–52 was Hound Dog, a large winged strategic weapon which manoeuvred like an aircraft in delivering its thermonuclear warhead to targets up to 700 miles distant. The carrier is a B–52G, whose engines were assisted on take-off by those of the missiles*

fit several hundred fuselages and centre sections they had underway with Lancaster outer panels. The first Lancaster was actually a rebuild of an old Manchester I with the triple tail, but when it emerged at the end of 1940 as the Manchester III it was given a completely new serial number, BT308/G—the suffix letter signifying a special aircraft not to be touched by ground crew without authority from someone who knew all about it.

That is almost the end of the story, because the first flight, by Capt H. A. 'Sam' Brown at Ringway on 9 January 1941, demonstrated that the new four-Merlin bomber was a real winner. Brown afterwards said he had felt like rolling it, and later the 'Lanc' was shown to be highly aerobatic. Measured performance was startlingly better than prediction, and Chadwick was at a loss to account for it. After only two weeks BT308/G went to Boscombe Down, where eventually a classic report emerged, opening with 'This aircraft is eminently suitable for operational service'. (Another report, on a different type, began: 'Entry to this aircraft is somewhat difficult. It should be made impossible'.)

Little more had now to be done but boost production of the Lancaster. The second prototype (DG595) was almost indistinguishable from the eventual production machine. The first production aircraft (L7527) had, like 243 others from Avro and 57 from Metrovick, begun life as a Manchester and had the latter's shallow windows along the centre and rear fuselage. By 1942 Lancasters were in full production at Avro Chadderton and other factories (later at Yeadon, with major contributions by Langar and Bracebridge Heath), Armstrong Whitworth, Metrovick, Vickers-Armstrongs and Austin Motors, output rising to 293 a month, plus the equivalent of 28 in spares.

Armament at first comprised ten 0·303 in Brownings in nose, dorsal, ventral and tail turrets. The ventral turret was seldom used, and was soon dispensed with. The dorsal (mid-upper) turret, which was better than that on the Manchester, was soon surrounded by a large fairing topped by 'taboo tracks' on which ran a roller that lifted the guns high in the fore and aft directions to avoid damage to the aircraft when they fired. Boxes in mid-fuselage housed 10000 rounds for the tail turret, and one-fifth as many for the mid-upper. All three hydraulic turrets were by Frazer-Nash, and the only changes to the armament before 1945 were small, such as the removal of the Perspex from the back of the tail turret to improve vision. Normal maximum bomb load was 14000 lb,

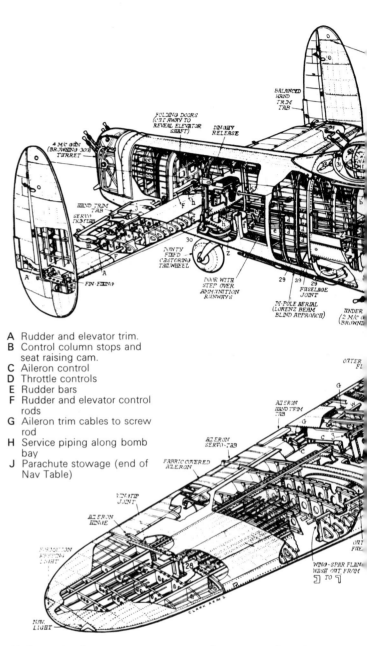

A Rudder and elevator trim.
B Control column stops and seat raising cam.
C Aileron control
D Throttle controls
E Rudder bars
F Rudder and elevator control rods
G Aileron trim cables to screw rod
H Service piping along bomb bay
J Parachute stowage (end of Nav Table)

K Oxygen bottle stowages
L Observer's window blister
M Bomb lock units in floor
N Longeron joint flanges and holes
P Spar flange reinforcement
Q Hydraulic reservoir
R Signal pistol
S Armoured doors
T Rest bunk and 15 oxygen bottles underneath
U Spar webs extended into former frames
V Spar flanges
W Flap op. cylinder and op. rods
X Reconnaissance flares
Y Flare chute shown stowed *and* in position
Z Tail gun ammunition magazine and runways

a Under-turret magazines
b Top turret magazines
d Vacuum flasks stowages
e Dead-man's handle (puts rear turret fore and aft to extricate gunner through sliding door)
f Elsan lavatory
g Tailwheel leg spigoted into tailplane
h Tailplane halves joints
j Elevator trim screw rod and cables
k Tailplane fix to fuselage
m Elevator hinge bracket
n Bomb door op. jack and mud brushes (and at front end).
p Hinged leading edge
q Starboard fuel tank (580 gal) space
r Glycol tank
t Undercarriage and motor bracket
w U c radius rod and jack anchorages
x Fuel tank structure (swash-plate former plates, stringers, plating and bulletproof skinning).
y Fuel tank support strap
z Wing trailing section spar (bolted to wing rear spar)

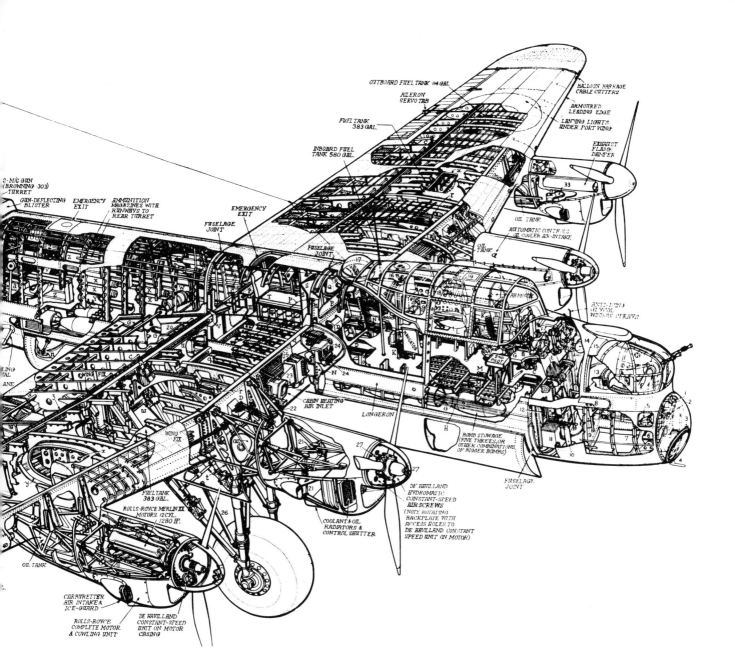

1 Navigation light	19 Curtain
2 Bomb aiming sight	20 Dinghy stowage (starboard wing)
3 Flat window (no distortion) and glycol anti-icing spray pipe	21 Radiator control jack and rods
4 Air-speed pressure head	22 Fuel cocks (remote controlled)
5 Glycol pump for '3'.	23 Hot glycol pipes into cabin heater
6 Bomb aimer's body rest	24 Worm drive (cabin air heat controls) and air overflow
7 Emergency exit	25 Service pipes along leading edge
8 Ventilator	
9 Camera (through floor)	26 U/c door op. link rod
10 Pump	27 Spinner and back plate fixing to airscrew hub
11 Glycol tank (window spray) and step	28 Wing-tip joint
12 Bomb aimer's squint into bomb bay	29 Downwards identification lamps
13 Detail of front turret mounting ring	30 Tailwheel leg hinge
14 Compressed air bottle	31 Taboo track and rollers
15 Pilot's glycol pump (cockpit window spray).	32 Aerial spring suspension
16 D.F. loop	33 Carburetter air intake junction (up to carburetter)
17 Astro-dome	
18 Rubber headroom buffer (cut away to show half-framed jointing). Note bullet-proof glass panel above	

This was probably the finest of all Clark's wartime cutaway drawings. It was almost unique in that era to lay a complex aircraft bare so completely. Features include the early, narrow-chord propellers; fuselage windows; and the ventral turret (the only one needed, and the only one soon left off). One of the remarkable features of the Lanc was how similar were the first and last

SPECIFICATION

Lancaster I

Engines: four 1460 hp Rolls-Royce or Packard Merlin 20 or 22 (Mk II only: four 1650 hp Bristol Hercules VI, 14 cylinder two-row, sleeve-valve radials).

Dimensions: span 102 ft (31·1 m); length 69 ft 4 in (21·1 m); height 19 ft 7 in (5·97 m).

Weights: empty 36 900 lb (16 705 kg); loaded 68 000 lb (30 800 kg); overload with 22 000 lb bomb 70 000 lb (31 750 kg).

Performance: maximum speed 287 mph (462 km/h) at 11 500 ft (3500 m); cruising speed 210 mph (338 km/h); climb at maximum weight to 20 000 ft (6095 m) 41 minutes; service ceiling 24 500 ft (7467 m); range with 14 000 lb (6350 kg) bombs 1660 miles (2675 km).

Left: *This photograph was taken in the late 1960s at the Boeing Wichita division in Kansas. In the background are operational B–52G and H bombers at McConnell AFB, all of which have since come over the fence for rework (there is no longer a SAC manned-bomber unit at Wichita). In the foreground is a B–52D, a tall-tailed oldie, being rebuilt with the Big Belly modification to enable it to carry up to 90 bombs of 750 lb (actual weight, about 825 lb)*

Above: *The view the boomer (the operator of the refuelling boom in a KC–135 tanker) sees as he pumps juice into a Big Belly B–52D toting external triplets of iron bombs. At 1000 gallons per minute, fast enough to fill a car in one second, a KC could pump for 30 minutes and still get nowhere near filling a dry-tanks B–52G or H*

Everything about the Lancaster looked exactly right. Virtually all the improvements had been done with the Manchester One of the last users of the Lancaster was the Royal Canadian Air Force. Victory Aircraft at Malton, Toronto, made 430 Mk X Lancs, with Packard-Merlin engines, and after 1945 many were refurbished as coastal reconnaissance and anti-submarine patrollers. This example shows some of the changes, with turrets removed, de-icer boots fitted

and the official version that 'the target had to be attacked by day 'in order to cause sufficient damage' hardly stands up. Bert Harris's philosophy was always to clobber the whole city, taking any diesel factories there might be with it. Ever since, observers have engaged in a fierce debate, some saying that the US method of properly aimed pinpoint attacks was superior, while others—vehemently including Harris—adhere to the traditional Trenchardist view that simply pouring HE and incendiaries on to whole cities was the most effective way of winning the war. The funny thing is, had every Bomber Command 'heavy' been equipped to receive the Oboe navaid, which could have been modified to handle many aircraft at once, every bomb could have been aimed as accurately as those on the gallant Augsburg mission.

As it was, thousands of Lancs droned nightly across a Germany that became more deadly every week. Bomber Command used outstanding techniques of programme management, operational research and Britain's unrivalled electronic technology to confuse and defeat every wile of the Luftwaffe. But we did many odd things. Most Lancasters broadcast their precise location throughout their mission by carrying and using their H_2S mapping radars, which in the end became valueless, because Pathfinders put down markers along the outward course and over the target itself, so that the main-force aircraft hardly needed a navigator at all. Even worse, from 1943 Bomber Command was the recipient of vast numbers of Monica rear-warning radars, with a dipole aerial just below the rear turret, which were intended to warn of the presence of night fighters but gave so many false alarms by picking up other heavies in the bomber stream that the orange and red panel lights were soon ignored. If this warning had been switched off completely it would not have done much harm, but the crews were told to use it and the Luftwaffe developed a passive receiver tuned to Monica (Flensburg) which could home on to a Lanc from 130 miles away.

Worst of all, there appeared to be no attempt to do anything about the growing depredations of the formidable night fighters. From mid-1943 these were increasingly fitted with upward-firing cannon, the standard interception finishing with the night fighter in close formation under the bomber. The perfect no-deflection shot could be aimed so accurately that an *Experte* could pump his 20 mm and 30 mm shells exactly into the wing spars between the left engine nacelles and nobody on board the bomber could do anything about it. The fighter could not be seen, no gun could be brought to bear on it as the

though by far the most common load was one 4000 lb 'cookie' and eight SBCs (small bomb containers) with 4 lb incendiaries. Even with the maximum load, a range of 1660 miles was possible at 210 mph, with an over-target height above 20000 feet. But it took time to climb to that height, and for the Ruhr or closer targets the first 10000 feet had to be gained even before setting course.

The Lancaster I had Merlin XX engines giving a maximum of 1460 hp at 6000 feet, with 1280 hp for sea-level takeoff. First deliveries went not to the 97th Foot (they were second) but to No 44 (Rhodesian) Squadron, previously with Hampdens. The build-up was rapid, though hiccups were caused by dangerous structural problems chiefly affecting the wing-tips and upper wing skins. On 17 April 1942 a formation of 12 of the new bombers was sent to the MAN diesel works at Augsburg, flying at 'nought feet' in daylight. Nobody ever explained this extraordinary mission, which suffered a 58 per cent loss, with the five survivors all damaged,

Designed to carry nuclear weapons in the high stratosphere, the Hawker Siddeley Vulcan suddenly found itself in 1963 in a mainly conventional high-explosive role at tree-top height. The new camouflage paint was more obvious than the

internal modifications and new equipment intended to prolong structural life and make it easier to penetrate hostile defences

50 Sqn aircraft and a view across Swinderby which will bring a lump to the throat of the thousands who still remember the green grass and black runways of those stirring times

ventral turret had been scrapped in 1942, and the three gunners eagerly scanned the sky everywhere else.

None of these things reflect on the Lancaster but only on Bomber Command's inexplicable policies. So what about the Lanc? While the main manufacturing consortium made 3425 Mk Is, most with the Merlin 22 or 1640 hp Merlin 24, Armstrong Whitworth delivered 300 Mk II with the 1735 hp Bristol Hercules XVI and many other changes (some had the ventral turret), which were faster but burned fuel more quickly and were not able to achieve quite the same over-target height. The Mk II, used mainly by the Canadians, was an insurance against engine shortage. In 1940 it had been decided that Rolls-Royce, which rejected shadow factories making their products, could not deliver enough

Merlins. In the First World War the company's colourful general manager, Claude Johnson, had said 'I will go to prison rather than let others build our engines', and he had his way. In 1940 'Hs' maintained this principle, but he lost out eventually and the Merlin went into production in the summer of 1941 at Packard, Detroit. The Lanc also went into production at a specially formed company, Canada's Victory Aircraft at Malton, Toronto, taking engines from Packard. British aircraft with Packard engines were designated Lancaster III, 3039 being built, but before long the American Merlin, with the Hamilton paddle-blade propeller, began to appear on overhauled Mk I aircraft, which lead to a complicated situation; Victory-built aircraft were designated as the Lancaster Mk X.

Other Lancaster versions included the IV, to

Specification B.14/43, that became the post-war Lincoln; the V was a related type with the Merlin 85; the VI saw limited service as a high-performance Pathfinder, Master Bomber and ECM platform, with tail turret only, extensive new equipment and the two-stage Merlin 85/87; and the VII succeeded the III as the standard bomber in 1945, with a Martin twin-0·5 in mid-upper turret, mounted further forward, and the capacious Rose twin-0·5 in tail turret that was also installed on the final Mk IIIs. Total production, discounting spares, was 7366, of which 422 were built at Malton.

Of many special installations the most famous was that of the Upkeep conversion which carried the Barnes Wallis mine devised to breach the German dams. This was a 9250 lb spinning cylinder driven by a hydraulic motor at 500 rpm so that when dropped it would skip across the calm water of a German reservoir upstream of the dam. The story of how Guy Gibson formed 617 Squadron and breached the Möhne and Eder dams, and damaged the Sorpe, is now legendary and has been told many times.

By 1944 other Mk I (Special) aircraft were converted to carry first the 12000 lb Tallboy bomb, which sank the *Tirpitz*, and finally the 22000 lb Grand Slam (another Wallis design) which fell at supersonic speed and shook its targets to pieces by detonating deep underground. Experimental rebuilds included the saddle-tank long-range aircraft intended for Tiger Force in the Far East and LL780/G which had upper and lower Bristol gun turrets, each with two 20 mm Hispanos aimed by a gunner in the extreme tail.

The Lancaster was the supreme expression of the classic British area-flattening heavy bomber. Simple and quick to build and maintain, amazingly durable, effortless to fly, and capable of carrying unbelievably heavy loads, it was exactly the right machine at the right time. Coastal Command retired its last MR.3 on 15 October 1956, and the Royal Canadian Air Force and French Aéronavale went on using them for a decade. Even today, the Lancaster's basic design endures in the AEW Shackleton.

The Lancaster shown below is an Armstrong Whitworth-built Mk I, representative of the great mass of true Lancs that inherited no Manchester features, and the yellow bars on the fins proclaim NG358 to be a lead aircraft equipped with the Gee-H pecision navaid. LS was the code of 15 Sqn, based at Mildenhall. No 15 had previously been the second unit to receive the mighty Stirling, the RAF's first four-engined bomber

This striking-looking aircraft is an SF37, the overland reconnaissance version of the Swedish Viggen. Capable of more than twice the speed of sound at high altitudes, the SF37 is more often found at tree-top height, using every trick in the book—including the worst possible weather—to try to evade hostile defences as its cameras, infra-red and side-looking radar systems gather as much information as possible. Visibly distinguished by its longer, more pointed nose, the SF37 is one of the dominant class of modern warplanes which look like fighters, and are often called fighters by the media, but which do their best to avoid encounters with enemy aircraft. Examples of tactical aircraft in this class are the MiG–27, Su–19, Jaguar, Tornado, A–4 Skyhawk, A–7 Corsair, Fiat G91 and General Dynamics F–111. They are today's bombers—yet the term bomber is beginning to sound somewhat dated

126

De Havilland Mosquito

Though one of the greatest aircraft ever created, the de Havilland Mosquito happened not because of official thinking and planning, but in spite of it. As with Whittle and his new jet engine, nobody wanted to know until a few far-sighted people had achieved the 'impossible' in the face of expert official opinion against it. The mind boggles at the idea that such things can come about, and the answer must lie in the tradition in Britain that many decisions are taken not by real experts but by brilliant amateurs. Fortunately the Mosquito managed to survive officialdom, and I am glad myself that it did, not only because it did as much as any aircraft to help win the Second World War, but also because I knew the 'Mossie' (pronounced Mozzie) far better than any of the other great bombers in this book.

Despite the fact that in 1924 the Air Ministry had issued an order prohibiting the use of wood for any primary structure for British military machines, the directors of the de Havilland Aircraft company had, by 1938, firmly come to the conclusion that a case could be made out for a new all-wood bomber of advanced design. One ponders on their motivation. My view has always been the pragmatic one that by 1938 the rearmament programme was at last getting under way, and contracts that by any previous standard were gigantic were going to all de Havilland's rivals for new all-metal, stressed-skin machines. Hatfield had little experience of this, so how could their wood-shavers compete? It could not do any harm to make out a case for construction in wood, but to suggest a bomber so fast it needed no defensive armament was

A beautiful portrait of a beautiful aeroplane. Taken by that master of the airborne camera, Charles E. Brown—and passed by the censor on 16 November 1944—it shows a PR.XVI with two-stage engines and paddle-blade props

radical enough; to propose to build it of wood almost made it a bad joke. And anyone who disagrees had better study what happened.

Arthur Hagg, who had designed the superbly graceful D.H.91 Albatross, told me the original idea was an Albatross bomber. In fact the Albatross was one of the least successful aircraft ever built, despite its graceful appearance, and much of the trouble was attributable to its structure. Hagg was actually no slouch with metal structures, and later designed the Ambassador, so if only de Havilland's board had taken the plunge into stressed skin in January 1938—they had stuck one toe in with the Flamingo—we might have had a better Mosquito a year sooner. As it was, according to C. C. Walker, 'We had for so long been outside the ring of Ministry designers that they did not seem to take us very seriously'.

Walker and Sir Geoffrey de Havilland had gone to the Air Ministry in October 1938 with plans and specifications, not for a bomber Albatross, but for a far better concept, a neat two-Merlin bomber with a crew of two. All the top DH men asked every RAF officer they met for his opinion on bombers without rear defence but faster than enemy fighters. This was a tricky one for them to answer, and in 1938–39 RAF officers faced with a totally radical idea tended to give an official reply favouring the *status quo*. But at least it made many people give the matter some thought, which is more than could be said for the Air Ministry. Despite gathering war clouds, no action whatsoever was taken regarding the DH proposal. Instead the company was asked whether it would tool up to build wings for an existing bomber, probably the Halifax!

War came on 3 September 1939. A week later de Havilland, Walker and others were back at Air Ministry. They were told that the supplies of aircraft materials, especially light-alloy extrusions, would not suffice even for existing programmes. But the Hatfield team reminded the officials that their proposal would involve a whole new industry, using wood. They also pointed out, with plenty of figures to back it up, that their unarmed fast bomber would deliver a greater tonnage of bombs per thousand man-hours of construction, maintenance and flying than any existing bomber. But even at that time voices could cry in the wilderness without success. The Hatfield team again met polite disinterest. Few of the officials wanted even to comment, but someone asked: 'Suppose the Germans build faster fighters?' One man alone had the sense and authority to take action, Air Marshal Sir Wilfrid Freeman, Air Member for Development and Production. His far-reaching power made him many enemies as well as friends, but even the former respected the titanic job he did to help win the Second World War.

On 1 January 1940 de Havilland and Walker went up to Harrogate, whence the production directorates had been evacuated, to see Freeman and get the project started. A few days later it was under way as the D.H.98 to the specification B.1/40 which was then being written by John (later Sir John) Buchanan. Freeman's stature showed in his authorizing the skipping of whole stages of the normal operational procedures; this was clearly going to be another Whittle, either a flop or a fantastic winner, and the quicker they could find out which the better. Design and engineering went ahead day and night at Hatfield and nearby Salisbury Hall, by a team numbering about 140, and progress was amazingly swift. Then came disaster to the campaign in France, followed by Dunkirk, and the dynamic 'Beaver' (Lord Beaverbrook) became Minister of Aircraft Production. There followed sweeping decisions, with five (largely obsolescent) types given super-priority status. The D.H.98 was cancelled, but work on the prototype, now named Mosquito, did not stop. Shocked de Havilland argued, and Patrick (later Sir Patrick) Hennessey, who had come from Ford to take over production from Freeman, eventually agreed on a plan that allowed work to continue: 1 prototype to meet the deadline of November 1940 followed by 49 unarmed bomber-reconnaissance aircraft to complete the project. But a programme of 50 aircraft was nonsense in 1940, and Air Ministry again cancelled it. However, this time Beaverbrook himself reinstated it (amazingly) and meanwhile the most beautiful and exciting aeroplane I can think of had taken shape at Salisbury Hall. Trucked to Hatfield on 3 November 1940, it was put together, sprayed glossy 'training yellow', given the serial W4050, and flown by Geoffrey de Havilland Jr on 25 November. The new prototype was superb, and Geoffrey's handling and showmanship made full use of it. According to Walker 'When they saw it fly, even the RAF understood what the Mosquito was all about'.

This long introduction just goes to show what an uphill struggle a good idea has in Britain; maybe the result is a filtering process that sifts the grain from the chaff, but much of the obstruction is just sand in the works. Even after the splendid Mosquito had flown, the officials tried to do what they could to kill the idea. Unable to believe in an unarmed bomber, they decreed that only 20 could be bombers; the rest had to be fighters. Fine, but then much effort was wasted in trying to lumber these with four-cannon turrets. Then the order was again changed with 28 bombers being converted to fighters, and 19 to photo-reconnaissance. What was really happening was that the Mosquito was suddenly emerging as an aircraft which everyone wanted, one which could fly every kind of mission.

Flight development was swift, the only major external change being to extend the engine nacelles and divide the flaps into inner and outer sections, and the engine intakes and a few other details were also changed. The entire airframe was wood, except for a few joints, the engine mounts and the rubber-in-compression landing gear. For the wings the ply skins formed a double shell, with spruce stringers between; the fuselage was basically a ply/balsa/ply sandwich. The 1460 hp Merlin 21s were cooled by radiators in ducts forming the leading edge of the inboard wings giving, not drag, but a net thrust. The wing was mounted at shoulder level, with a bay in the fuselage under it carrying four 500 lb bombs. Pilot and navigator sat side-by-side immediately ahead of the main spar, with a transparent nose for visual bombing.

The first Mossies to reach the RAF were Mk I photo-reconnaissance aircraft, and on the first operational sortie, on 20 September 1941, one photographed French naval bases as far south as Bordeaux, was chased by three Bf 109s and outpaced them. The speed of the Mosquito had astonished Boscombe Down earlier in the year on its first official trials. Nobody believed the figures at first, because, with the same engine and twice the weight and wetted area the aircraft was 20 mph faster than a Spitfire. I can recall flying down the straight railway line to Ashford having a race with a new Hurricane on test from Langley and holding it with one prop feathered.

From the start the RAF were excited about the Mosquito, and when 105 Squadron at Swanton Morley began to receive the B.IV bomber on 15 November 1941 they were the envy of everyone. The first bomber operation by Mosquitoes was a trip by four of 105 Squadron to Cologne on the morning after the first 1000-bomber raid on 31 May 1942, but the new stinger first hit the headlines on 22 September 1942 with a daring pinpoint raid by four aircraft on the Gestapo headquarters in Oslo. The building was in the city centre and would have been destroyed had the RAF had proper bombs, for one hit and failed to explode, and four hit, went out through the far wall and then exploded. Navigation was outstanding, but one aircraft was caught and hit by an Fw 190. Another 190 crashed near Oslo (the Air Ministry did not dispel the Luftwaffe's belief it had been

1 Starboard navigation light
2 Detachable wingtip
3 Starboard formation light
4 Resin lamp
5 Wing structure
6 Starboard aileron
7 Aileron trim tab
8 Aileron control linkage
9 Flap outer section
10 Flap jack inspection/access panel
11 Starboard outer fuel tanks, 24 Imp gals (109l) outboard/34 Imp gals (155l) inboard

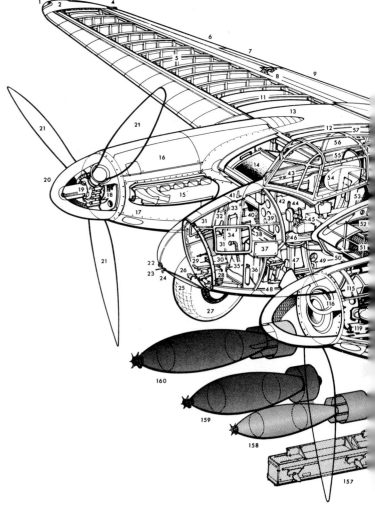

SPECIFICATIONS

Types 1 to 43
Engines: (Mks II, III, IV and early VI) two 1230 hp Rolls-Royce Merlin 21 or (late FB.VI) 1635 hp Merlin 25: (Mk IX) 1680 hp Merlin 72; (Mk XVI) Merlin 72 or 1710 hp Merlin 73 or 77; (Mk 30); 1710 hp Merlin 76, (Mk 33) 1640 hp Merlin 25; (Mks 34, 35, 36) 1690 hp Merlin 113/114. Many other variants had Merlins made by Packard.
Dimensions: span (except Mk XV) 54 ft 2 in (16.5 m); length (most common) 40 ft 6 in (12.34 m); (bombers) 40 ft 9½ in; (radar equipped fighters and Mks 34—38) typically 41 ft 9 in; (Mk 39) 43 ft 4 in); height (most common) 15 ft 3½ in (4.66 m).
Weights: empty (Mks II—VI) about 14100 lb; (Mks VIII—30) about 15200 lb; (beyond Mk 30) about 15900—16800 lb, maximum gross (Mks II and III) around 17500 lb; (Mks IV and VI) about 22500 lb, (later night fighters) about 20500 lb but (HF.XV) only 17395 lb; (Mks IX, XVI and marks beyond 30) typically 25000 lb (11340 kg).
Performance: maximum speed, from 300 mph (TT.39 with M4 sleeve) to 370 mph (595 km/h) for early night fighters, 380 mph (612 km/h) for III, IV and VI, 410 mph (660 km/h) for IX.XVI and 30: and 425 mph for 34 and 35: service seiling, from 30000 ft (9144 m) for low-rated naval versions to 34500 m (10520 m) for most marks, to around 40,000 ft (12190 m) for highblown versions, with Mk XV reaching 44000 ft (13410 m); combat range, typically 1860 miles (2990 km), with naval TFs down at 1260 miles and PR.34 up at 3500 miles.

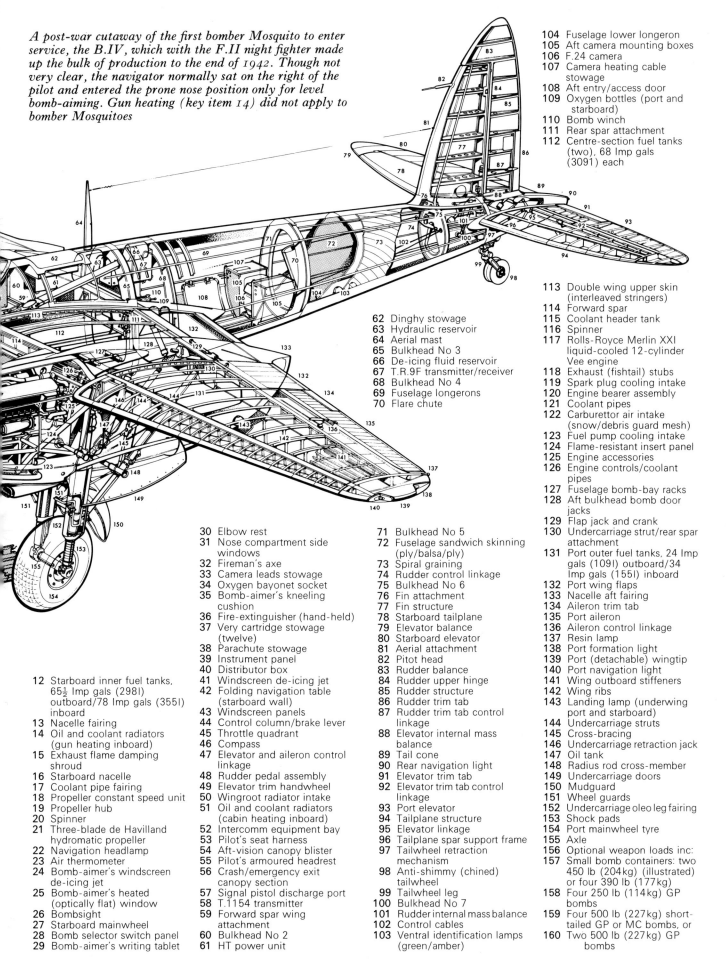

A post-war cutaway of the first bomber Mosquito to enter service, the B.IV, which with the F.II night fighter made up the bulk of production to the end of 1942. Though not very clear, the navigator normally sat on the right of the pilot and entered the prone nose position only for level bomb-aiming. Gun heating (key item 14) did not apply to bomber Mosquitoes

104 Fuselage lower longeron
105 Aft camera mounting boxes
106 F.24 camera
107 Camera heating cable stowage
108 Aft entry/access door
109 Oxygen bottles (port and starboard)
110 Bomb winch
111 Rear spar attachment
112 Centre-section fuel tanks (two), 68 Imp gals (309l) each

62 Dinghy stowage
63 Hydraulic reservoir
64 Aerial mast
65 Bulkhead No 3
66 De-icing fluid reservoir
67 T.R.9F transmitter/receiver
68 Bulkhead No 4
69 Fuselage longerons
70 Flare chute

113 Double wing upper skin (interleaved stringers)
114 Forward spar
115 Coolant header tank
116 Spinner
117 Rolls-Royce Merlin XXI liquid-cooled 12-cylinder Vee engine
118 Exhaust (fishtail) stubs
119 Spark plug cooling intake
120 Engine bearer assembly
121 Coolant pipes
122 Carburettor air intake (snow/debris guard mesh)
123 Fuel pump cooling intake
124 Flame-resistant insert panel
125 Engine accessories
126 Engine controls/coolant pipes
127 Fuselage bomb-bay racks
128 Aft bulkhead bomb door jacks
129 Flap jack and crank
130 Undercarriage strut/rear spar attachment
131 Port outer fuel tanks, 24 Imp gals (109l) outboard/34 Imp gals (155l) inboard
132 Port wing flaps
133 Nacelle aft fairing
134 Aileron trim tab
135 Port aileron
136 Aileron control linkage
137 Resin lamp
138 Port formation light
139 Port (detachable) wingtip
140 Port navigation light
141 Wing outboard stiffeners
142 Wing ribs
143 Landing lamp (underwing port and starboard)
144 Undercarriage struts
145 Cross-bracing
146 Undercarriage retraction jack
147 Oil tank
148 Radius rod cross-member
149 Undercarriage doors
150 Mudguard
151 Wheel guards
152 Undercarriage oleo leg fairing
153 Shock pads
154 Port mainwheel tyre
155 Axle
156 Optional weapon loads inc:
157 Small bomb containers: two 450 lb (204kg) (illustrated) or four 390 lb (177kg)
158 Four 250 lb (114kg) GP bombs
159 Four 500 lb (227kg) short-tailed GP or MC bombs, or
160 Two 500 lb (227kg) GP bombs

12 Starboard inner fuel tanks, 65½ Imp gals (298l) outboard/78 Imp gals (355l) inboard
13 Nacelle fairing
14 Oil and coolant radiators (gun heating inboard)
15 Exhaust flame damping shroud
16 Starboard nacelle
17 Coolant pipe fairing
18 Propeller constant speed unit
19 Propeller hub
20 Spinner
21 Three-blade de Havilland hydromatic propeller
22 Navigation headlamp
23 Air thermometer
24 Bomb-aimer's windscreen de-icing jet
25 Bomb-aimer's heated (optically flat) window
26 Bombsight
27 Starboard mainwheel
28 Bomb selector switch panel
29 Bomb-aimer's writing tablet

30 Elbow rest
31 Nose compartment side windows
32 Fireman's axe
33 Camera leads stowage
34 Oxygen bayonet socket
35 Bomb-aimer's kneeling cushion
36 Fire-extinguisher (hand-held)
37 Very cartridge stowage (twelve)
38 Parachute stowage
39 Instrument panel
40 Distributor box
41 Windscreen de-icing jet
42 Folding navigation table (starboard wall)
43 Windscreen panels
44 Control column/brake lever
45 Throttle quadrant
46 Compass
47 Elevator and aileron control linkage
48 Rudder pedal assembly
49 Elevator trim handwheel
50 Wingroot radiator intake
51 Oil and coolant radiators (cabin heating inboard)
52 Intercomm equipment bay
53 Pilot's seat harness
54 Aft-vision canopy blister
55 Pilot's armoured headrest
56 Crash/emergency exit canopy section
57 Signal pistol discharge port
58 T.1154 transmitter
59 Forward spar wing attachment
60 Bulkhead No 2
61 HT power unit

71 Bulkhead No 5
72 Fuselage sandwich skinning (ply/balsa/ply)
73 Spiral graining
74 Rudder control linkage
75 Bulkhead No 6
76 Fin attachment
77 Fin structure
78 Starboard tailplane
79 Elevator balance
80 Starboard elevator
81 Aerial attachment
82 Pitot head
83 Rudder balance
84 Rudder upper hinge
85 Rudder structure
86 Rudder trim tab
87 Rudder trim tab control linkage
88 Elevator internal mass balance
89 Tail cone
90 Rear navigation light
91 Elevator trim tab
92 Elevator trim tab control linkage
93 Port elevator
94 Tailplane structure
95 Elevator linkage
96 Tailplane spar support frame
97 Tailwheel retraction mechanism
98 Anti-shimmy (chined) tailwheel
99 Tailwheel leg
100 Bulkhead No 7
101 Rudder internal mass balance
102 Control cables
103 Ventral identification lamps (green/amber)

shot down) and a whole gaggle of 190s were outpaced on the full-throttle return journey. Subsequently, Fw 190s had ample advance warning of BOAC Mosquitoes flying on civilian services to Stockholm, but casualties were infrequent.

In the spring of 1943 deliveries began of the B.IX, with the two-stage Merlin 72/73 or 76/77 and many other changes including, usually as a modification, a bulged bomb bay carrying a 4000 lb bomb. Many had H_2S radar and the PFF (Pathfinder Force) aircraft had the Oboe precision navaid, first used by the Mk IV in 1942. From the start of 1943 Mosquitoes were the standard aircraft for Master Bombers and for the increasingly clever and complex systems of precision target-marking. The main bomber version in the final year of war was the B.XVI with the same high-blown engines, paddle-blade propellers and a pressure cabin. The equipment carried revives exciting memories and underlines Britain's unrivalled progress with wartime electronics (Oboe, H_2S Mk VI, Monica, Boozer, Album Leaf and Fishpond) still with immense loads of fuel, a 4000 lb 'cookie' and an over-target speed of 408 mph at 28 500 feet, rising to 419 mph after dropping the bomb. The XVI sometimes operated at weights almost 10 000 lb heavier than the early versions. The final bomber, the B.35, was even more powerful and versatile and had Merlin 113/114 engines, but was only just in time for wartime service.

Exploits of Mossie bombers are incredibly diverse. They dropped every kind of bomb up to 4000 lb, made attacks with special anti-ship weapons, sowed mines, fired rockets and placed 4000-pounders inside railway tunnels. Night after night forces of 50 to 100 would make the trip to Berlin, dropping 4000-pounders, just to deny the enemy rest. The de Havilland-Canada plant at Toronto built several sub-types, beginning with the B.XX, all fitted with

Above: *VP181 was a Mosquito B.35 built by Airspeed at Portsmouth. It is shown after conversion around 1950 to TT.35 (target-tug) standard*
Foot of page: *W4072 was the last of the original batch of nine aircraft originally styled PR.I and converted into bombers designated B.IV Series I. To speed delivery in early 1941 they had the original short nacelles, but the increased-span wing of all Mosquitoes except the prototype, W4050*

Packard-built Merlins, while de Havilland Australia at Bankstown built a further series beginning with the FB.40, again all with Packard engines. The FB.40 was a variant of the British FB.VI, itself a derivative of the original fighter Mk II.

The fighter variants of the Mosquito deserve brief coverage, even though this is a book about bombers, because the fighter and fighter/bomber versions outnumbered the others. Most had a flat, bullet-proof windscreen, four 20 mm Hispanos under the floor and, instead of the ventral door of the bomber and PR types, a side door on the right. The crew member in the right-hand seat in the FB.VI was the navigator. As well as the cannon this model had four 0·303 in Brownings in the nose and carried bombs or tanks under the wings, supplementing a normal load of two 500 lb (later two 1000 lb) in the rear bomb bay. But many Mosquitoes were

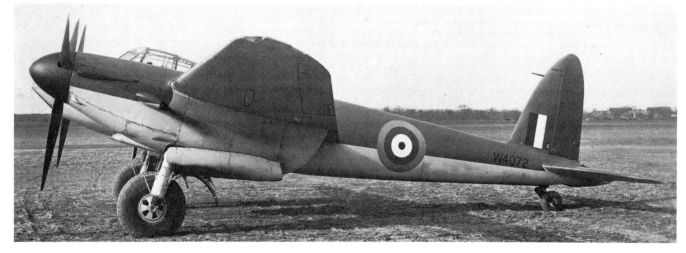

Above: *DZ353, one of the original B.IV bombers of 105 Sqn, photographed during the press visit in December 1942*
Below: *Another photograph taken during the same memorable visit to the base of 105 Sqn, Marham in Norfolk. A-Able, in the foreground, had previously flown three trips with 139 Sqn, the other pioneer Mossie unit, but was shot down days after the picture was taken. E-Easy lasted until 8 June 1944; P-Peter was the only one of this line-up not to be lost in action*

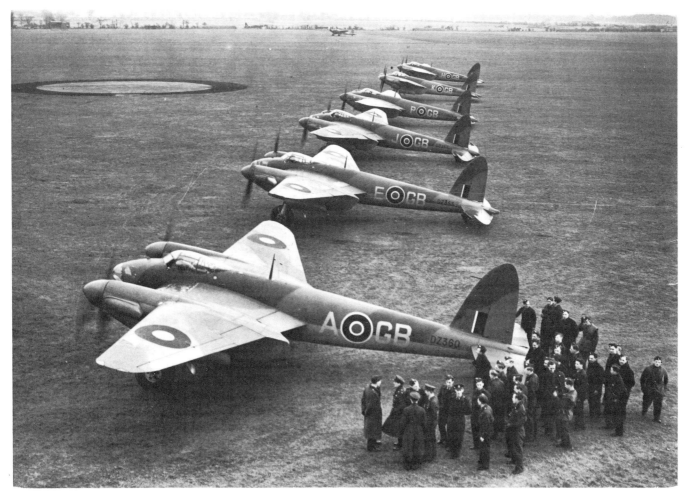

night fighters, with radar, and in these a radar observer occupied the right-hand seat, who studied his dimly-lit indicators and translated what he saw into immediate and precise orders to his pilot.

The original fighter, and at 17700 lb almost the lightest of all Mosquitoes, was the F.II, first flown (W4052) on 15 May 1941. Painted black, with roundel-red serial numbers, these almost futuristic machines had AI.IV or V radar with the old-type array of fixed but switchable dipole aerials, a harpoon transmitter on the tip of the nose and vertical elevation and azimuth aerials on the wingtips, though other arrangements were used. These gave a tricky pair of images, with flickering 'grass' amongst which the observer had to search for the tiny spike that meant a target. Later fighters had the centimetric AI.VIII, with an oscillating scanner in the blunt nose instead of the machine guns, and a single circular display interpreted in quite a different way. Other versions had the AI.10 (SCR–720) American radar with yet other kinds of display, and de Havilland not only achieved a superb installation of this excellent radar but also devised a 'bull' nose which was capacious enough to house any of the available AI scanners. The FB.VI, already mentioned, was a multi-role attack machine with no radar, while one of its main users, Coastal Command, also operated the Mk XVIII with a 6-pounder gun for knocking

Top: *V-Victor of Coastal Command's 235 Sqn, an FB.VI, has all eight rockets in flight, having lined up with cannon fire on a steamer in Stongfjord, Norway, on 19 September 1944* Above: *Here seen without drop tanks, the B.35 was the final mark of Mosquito bomber*

holes in shipping or indeed in U-boats, which by 1943 stayed much on the surface and carried so much flak they stood a good chance against anything other than a Mk XVIII Mosquito. The Mk XV was a special, light-weight pressurized fighter with extended, pointed wings, designed for stratospheric interceptions that, in the event, were seldom needed.

Altogether there were 7781 Mosquitoes, and my own favourite was the highest performer of all, the PR.34 long-range reconnaissance model, carrying 1267 gallons of fuel. It was a good thing indeed that the persistence of de Havilland wore down the disinterest of the customer, and not vice versa.

Boeing B-29 Superfortress

I once had to answer the question: 'Which aircraft showed the biggest technical advance in all history? It was a difficult choice, but I finally picked the B–29. In terms of technical achievement it far transcended everything that had gone before, though in some ways the German A–4 'V–2' rocket, which ran parallel in timing, ran it close, but it was hardly an aircraft. In at least a dozen areas the B–29 broke completely new ground, and in everything except its electrical system voltage, it pushed far beyond the boundaries of existing knowledge and experience. There is a general rule that when building a new aircraft it is permissible to introduce one or two new features but never too many; for example, do not produce a new type of aircraft which has new engines as well. But Boeing have always had a reputation for sticking their necks out; the only old thing on the B–29 was the maker's name.

The B–29 was a truly dramatic advance in technology and ideas incorporated in it were

used in all subsequent large piston aircraft, many of them being carried over into the jet era. And in spite of being so much ahead of its time, the B–29, instrument of horrifying destruction as it was, was one of the most wonderful aircraft in the sky. It might easily have been very dangerous because it was so extremely highly loaded and in addition was packed with complex things to go wrong. Instead every B–29 pilot I ever met always had time to stop and chat admiringly about it, and his memories were filled with respect for the most graceful, willing, efficient and capable bomber the world had then seen.

Everyone who knows anything about aviation knows the B–29 dropped atom bombs on Japan in 1945. I once asked an RAF audience when they thought the programme for this exercise started, and the general consensus was in 1942 or 1943. In fact the year was 1938, and it says much for the farsightedness and sheer nerve of Chief of Staff General Oscar Westover that it

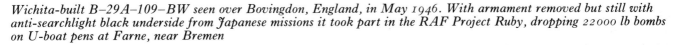

Wichita-built B–29A–109–BW seen over Bovingdon, England, in May 1946. With armament removed but still with anti-searchlight black underside from Japanese missions it took part in the RAF Project Ruby, dropping 22000 lb bombs on U-boat pens at Farne, near Bremen

135

began at a time when Congress was refusing funds for the B–17, and for his successor in January 1939, 'Hap' Arnold, who set up a nationwide manufacturing programme on a gigantic scale long before the prototype flew. Important aircraft do not happen overnight, yet even today one finds politicians who would— so they say—willingly cancel new combat aircraft in the belief that such a weapon could suddenly be produced out of the blue in any emergency. The B–29 took six years to perfect; today's warplanes generally take longer.

Developing the B–29 was a herculean task, with false starts and urgent rethinks resulting from lessons learned in the first months of the

sections of the B–29 to a completely new Navy plant (built for the cancelled Sea Ranger programme) a few miles away at Renton. Further assembly lines were in three of the largest new plants in the nation, one at Wichita, Kansas, managed by Boeing, one at Omaha, Nebraska, managed by Martin, and the third at Marietta, Georgia, managed by Bell. Further large-scale production of airframe assemblies took place at the new Cleveland plant of the Fisher Body division of General Motors, which made all the engine nacelles. The engine chosen was the biggest available, the 2200 hp Wright Duplex Cyclone R–3350–23 with two General Electric turbochargers mounted in the sides of

This breathtaking picture needs to be big. Taken at Renton in the summer of 1944, it affords a comparison between two of the greatest bombers of the Second World War. These B–29s are not from the first production block; they have the four-gun forward dorsal turret, which was chosen in late 1942 as a result of combat experience with the B–17

Second World War. By February 1940 Boeing had built their third mock-up and arrived at the Model 345, significantly more advanced than its predecessors. In August 1940 the Army Air Corps provided funds for two (later three) prototypes, and the first, 41–002 and painted olive drab, flew on 21 September 1942. But by this time a few things had happened. In January 1942, a month after Pearl Harbor drew America into the war, orders had been signed for 14 YB–29s and 500 B–29A Superfortresses, and by September the total had reached 1664. To build them, and thousands yet to be ordered, the biggest aircraft-manufacturing pool ever organized was planned in six weeks and put into operation in less than a year, mostly using colossal factories built in virgin territory. Seattle, the Boeing headquarters, continued to pour out B–17s but also tooled up to deliver major

each nacelle, driving 16 ft 7 in Hamilton four-blade propellers.

Aerodynamically one marvelled at the Boeing 117-section wing, with an aspect ratio of 11·5 and bristling with radical things that today are commonplace. The structural loadings throughout were dramatically higher than in any previous aircraft, and the inboard wing-box skin thickness of 0·64 inch was more than double that of any previously tried. Revolutionary, too, were the enormous flaps, a modified Fowler type, screwed out electrically to add one-fifth to gross wing area and overcome the unprecedented wing loading of 71·9 lb/sq ft at design weight of 124000 lb and 81·1 lb/sq ft at take-off on the first combat mission. For comparison, the wing loading of a typical B–17 was 35 lb/sq ft. Nothing is more critical in aeroplane design than wing loading, and this aspect of the B–29

136

caused more concern than any other. In the years when the irrevocable decisions were taken, nobody knew for sure that such a wing loading would be compatible with the use of operational airstrips or even safe to fly at all.

Boeing, alone of the world's planemakers, had extensive experience with pressure cabins. So great was the planned performance of the B-29 that the whole crew of ten would have to ride in pressurized compartments. One formed the forward fuselage, accommodating the bombardier in the Plexiglas nose, the pilot and co-pilot side-by-side with an aisle between, the navigator facing ahead behind the pilot, and the flight engineer (sometimes two) facing aft

o·5 in. This advanced system eventually worked well, with each turret always under the direction of one gunner only (though control could switch), with secondary control links to enable sight stations to direct other turrets should the original gunner be wounded. In 1942, when the Luftwaffe found the best way to attack a B-17 formation was head-on, the decision was taken to fit a new forward upper turret with four o·5 in guns. This had great punch but added a great deal of weight and completely obstructed the forward fuselage with a large ammunition magazine, round which a portly crew-member could not pass.

For a pilot, the Superfort was a new experience

behind the co-pilot, with the radio operator behind him. Under the centre of the fuselage were two enormous bomb bays, separated by a very strong ring section, built integral with the wing box and forming the structural heart of the B-29. An electric sequencing switch released bombs alternately from the front and rear bays to preserve the c.g. position. Above the wing box ran a pressurized tunnel through which crew members could crawl to the second crew compartment well behind the wing, just aft of the rear weapons bay, where three Plexiglas bubbles served as sighting stations for three gunners. These were linked electrically to four turrets. The top bubble controlled either or both the upper turrets, the side bubbles the lower rear turret and the nose one (bombardier) the lower forward turret, all with two o·5 in guns. In the extreme tail sat a rear gunner, in a separate pressurized compartment, with a sight controlling a barbette with one 20 mm cannon and two of

indeed. A Blenheim I or He 111 pilot might not have found it strange to sit in the nose formed from a great glass hemisphere, but pilots experienced on the B-17 looked in vain for some kind of structure they could line up ahead of them with the horizon, and eventually found themselves flying on instruments, even in bright sunshine.

The B-29, more than any previous aircraft in history, was an aircraft where a team worked together and did things by the book. That does not mean that previous bombers like the B-24 could be flown how they liked, but the B-29 had long lists of vital actions that needed a whole crew to perform, long checklists that had to be read on the R/T, and precise sequences of action performed by the co-pilot or engineer on the direct command of the captain. So far as I know, the B-29 was the first bomber that could not be flown solo. For anyone to attempt this five pairs of hands would have been needed, the seat harness would be permanently undone, and the pilot would have had to leap all over the forward fuselage. The takeoff and landing speeds were getting on for the 200 mph cruising speed of a B-17.

Deliveries of production aircraft, from Wichita, began in July 1943. Crews were excited, challenged, frightened, baffled and sometimes elated. Maybe the biggest genuine disappointment was aircraft range. By this time the decision had been taken to send all B-29s to attack Japan, chiefly because the distances involved were extremely great. Boeing had given impressive guarantees on range, but for some reason the first crews did not know how to realize the performance in practice. Crews in the US Midwest tried to simulate raids on Tokyo, starting in theory from yet-to-be-captured strips in the Marianas, flying practice missions to Havana, which looks a bit like Tokyo only smaller. They found they could not fly a mission a mere 1500 miles each way, with no bomb load! Only gradually did the USAAF learn what the RAF (certainly the PRU pilots in lone Mossies and Spits) had known for years:

Reduce the revs, and boost the boost;

You'll have enough petrol to get home to roost.

Almost unbelievably, the air miles per gallon were increased over a period of three months by 100 per cent! Yet when the first crews of the 58th Bomb Wing flew their great birds across the Atlantic, across Africa and to bases in India in the spring of 1944, they were still frighteningly deficient in almost everything save basic flying skill and guts. Just how to turn a B-29 into an efficient fighting ship had still to be learned, and how to make its umpteen thousand parts work at maximum efficiency was also a problem. Engine fires, invariably caused by overheated upper-rear exhaust valves, became a real menace. The de-icers, propellers, Plexiglas demisting, radio/navaids and many other things gave considerable trouble, and not a few crews either just found it all too much or crashed or disappeared without leaving an explanation. And, of course, the B-29 was very much on the limit of usable runway length and strength, and also needed an unobstructed climb path at a flattish angle, because at maximum weight the speed had to build up to about 200 mph before any climb at all was possible.

On 5 June 1944, as a million men in Operation Overload girded their loins for the greatest mission in history, a handful of men at 31000 feet on the other side of the world dropped the first bombs to leave the Superfortress, in anger, on a marshalling yard at Bangkok. Gradually attacks built up in strength and diversity. Superforts struck further afield, up to 2000 miles from base, while others crossed 'The Hump' and began operations from deep in China against the Japanese mainland. The first was flown from Chengtu on 15 June 1944 against a big steelworks at Yawata. The intention had been to use the Superfort's new radar bombing system to attack by night, but point targets, even as big as a steelworks, were too difficult and raids had to be made by day. It was all terribly demanding. Just flying fuel, bombs and provisions for the B-29s and their crews over The Hump needed a mighty fleet of C-47 and C-46 transports, which suffered from the lack of navaids, bad weather and unyielding mountains. In the harsh environment in which they operated, B-29s tended to wear out and give fresh troubles. It was at this time that it was realized that a hot and high airstrip could easily mean an aborted mission, simply because running up to, say, 1200 rpm to check the magnetoes caused swift overheating. Soon the standard drill was: open up and begin the takeoff, and check the mags on the way!

From the start the B-29 had been designed to operate unescorted. By the second half of 1944 the B-29 crews could see what a difference an escort made over Europe; but their situation in the East was different. Though the B-29 losses continued to mount, they were seldom caused by enemy action. Crossing Japan at 300 mph at 31000 feet or even higher, there was not very much to fear from the defences. Just a few lucky hits were achieved with heavy flak, but the Japanese 'triple A' (anti-aircraft artillery) was like a holiday compared with that of Germany. One or two fighters might appear, but they seldom accomplished much. Not surprisingly, for one should ponder for a moment on the courage of a fighter pilot straining to reach a formation of B-29s bristling with heavy machine guns and cannon, all precisely aimed by men in snug, comfortable, warm seats, knowing that at full throttle in a fighter one's closing speed on the enemy would be about walking pace. Most Jap interceptors simply could not get anywhere near the B-29s and so lived to return to earth. Before long many of the American aircraft had been stripped of all except the tail guns and called B-29B, thereby being enabled to fly further, faster and higher.

On 21 November 1944 the first mission was flown by the newly formed 20th Air Force from the new strip on the newly captured Marianas. This first sortie was from Saipan, but soon B-29s from Guam and Tinian swiftly built up to a mighty crescendo against Japan. It should not be thought there were just a few B-29s at the end of the war. The number built by VJ-Day was 3667, and by 1945 the number in the Marianas alone equipped 20 Bomb Groups sending 450 to 500 aircraft on each mission. Experience dramatically reduced the navigational errors on the long, high-altitude missions, cut the aborts and crashes, and stretched out the range still further, until long missions were being flown with the design maximum bomb load of 17500 lb. Increasingly, the vast bomb bays were loaded up with incendiaries, and on 9 March 1945 the bold decision was taken to stay at low level for a coming mission and thus carry full bomb load. The target was Tokyo, and that night more people died—about 84000 —than in any other air attack before or since. About another 100000 were injured, and when an F–13 photo-reconnaissance version of the B–29 flew across next day it found about 16 square miles of the city completely burned out. The B–29s dropped over 100000 tons of incendiaries on Japan, as well as sowing mines in Japanese waters. Finally, two aircraft were rebuilt in June–July 1945 to carry the atomic bombs. On 6 August 1945 Col Paul Tibbetts and crew, flying *Enola Gay* of the 345th BS, dropped a fission weapon of 20 kilotons nominal yield, called 'Little Boy', on Hiroshima. The air-burst wrecked the heart of the city and killed around 70000. On 9 August the other machine, *Bockscar*, dropped 'The Fat Man' on Nagasaki. On 15 August the war was over, without the bloody invasion that had till then seemed inevitable.

Subsequently the B–29s went on to a whole series of new careers. They were modified for almost every kind of large military task imaginable, while the Soviets refused to return three that had force-landed in their territory after bombing Japan, put the B–29 into mass-production as the Tu–4, and used the same technology in the subsequent series of Tupolev jet and turboprop bombers and transports. Back at Seattle, Boeing developed the B–29 into the high-performance B–50 and the civil Stratocruiser. In March 1950 the first of 88 Washingtons (RAF name) arrived in Britain to help the RAF overcome the fact that nobody had provided it with any modern bombers. Around 1952, as a young staff-man on *Flight*, I covered an exercise in an aircraft of this type belonging to 90 Squadron, and what a wonderful improvement in comfort over the Lanc! But I am told the B–29 combat missions sometimes lasted 15 hours. You really need comfort for that.

Taken in January 1951, this picture shows the B–29A in action for the second and last time, over North Korea. In this prolonged and bitter war the B–29 played a central role in bringing the opposing sides to the peace talks at Panmunjom in 1953

English Electric Canberra

Cerulean Blue, similar to wartime PRU Blue, was the colour of VN799, the original English Electric A.1 which first flew on a Friday the 13th 1949

How does one create a superior jet bomber or, for that matter, any other type of aircraft? In the years following the Second World War the US Air Force unveiled six jet bombers of the most advanced design imaginable. All were bigger and much heavier than the average four-engined 'heavy' of the recent war, and some had such unprecedented features as sharply swept wings and tail, pod-mounted engines, tricycle landing gear, inbuilt rocket motors, braking parachutes and, in one case, a near-perfect all-wing layout. They did not happen overnight; designs had started in 1943, and drawings were being released to the shops in 1945. By comparison, Britain was late starting. When a jet bomber did appear, in May 1949, it was unexpectedly small and seemed quite conventional. Against the fantastic Americans it seemed to have no chance. Yet today, almost 30 years later, this small and ordinary machine is as busy as it can be, not only in the RAF and other air forces around the globe but also in the US Air Force, while the futuristic Americans have long since retired to museums.

In this brief chapter I want to pay tribute to the Canberra, which bids fair to be the longest-lasting bomber in history. There is an element of luck in this. I doubt if even W. E. W. 'Teddy' Petter, who led the design team, had the slightest notion that by the very process of making Britain's first jet bomber as straightforward as possible he would not only avoid trouble at the start, but also give it qualities to sustain its cost/effectiveness for a life of about 40 years.

During the Second World War, English Electric's Aircraft Division in Preston had built more Handley Page Hampdens and more Halifaxes than any other company, but they had virtually no design staff. In 1945 they were in production with the new Vampire jet fighter, getting used to a new level of flight performance, but it was still someone else's aeroplane. Petter arrived from Westland and set up a design office in the former bus garage of Barton Motors in Corporation Street. Soon he had Specification B.3/45 to work to, calling for a 'two-seat high-altitude bomber equipped with jet engines and a radar bombsight'. That was almost all the document said, because the Ministry of Aircraft Production did not yet know what to ask for. It simply suggested the bomb load of a Mosquito (4000 lb) and radius of action of a Lancaster (800 miles). Both figures were about one-third of what was being demanded for the future USAF Strategic Air Command.

Petter had come to some basic conclusions while he was at Westland. One was that the Mosquito concept was right for a jet bomber, turrets or other defensive armament being not worth while. Another was that the design should be aerodynamically as clean as possible, and he hoped to propel it by a single large turbojet of 13000 lb static thrust which would just fit the circular-section rear fuselage. A third was that, unlike the B–29 and the new crop of American jet bombers, the wing should be of generous area to give the lowest practical wing loading. Such a choice would result in a bomber having outstanding takeoff and landing, exceptional ceiling, and manoeuvrability at all heights. The thing that worried him most was the radar bombsight, and in this he was fully justified.

Chief test pilot Wing Commander R. P. Beamont—who is invariably called Bee by his friends and Roly (which he abhors) by the media—took VN799, the turquoise-blue prototype, into the air on Friday the 13th May, 1949. From that moment, the Canberra was recognised as probably the most sweetly manoeuvrable bomber in the modern world. The broad wing made it possible with only modest engine thrust to leap off the ground and go into a roll or a tight turn within the airfield boundary, all with consummate ease. Even then the full implications were not realised, and many critics said it ought to have slim, swept wings and weigh twice as much. Petter never wavered from his objective of creating a jet bomber that any service pilot could fly, any runway could accommodate, any factory could build and any air force could afford to buy and maintain.

He failed in his bid to fit one big fuselage-mounted engine, but 30 years ago two of Rolls-Royce's axial Avons were hardly second best to anything, however they were mounted. Sticking to his search for cleanliness, Petter put them inside the wing ahead of the front spar in simple nacelles. The radar bombsight failed to appear, and at the eleventh hour Petter had to accommodate a bomb aimer by redesigning the pressurized forward fuselage with a transparent nose which could be used for old-fashioned sighting. But he still improved on the specification by making provision for two triple clusters of

John Yoxall, who had been chief photographer of Flight *since 1910, took this study of Canberras in 1955, at about 30000 feet over The Wash. The aircraft are B.2 bombers from 100 Sqn*

1000 lb bombs, or a variety of other stores. Best of all, the all-round performance was not just as good as, but in many respects better than, that of the RAF's latest Meteor or Vampire jet fighters. Around January 1951 deliveries began to 101 Squadron at Binbrook. First deliveries had glossy black sides and undersurfaces, but these were soon changed to grey-blue. Going on exercises in these early Canberra B.2 bombers was about the most pleasant thing one could imagine. Even when the RAF later received Canadian-built Sabre fighters, their pilots found the Canberras by no means easy to intercept.

The only serious problems were crashes caused by pupils overshooting in poor visibility and becoming confused by 'seat of the pants' flying, to which they were not used, misreading horizons (due to sustained acceleration causing gyro errors) and lack of true visual reference points beyond the goldfish-bowl canopy. These problems were eventually cleared up by the T.4 version with side-by-side dual controls. Other early marks included the PR.3 photo-recce, B.6 with more fuel and more powerful engines, PR.7 (camera-PR version of B.6) and B(I).8, the last being a useful multi-role two-seater with the pilot under a fighter-type canopy offset to the left, a weapon bay with three bombs at the back, and four 20 mm cannon and a vast amount of ammunition in the front. Most versions had provision for under-wing bombs or missiles and wing-tip tanks, raising the loaded weight from

A cameraman from Picture Post *visited RAF stations in May 1952 to prove that the RAF was all right, and not— as scare-mongers would have it—inadequately equipped. This view of nearly the entire initial batch of B.2 Canberras is impressive, but to allay public fear by proclaiming 'nearly all the fighter squadrons now have the latest mark of Meteor' shows how disastrous things really were*

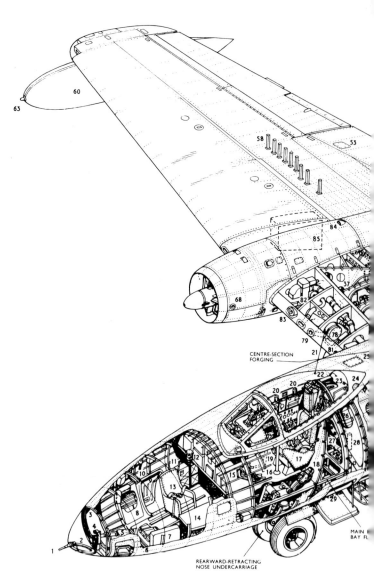

REARWARD-RETRACTING
NOSE UNDERCARRIAGE

Dick Ellis, who still draws cutaways in the Flight *offices, managed to nip through the Ministry security screen with this illustration in 1951. A matter of weeks later a new D-notice grading system put the Canberra B.2, subject of this drawing, on the Part-Publication list, meaning that cutaways were prohibited. But this particular horse had already left the stable*

1	Pressure head	24	Inflatable canopy seal
2	Optically flat window	25	Access to fuel bay and vent galleries
3	Bombing control panel		
4	Bombsight	26	Hydraulic reservoir
5	Prone bombing position	27	Batteries
6	Under-floor armour	28	Front bomb-door jack
7	Bombing computer	29	Port equipment bay
8	Wind-break door	30	Bomb doors
9	Crew-entry door	31	Bomb-door rollers
10	Crash axe	32	Fuel booster pump
11	Door jettison handle	33	Fuel tank skin
12	Signal pistol	34	Fuselage keel structure
13	Navigator's seat	35	Loop-aerial hatch
14	Navigator's table	36	Camera
15	Rudder pedals	37	Extinguisher bottle
16	Control column	38	Bomb-bay bulkhead
17	Martin-Baker Mk 1C seat	39	Camera hatch
18	Pressure bulkhead	40	Elevator and rudder control-rods
19	Navigator's take-off seat		
20	Canopy-jettison bolts	41	Aerial
21	V.H.F. whip aerials	42	Fuel vent-pipe outlet
22	Demister unit	43	Tail bumper
23	Canopy-jettison ram	44	Rear bulkhead

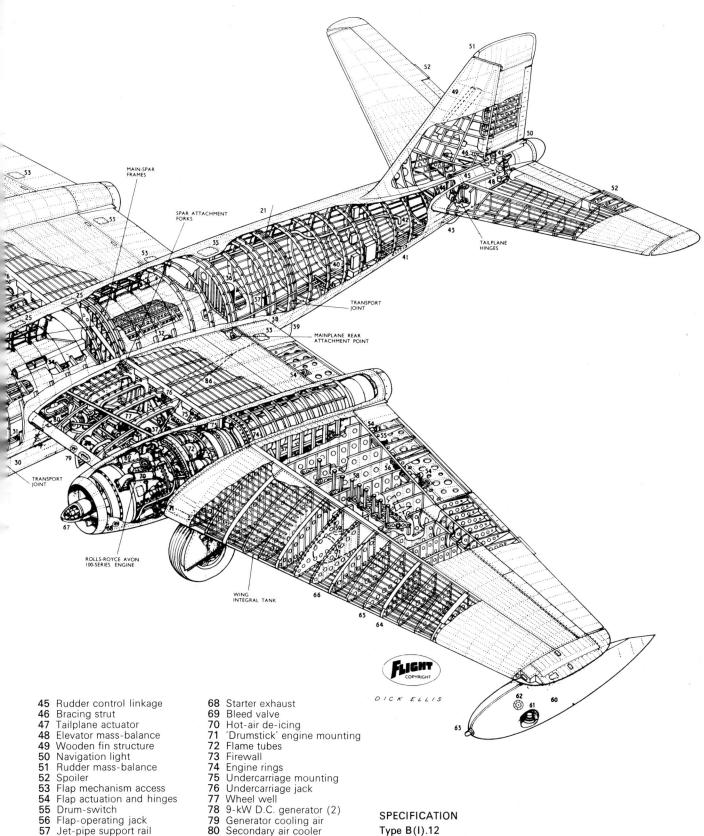

DICK ELLIS

45 Rudder control linkage	68 Starter exhaust
46 Bracing strut	69 Bleed valve
47 Tailplane actuator	70 Hot-air de-icing
48 Elevator mass-balance	71 'Drumstick' engine mounting
49 Wooden fin structure	72 Flame tubes
50 Navigation light	73 Firewall
51 Rudder mass-balance	74 Engine rings
52 Spoiler	75 Undercarriage mounting
53 Flap mechanism access	76 Undercarriage jack
54 Flap actuation and hinges	77 Wheel well
55 Drum-switch	78 9-kW D.C. generator (2)
56 Flap-operating jack	79 Generator cooling air
57 Jet-pipe support rail	80 Secondary air cooler
58 Air-brake drag channels	81 Camera gun
59 External stores pylon	82 Accessory gearbox
60 Jettisonable fuel tank	83 Hydraulic pump (2)
61 Drain valve	84 Engine-ring cooling air
62 Filler cap	85 Fuel collector box
63 Navigation light	86 Gun-pack
64 Main wing rib	
65 Secondary rib	
66 Nose beam	
67 Triple-breech starter	

SPECIFICATION

Type B(I).12

Engines: two 7500 lb (3402 kg) thrust Rolls-Royce Avon 109 single-shaft turbojets.
Dimensions: span 63 ft 11½ in (19·5 m); length 65 ft 6 in (19·95 m); height 15 ft 7 in (4·72 m).
Weights: empty 23173—27950 lb (10400—12700 kg); loaded 43000 lb (19504 kg); maximum permissible 56250 lb (25515 kg).
Performance: maximum speed 580 (933 km/h) at 30000 ft (9144 m) or Mach 0·83; initial climb at maximum weight 3400 ft (1036 m)/min; service ceiling 48000 ft (14630 m); range (typical mission at low level) 805 miles (1295 km); ferry-range 3030 miles (5842 km).

143

Two of today's Canberras are the T.17 (top) and TT.18, both rebuilds of old B.2 bombers. The T.17, operated by 360 Sqn (combined RAF/RN crews) at Cottesmore, is an ECM trainer filled with clever electronics. The TT.18, operated by 7 Sqn at St Mawgan, carries the Flight Refuelling Rushton target system, and it is a testimony to the accuracy of the Rapier SAM that it has always hit the target and never the Canberra

around 46000 lb to 56250 lb.

While production of the B.2 and B.6 was speeded by bringing in Avro, Handley Page and Short, with an uneconomic separate production line at each plant, further production began at the Government Aircraft Factories at Fishermen's Bend, Melbourne. A major factor in ironing out problems in this unexpectedly widespread manufacturing complex was the original lofting scheme whereby every airframe part was reproduced actual size on thin but substantial metal plates. These undistortable plates, used in place of conventional drawings, were flown out to Australia and there was no trouble at all. And in 1951 further sets were flown out to The Martin Company, Baltimore, Maryland. One of the great American plane-makers, Martin had produced an aircraft seemingly far more advanced than the Canberra, the triple-jet XB–51. But—almost contrary to the laws of nature—it was the little British machine that the US Air Force picked to fly tactical intruder missions. As a result the B–57 family emerged as a fresh series of Canberras, ultimately to give distinguished service throughout the conflict in SE Asia and to be rebuilt by Convair

as the RB–57F with wings of almost twice the span and and TF33 turbofan engines.

English Electric became part of British Aircraft Corporation in 1960, which in 1977 was swallowed by the nationalized monolith British Aerospace. But at the Preston (Warton and Samlesbury) factories the sons of the men who built the first Canberra are refurbishing large numbers of these useful aircraft for an astonishing diversity of customers and uses. Back in the 1950s, various marks were sold to many air forces, and almost all not only still use Canberras but have come back for more. In the RAF, joined now by the Royal Navy, mark numbers have now reached 22, later versions including electronic warfare platforms, special electronic trainers, target tugs and the extra-high-altitude PR.9 with more power and a revised airframe. Foreign customers usually specify less exotic bomber, reconnaissance, intruder and trainer sub-types, and increasingly these are ex-RAF or other aircraft, rebuilt for a fresh career. All of which goes to show that, if you want a real winner which will last for 40 years, start off by making it a wee bit old-fashioned.

144

Boeing B-52

In the story of the B–17 the point was made that the United States is thousands of miles from possible adversaries. Before the Second World War the distance was sufficiently great to rule out direct bombing attack, but after that conflict aircraft development had altered the situation. In 1941 work had begun on a gigantic strategic bomber able to fly a return mission from North America to Germany. After the war, as the Convair B–36, this entered service with the newly formed US Air Force Strategic Air Command (SAC). In most ways the biggest bomber in history, it had six of the most powerful piston engines driving 19-foot pusher propellers, and later was boosted to greater over-target speeds and heights by two pods containing four jet engines. It was a great aircraft, and the centre of a lively debate at political level. The Navy liked power, and this was personified in the new *Forrestal*-type super-carriers. The upstart Air Force also liked power, and this was personified in the globe-girdling B–36. As both programmes cost billions of dollars the *Forrestal* and B–36 became such bitter foes that sometimes the men in dark and light blue forgot all about the

problem of the Soviets and the chilly Cold War.

In the early 1950s the monster B–36 was the only way SAC could create what became known as a 'credible deterrent'. Along with the shorter-range B–47 it was real enough, and certainly deterred most would-be aggressors apart from the army of North Korea, but an over-the-target speed of 435 mph at 40000 feet was nothing like enough. A jet could do much better on both counts, but jets could not fly far enough. Even the splendid B–47, whose aerodynamic drag was an unprecedented 25 per cent lower than prediction, could not fly a SAC mission from within the USA to Soviet territory, even with the new technique of flight refuelling. There was thus great pressure on the US industry to produce an intercontinental jet bomber.

As early as April 1946 Boeing had been working on the XB–52, which had four powerful turboprops. Turbojets burned up fuel too quickly, and the complex and troublesome turboprops in the 8000-horsepower class seemed the only answer. It seemed for a while that salvation lay with the engine firm of Pratt &

A unique photograph showing a B–52C, with full flap, in formation with one of the last airworthy B–17s (it is a real picture, not a montage)

Whitney. Helped by Rolls-Royce into the gas-turbine business, they started work in 1947 on a completely new two-shaft turbojet, which eventually became the J57 and was much like Britain's Olympus, which had the same timing. Its advanced design gave it a high compression ratio, leading to better fuel economy, and it was soon the centre of attraction for designers of fighters, bombers and future civil airliners. However, even this engine seemed to be unable to fly the very long SAC missions, and work went ahead on a turboprop version, the T57. Much later this powerful turboprop was the basis around which the USAF planned a giant freighter, the Douglas XC–132; but the onward march of engine technology finally permitted an escape from the propeller into today's world of big turbofans, and instead of the XC–132 the USAF bought the jet-engined Lockheed C–5A Galaxy.

But what about the bomber? Back in October 1948 Boeing, though committed to the T57-turboprop bomber, were asked by the USAF if they would submit a study for one powered by jets. This was because, compared with improved models of the B–36, the turboprop did not offer much extra speed or height, and was actually inferior in range. The USAF did not believe there could be a strategic jet bomber, and was quite taken aback when Boeing's team at Wright Field said their study would be delivered the following Monday! The far-sighted planemaker had already completed a detailed study for a 'medium bomber' (a B–47 replacement) with four J57 engines of 8500 lb thrust. By simply scaling this design up to have eight of these engines, with two engines in each pod instead of one, the result looked interesting. A week later the designation XB–52 had been transferred to the new eight-jet aircraft, the Boeing 464. Boeing coined an obvious name for it: the Stratofortress.

To provide competition and a comparative yardstick, Convair was awarded a contract for the YB–60, a B–36 rebuilt with swept wings and tail and the same eight J57 engines. This in fact was even larger than the B–52, but despite some apparent advantages—especially in reduced cost and technical risk—the superiority of

In the early 1950s the journal Flight *published numerous cutaway drawings of a rather novel kind. It happened almost without our being aware of it. Like most people in aviation I was an enthusiast, and it was only natural that, in a huddle with such fine artists as Arthur (Art) Bowbeer and Frank Munger, we should have devised what we called the 'probe'. This was a cutaway of an aircraft still secret, prepared without external collaboration or access to the real thing. A few probes, such as this of the first production B–52, were drawn with a ballpoint pen*

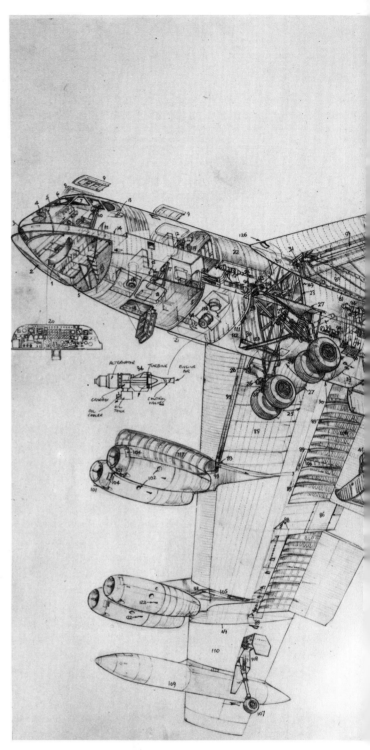

SPECIFICATIONS

Types B–52 to B–52H
Engines: (B–52F, G) eight 13750 lb (6238 kg) thrust (water-injection rating) Pratt & Whitney J57–43W two-shaft turbojets; (B–52H) eight 17000 lb (7711 kg) thrust Pratt & Whitney TF33–3 two-shaft turbofans.
Dimensions: span 185 ft (56·4 m); length 157 ft 7 in (48 m); height 48 ft 3 in (14·75 m); (B–52G, H) 40 ft 8 in (12·4 m).
Weights: empty 171,000–193,000 lb (77200–87100 kg); loaded 450000 lb (204120 kg) (B–52G, 488000 lb, 221500 kg; B–52H, 505000 lb, 229000 kg).
Performance: maximum speed about 630 mph (1014 km/h) at over 24000 ft (7315 m); service ceiling 45000–55000 ft (13720–16765 m); range on internal fuel with maximum weapon load (C, D, E, F) 6,200 miles (9978 km); (G) 8500 miles (13680 km); (H) 12500 miles (20150 km).

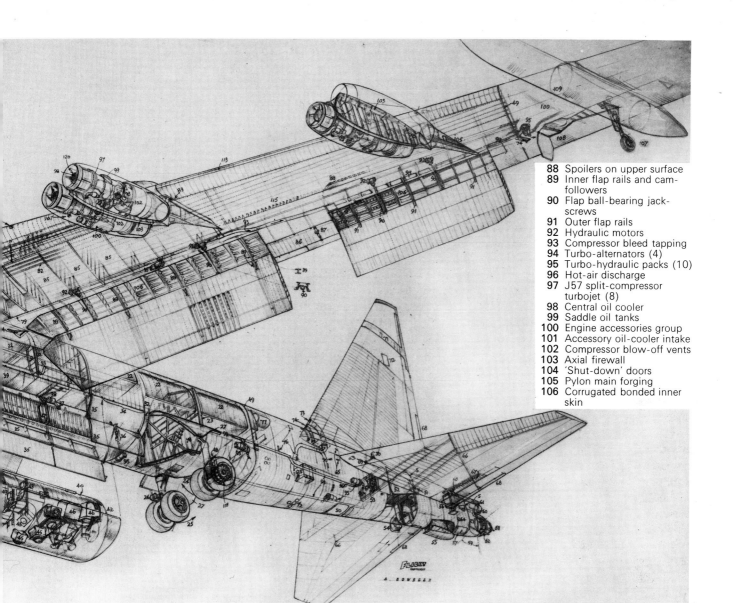

the 'clean sheet of paper' Boeing bomber carried the day. Tex Johnston and Col. Guy M. Townsend flew the extremely impressive YB–52 (second prototype, but first to take the air) from Boeing Field, Seattle, on 15 March 1952. As with the B–47 flight test programme, the development flying was centred at Larson Air Force Base at Moses Lake, in central Washington, where there was a 10000 foot runway, good facilities and no community relations problems with eight of the noisiest and smokiest engines ever hung on one airframe.

Though clearly related to the B–47, the new bomber was different in many respects apart from sheer size. Far more of the fuel was carried in flexible cells inside the wing. Instead of three men in line under a large teardrop canopy there were two pilots in tandem under a multi-pane roof and four crew-members elsewhere, one being a gunner in the extreme tail. The bomb bay was enormous, and though sized to a thermonuclear weapon or a 27000 lb load of conventional bombs, in fact had volumetric capacity for much heavier loads. A scheme was devised whereby, in a strategic reconnaissance version, the RB–52B, the bomb bay would be occupied by a pressurized cabin housing a crew of two and a tightly packed array of cameras, electronic sensors and ECM (electronic counter-measures). The 200-ton weight of the monster rested on four twin-wheel trucks which retracted diagonally to lie in compartments ahead of and behind the weapon bay. A unique feature was that for landing in strong crosswinds the front and rear trucks could all be slewed to line up with the runway while the rest of the aircraft crabbed along diagonally. Small outrigger landing gears under the outer wings gave a clue to the fuel load: with full tanks they pressed firmly on the ground, but on landing after a long mission the wheels stayed suspended in mid-air.

From stem to stern this mightiest of bombers brimmed with technical interest. The flight controls had the innovation of small inboard ailerons between the giant flap sections, the chief lateral controls being spoilers on the upper surface. The 'all-flying' tail was operated hydraulically, but with narrow manual-tab elevators on the trailing edge for immediate pilot control. The 48-foot fin hinged over to the right to reduce the height for entering hangars, and carried on its trailing edge a narrow manual-tab rudder. Perhaps the most intriguing feature of all was that, instead of being shaft-driven, accessories such as the electric generators, hydraulic pumps and similar items were mounted on air-turbine packages in various parts of the fuselage, driven by hot high-pressure air ducted

along steel pipes leading from the engines.

The production B–52B entered service with the 93rd Bomb Wing at Castle AFB, California, on 29 June 1955. By this time the flight deck had been rearranged with both pilots side-by-side as in a transport. They had ejection seats slightly angled to clear the mighty fin, while the bombardier and radar operator could eject downwards; the tail gunner, with a radar-directed barbette carrying four 0·5 in guns, could unlatch the whole rear end and drop clear. The engines by this time had been developed to give 12500 lb thrust with water injected from a 360-gal tank in the rear fuselage, but at this thrust the noise soon caused cracks to appear in the flaps. Under the outer wings were 833-gal non-jettisonable tanks, and in the roof behind the flight deck was a receptacle for the Boeing Flying Boom for flight refuelling. To support the SAC jet-bomber force, Boeing was awarded extremely large contracts for the KC–135 Stratotanker, derived from the company-funded 707 prototype, which unlike the Boeing KC–97 tanker could meet the bombers at their operational speeds and heights.

It seems hardly credible today, but in 1957 Boeing's Seattle and Wichita plants were delivering 20 B–52s and 20 KC–135s a month, as well as keeping pace with the fast-growing civil 707 output. And to show the pace of inflation, when this tempo of production was reached a B–52 cost only about $6 million, which today would not buy a fighter; the B–1 bomber would have cost over $70 million. The manned-capsule RB–52 was soon dropped, and after delivering 50 B–52B bombers Boeing delivered 35 B–52Cs and 170 B–52Ds with enormous 2500-gal underwing tanks, strengthened structure and, in the D, the MD–9 tail fire-control system. Then came 100 E models, with the completely new ASQ–38 navigation/bombing system, and 89 B–52Fs with 13750-lb J57–43W engines with water supplied from tanks in the wing leading edge, and shaft-drive accessories making great bulges on the engine pods. The Seattle plant then ceased assembly but continued making the forward fuselage for the production line at Wichita. This continued with the B–52G, the most numerous version (193), in which a new integral-tank wing, the biggest made up to that time, housed 40000 lb more fuel. The whole aircraft was re-engineered, with new crew stations (nobody in the tail turret but ASG–15 fire control) and much later systems, though the only obvious visual changes were smaller under-wing tanks and a shorter, flat-topped fin. The final model, of which 102 were built by June 1962 (bringing the total

Above: *flight deck of one of the late-model (G and H) B–52s still in front-line service with SAC. The obvious difference, compared with an earlier B–52, is the prominent pair of display screens forming part of the electro-optical viewing system (EVS). This is fed by infra-red and TV sensors and gives much superimposed numerical data as well* Below: *B–52D as used in SE Asia.* Bottom: *B–52G*

programme to 744 aircraft), was the B–52H with TF33 turbofan engines giving 18000 lb thrust without water injection, which extended the miles per gallon by over 35 per cent, and ASG–21 fire control for a 'Gatling' gun giving a much better sting from the tail.

Other changes affected the loads carried. Back at the start of the programme, McDonnell designed the ADM–20 Quail, a miniature aircraft that fits the B–52 bomb bay. Over hostile territory it can be released, unfolding its aerodynamic surfaces, lighting its J85 jet engine and thereafter flying away whilst looking, on enemy radars, exactly like a B–52. Three can be carried, and these can do much more than merely dilute the defences by giving them four apparent targets instead of one, but details of active countermeasures are a sensitive area and cannot be given. In 1956 North American Aviation began work on AGM–28 Hound Dog, a big turbojet-engined missile carrying a thermo-nuclear warhead up to 750 miles, and many B–52s were given two Hound Dog pylons under the inner wings. In 1959–62 it was planned that

149

Top: *the first test hook-up between a G-model and a KC–135 tanker (also Boeing-built) in 1959*
Above: *taken around 1960 this shows a new G-model with drag-chute popped. The SAC squadrons in the background still have the B–47E*

these pylons should also carry pairs of an air-launched ballistic missile named Skybolt, which was also adopted as armament for the Vulcans of the RAF, but President Kennedy terminated this weapon and sold Britain Polaris instead. In 1966 Boeing started to develop a much superior ballistic missile, AGM–69A SRAM (short-range attack missile) which carries a similar warhead but is smaller, with a radar 'signature' little greater than a pistol bullet. SRAM can fly over 100 miles, is almost unstoppable, and can fly dog-legs or zoom on to its target from behind a hill to confuse the defences. Each B–52G or H can carry 20, all assigned to different targets; eight are on an internal rotary launcher like a giant revolver cylinder and the

other 12 are on the old Hound Dog racks.

In service the B–52 has demonstrated immense willingness and fantastic lifting capability, but its life has been hard. From the mid-1950s it was obvious that the only way to penetrate hostile airspace in future would be at the lowest possible level, trying to get under the region of surveillance by enemy radars. Coupled with the gruelling 'airborne alert' policy of the early 1960s to escape sudden enemy missile attack, the switch to low-flying in dense turbulent air soon resulted in severe structural problems, cracks and crashes, despite prolonged prior research. There followed successive rebuild and modification programmes, so extensive they have cost much more than the original price of the aircraft.

None of this was foreseen when the B–52 was designed, and neither was the Vietnam war in which substantial forces of D and F models operated from Andersen AFB on Guam, and later from Thailand, dropping heavy loads of conventional bombs. Long carriers were added to the wing pylons to carry a row of four triple 750 lb bombs (actual weight 825 lb) on each side, while the B–52D bomb bays were altered to carry 84 nominal 500 lb bombs (actual weight 580 lb), giving a total load of almost 70000 lb. Meanwhile the later Gs and Hs have been dramatically updated in equipment and given much new defensive electronics as well as an EVS (electro-optical viewing system) with chin turrets under the nose, that on the left housing a low-light TV and that on the right a forward-looking infra-red.

In 1955 the USAF planned to use this great bomber, the 'long rifle of the air age', for 12 years. In 1970, when its planned life had long since expired, experts wondered if the gallant old workhorses could last out until the B–1 entered service, which then was expected in 1975. Today, with sea surveillance added to their tasks, the B–52 squadrons of SAC look like flying on and on until the last tail comes off with fatigue! There are 19 wings equipped with 269 G and H models, which eventually will exchange their limited-shelf-life SRAMs for a longer-range ALCM (air-launched cruise missile), and about 80 B–52Ds which have been so patched up there is not much of the original left. Today the B–52 is unfairly being asked to do things that were unknown when it was designed. It has a radar signature like two barn doors, and trying to modify it so that it can survive in the face of modern defences has in my view passed the point where you encounter diminishing returns. But with the B–1 cancelled, we shall soon see the B–52 so laden with defensive electronics there is no room even for a little ALCM. That is how the US Congress appears to want it.

How the surviving B–52s look today. This is a B–52H, with EVS bumps under the nose, low-level camouflage and SRAM missiles

Hawker Siddeley Vulcan

Purists may ask "Why call the Canberra 'English Electric' and the Vulcan 'Hawker Siddeley'?" One could equally well call the latter the Avro Vulcan, because it was created by the team that built the Lancaster—except for technical director Roy Chadwick, the most vital cog of all, who in August 1947 was tragically killed in a crash caused by reversed aileron linkages. Modern politicians often appear not to appreciate that the development of major combat aircraft means a half-century programme. The Vulcan, which is now hardly modern, was begun in 1946 and will soldier on into the 80's, so we could call it a product of Avro, Hawker Siddeley or British Aerospace. However, to my way of thinking, names are trivialities; it is the hardware which is important.

Today, building a bomber to the British Air Ministry specification B.35/46 would be pretty straightforward. Issued in March 1947, it called for a bomber with 'at least twice the speed and twice the over-target height' of existing bombers such as the Avro Lincoln. This meant something like 600 mph at 50000 feet. For this, we would use a high aspect-ratio supercritical wing with little sweep, and would certainly adhere to the same traditional overall shape that has been increasingly the standard one for aeroplanes since 1908, but in 1947 nobody knew this. There was an overwhelming feeling that something new should be tried. Designers did not want to continue to fit jet engines in traditional airframes but to create radically new aircraft that could realise the full potential of the new form of propulsion. Germany had demonstrated some of the possibilities with swept and delta wings. Now Britain intended to create the 'ultimate' in strategic bombers, going all-out for the highest practical speed.

There were several reasons for this. One was the natural corollary of the acceptance of the unarmed bomber that relied on its performance for survival. It was thought that 600 mph at 50000 feet would make future bombers as immune to interception as the Mosquito had been. Supersonic aircraft had been discounted

by Britain, for political reasons, and the Minister of Defence said publicly that future fighters would have to fly faster than sound if they were going to be able to intercept what later became known as the British 'V' bombers because their names began with the letter V. He incorrectly predicted that the 'thunderclap hazard' would make it 'a very long time' before such fighters entered service with any air force. As for flak and missiles, these were going to be thwarted by the new bombers' altitude, which

while not necessarily above the projectiles' ceiling, would be high enough to prevent the likelihood of a hit. This reasoning, again quite wrong, was not explained.

There ensued possibly the most extraordinary episode in the history of defence procurement. The big and wealthy United States opted for one type of medium bomber, the B–47, which did more than was expected and of which more than 2000 were built. Impoverished Britain sank into a severe case of indecision, ordered production tooling for a straight-wing bomber built by Shorts (the SA.4 Sperrin) but only two of them were made, bought the slightly swept Vickers-Armstrongs Valiant in modest quantities (108), and ordered two more radical new bombers, the Handley Page Victor and Avro (Hawker Siddeley) Vulcan, in equally small numbers, which were to follow the Valiant a year or two later. In fact, all were ordered approximately at the same time, but Handley Page and Avro were repeatedly told that, as they were experimenting with something ex-

Above: *the third production Vulcan B.1 (XA891) in original silver finish*

Below: *Chichester is directly below this unique formation, pictured by Avro's Paul Cullerne on a photo sortie from the 1952 Farnborough airshow. Avro 698 No 2 leads the blue 707B and silver two-seat 707C, followed by the orange 707A No 2 and the 698 No 1 (red 707A No 2 is out of the picture)*

tremely bold and difficult it was going to take them a very long time indeed. Today design of such a bomber would not be difficult, but in the immediate post-war era engines burned a lot of fuel and Roy Chadwick, with the other chief designers, could not at first see a practical answer. He kept getting estimated weights about twice those stipulated, and eventually decided that the only way to make the aircraft light enough was to make it a tailless delta-wing type.

Such aircraft were so named because the plan shape of the wing is basically a triangle, like the Greek capital D, or delta. It is a good shape structurally, and one can use much thinner skins than in a highly stressed long and slender wing. The great chord (distance from wing leading edge to trailing edge) makes it easy to achieve a low thickness/chord ratio, and t/c ratio is one of the chief factors affecting the rise in drag near the speed of sound. With ordinary wings, reducing the t/c ratio makes the wing so thin that it becomes almost solid metal, and thus very heavy. Chadwick chose a vast delta wing which, because it was such a distance from the front to the back, was deep enough not only to house the engines but could even accommodate a tall man standing upright. One slight drawback was that engine performance suffered from the tremendous length of the inlet ducts and jetpipes, which was not a problem with the American bomber engines hung outside the aircraft in pods.

Wing Commander Roly Falk flew the Avro 698 prototype on 30 August 1952, just in time for the Farnborough air show. At that show Falk's demonstration of the new bomber was breathtaking. It was all-white, very big and of a dramatically new shape; and Falk had such confidence in it he did everything except a slow roll, though a year or two later he did that too, at low level. Technically the 698 was immensely promising, and eventually the production Vulcan B.1 entered service with the RAF 83 Squadron in September 1956. Powered by four Bristol

1 Dielectric nose 13 ft × 8 ft
2 Flight Refuelling probe
3 Radar scanner
4 Vent; cabin air discharge into bay
5 Front pressure bulkhead
6 Access hatch to nose
7 Rear pressure bulkhead, nosewheel beams on rear face

8 Jettisonable canopy
9 Production breaks
10 Pilot, co-pilot, Martin-Baker Mk 4 ejection seats
11 Flying-control assembly, toe brakes
12 Flying-control push-pull tubes
13 Feel-simulator input
14 Engine control-runs
15 Three non-ejecting seats, signaller, master-nav./air-bomber, second navigator
16 Working desk
17 Radio and radar racks
18 Ladder to pilots' deck
19 Visual air-bomber's prone position
20 Bomb-sight
21 Crew entry and lower-deck escape-hatch
22 Pneumatic actuating jacks
23 Ladder, ground equipment
24 Dinghy stowage in canopy fairing
25 Periscopes each side, external inspection
26 Ground rescue equipment; destructor to starboard
27 Cabin pressure and air-conditioning pack
28 Intake to 27 (starboard intake to 37)
29 Intercooler and turbine exhaust
30 Cabin-air feed and extractor duct
31 Dowty liquid spring, levered-suspension nosewheel unit
32 Magnesium-alloy casting
33 Breaker strut

34 Jack (4000 lb/sq in system)
35 Steering cylinder (internal final drive) ±47·5 deg.
36 Nosewheel door jacks
37 Equipment bay, hydraulics, pneumatics, electrics, electronics

38 Inverters (three)
39 Cooling air to 38
40 Boundary-layer bleed 'fence'
41 Boundary-layer duct and outlet
42 Three-position air brakes
43 Cam-track (brake surface angle)
44 Sprocket and chain drive, central motor
45 Roller guides
46 Weapons-bay door actuating cylinder
47 Concertina type doors
48 Subsidiary stores bay
49 Electrics bay
50 Access to 49
51 Five batteries
52 Vertical stiffeners on rear spar for fin loads
53 Rudder power control (Boulton Paul duplicated electric/hydraulic pack)
54 Cooling-air in
55 Cooling-air out
56 Access to 53
57 Tail bumper
58 Braking parachute box (starboard)
59 Streaming point for drag 'chute
60 Dielectric tail cone
61 Bifurcated engine-air intake
62 Engine air ducts through front spar

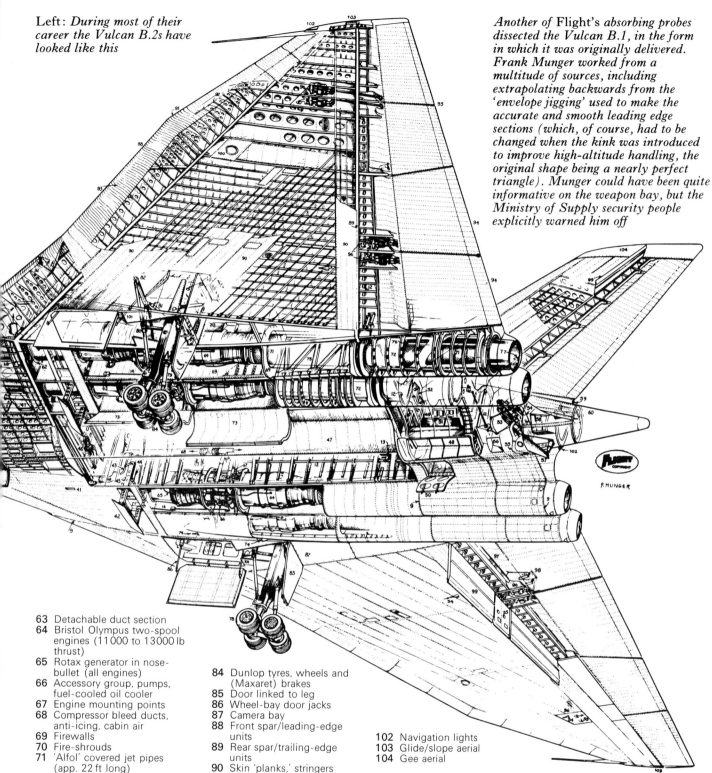

Left: *During most of their career the Vulcan B.2s have looked like this*

Another of Flight's *absorbing probes dissected the Vulcan B.1, in the form in which it was originally delivered. Frank Munger worked from a multitude of sources, including extrapolating backwards from the 'envelope jigging' used to make the accurate and smooth leading edge sections (which, of course, had to be changed when the kink was introduced to improve high-altitude handling, the original shape being a nearly perfect triangle). Munger could have been quite informative on the weapon bay, but the Ministry of Supply security people explicitly warned him off*

F.MUNGER

63 Detachable duct section
64 Bristol Olympus two-spool engines (11000 to 13000 lb thrust)
65 Rotax generator in nose-bullet (all engines)
66 Accessory group, pumps, fuel-cooled oil cooler
67 Engine mounting points
68 Compressor bleed ducts, anti-icing, cabin air
69 Firewalls
70 Fire-shrouds
71 'Alfol' covered jet pipes (app. 22 ft long)
72 Jet-pipe heat shroud
73 Engine access doors
74 Cool air to engine bays
75 Warren truss rib between jet pipes
76 Jet-pipe rail
77 Jet-pipe nozzle area adjusters
78 Dowty liquid spring bogie undercarriage
79 Shock absorber
80 Braking drag strut
81 Mainwheel retraction jack
82 Pivot points in wing structure
83 Internal light

84 Dunlop tyres, wheels and (Maxaret) brakes
85 Door linked to leg
86 Wheel-bay door jacks
87 Camera bay
88 Front spar/leading-edge units
89 Rear spar/trailing-edge units
90 Skin 'planks,' stringers attached
91 Drooped leading edge
92 Thermal anti-icing ducts
93 Corrugated inner skin
94 Elevators
95 Ailerons
96 Power-control jacks (see 53)
97 Irving-type pressure-sealed balance (and mass balance)
98 Hinges on upper surface
99 Honeycomb sandwich inspection panels
100 Landing lamps
101 Pressure refuelling points

102 Navigation lights
103 Glide/slope aerial
104 Gee aerial

SPECIFICATIONS

Type 698, Vulcan B.1, 1A, 2 and SR.2

Engines: four Rolls-Royce (originally Bristol, then Bristol Siddeley) Olympus two-shaft turbojets; for details see text.
Dimensions: span (1) 99 ft (30·18 m); (2) 111 ft (33·83 m); length (1) 97 ft 1 in (29·6 m); (2) 105 ft 6 in (32·15 m) (99 ft 11 in with probe removed); height (1) 26 ft 1 in (7·94 m); (2) 27 ft 2 in (8·26 m).
Weights: not disclosed; loaded weights probably about 170000 lb for B.1A and 250000 lb for B.2 and SR.2.
Performance: maximum speed (1) about 620 mph; (2) about 640 mph (1030 km/h) at height (Mach 0·97); service ceiling (1) about 55000 ft, (2) about 65000 ft (19810 m); range with bomb load (1) about 3000 miles; (2) about 4600 miles (7400 km).

Above: *RAF Waddington in February 1957, and 230 OCU (Operational Conversion Unit) is in business with the B.1. The nearest three are in anti-flash white*

Left: *the first production B.2 shows off its new wing on an early test flight on 7 September 1958. Note the small tailcone*

Below: *a production B.2 in the days of all-white finish with pale anti-flash markings*

Olympus two-shaft turbojets which first flew Vulcans at 9140 lb thrust and subsequently were up-rated to 11000, 12000 and finally 13500 lb, the new bomber had a crew of five, the two side-by-side pilots having fighter-type control columns and ejection seats and the other three crew members—usually two navigators and an air electronics officer—having ordinary seats lower down and behind. The neat weapon bay, sized to a supposed British nuclear weapon which proved later to be somewhat smaller, usually accomodated 21 ordinary bombs of 1000 lb each. Much of the airframe was of patented light-alloy sandwich construction, and Dowty supplied the main landing gear, each with eight small tyres, which I guarantee will delight any mechanical engineer.

This kind of attitude is not unusual after a takeoff by a B.2 at an air display, usually in a near-stall turn after an initial climb of unbelievable steepness. No other aircraft of this size and mass can be so effortlessly poled around the sky like a fighter

Quite early in development an aerodynamic 'buzz' at great heights was cured by slightly kinking the wing leading edge. In 1957 a Vulcan flew with a new wing which was so kinked and also extended in span, as to be almost an ordinary, non-delta shape. Its t/c ratio was even lower, the vast areas contained subtle curves that gave perfect results near the speed of sound at heights now considerably above 50000 feet, and the four powered wing controls were changed to elevons, instead of inboard elevators and outboard ailerons. Bristol startled engine rivals by pushing up the thrust of their great Olympus to 20000 lb, and the result was the Vulcan B.2, achieving a new level of flight performance while carrying a large Blue Steel stand-off missile and a very extensive array of navaids and defensive electronics. Entering service from July 1960, the Vulcan B.2 rapidly gained an outstanding reputation. Like its partner the B-52, it has had to soldier on into the modern era in which the original objective of flying fast and high has been completely forgotten, except on peaceful journeys between friendly nations.

In fact the whole design concept of past years was rendered obsolete even as these bombers entered service by the appearance of computerized radar air-defence systems, supersonic missile-armed interceptors and high-performance SAMs (surface-to-air missiles). By 1960 defence staffs had reluctantly concluded that the high-flying bomber—even a supersonic one—could no longer survive, and on May Day of that year this belief was reinforced by the shooting down over Sverdlovsk of Gary Powers and his very high-altitude U-2. So the Vulcan was given a terrain-following radar able to guide it up hill and down dale at treetop height in its attempts to penetrate hostile airspace 'under the radar'—a task which, in hilly country, or airspace watched by an airborne warning and control system (AWACS) aircraft, is impossible. Low-level missions are very tough on structures and crews, but the shape and construction of the Vulcan has enabled this fine machine to hold up wonderfully well. Even today a quick 'scramble' by a section of Vulcans is very impressive. The RAF still has about 74 of these aircraft in six squadrons, plus four specially equipped SR.2 (strategic reconnaissance) versions. The mileage Britain has got out of the Vulcan, in both senses of the word, is quite exceptional.

Saab Viggen

There are not many 'bombers' around in the modern world. This is because fundamental technical developments in aircraft structures, propulsion, systems and, especially, in nav/attack systems, have allowed aircraft that look like fighters to behave like bombers. Sometimes the process has gone so far that even the professionals have become confused, as when the USAF bought a new bomber for Tactical Air Command, mistakenly called it a fighter, and gave it the designation F–111. This confusion became even worse when the Secretary of Defense in 1960 thought it could also fly the fighter mission of the US Navy, and caused delays and wasted costs on an astronomic scale in the sincere expectation that he would save money. Now the strategic bomber version of this aircraft, which is called the FB–111A, is to be rebuilt for even greater ranges. This would be a marvellous chance to set the record straight and call the rebuilt bomber the B–2A—but instead they are likely to be designated FB–111H. They carry no gun or air-to-air weapon, as air fighting is just what they wish to avoid. So if you, the reader, are getting confused, you are in good company.

It is intended that this last chapter should show the kind of aircraft flying today's bomber missions. The Swedes, who have the best record of free-from-error defence procurement that I know of, asked for what they called System 37 in 1958 which was to be a next-generation weapon system to fly nearly all the missions of the Flygvapnet and be closely integrated with the Stril-60 air defence organisation. The result is a family of related aircraft named Viggen (Thor's hammer, or Thunderbolt). The aircraft abound in unusual features, many of which stem from the well-founded Swedish need for the ability to operate from country highways and other short strips. The RM8B engine gives very high thrust for takeoff, and the broad wing and flapped foreplane give exceptional lift, so that the Viggen fairly leaps off the ground and climbs steeply, from brakes-off to 33000 feet in less than 100 seconds.

Structure
1 Nosecone, slides forward on rails
2 Front pressure bulkhead
3 Bird-impact-resistant windscreen
4 Saab zero-zero rocket-powered ejection seat
5 Ejection levers, on both sides
6 Frangible automatically ejected canopy
7 Rear pressure bulkhead
8 Intake braces
9 Inspection panels (approx. 100 total)
10 Glass-fibre components (shaded)
11 Forged and machined alloy main spars
12 Titanium multi-bolt wing/fuselage attachment
13 Fabricated main frame
14 Redux-bonded leading edges
15 Bonded honeycomb panels (upper and lower surfaces)
16 Light alloy spars
17 Honeycomb control surfaces
18 Light alloy skin panels
19 Titanium ejector ring
20 Folding vertical fin
21 Provisional brake-chute housing (not used)
22 Glass-fibre cones

Air Systems
A1 Air conditioning and cockpit pressurisation bay
A2 Ram air intakes to electronics bay
A3 Cockpit venting ducts
A4 Electronics bay venting ducts

Powerplant
P1 Stainless steel engine intake
P2 Bifurcated ducts
P3 Boundary layer splitter plate
P4 Boundary airflow
P5 Svenska Flygmotor RM8 by-pass engine
P6 Forward mounting trunnions
P7 Single-point aft engine mounting
P8 Engine access panels
P9 Svenska Flygmotor afterburner
P10 Ejector intake sealing doors
P11 Electrical screw jacks (four)
P12 Thrust reverser plates (three) actuated by undercarriage compression
P13 Pneumatic thrust-reverser actuators
P14 Ejector air intake (open)

John Marsden, one of the leaders of today's team of Flight artists, could now prepare a comprehensive cutaway of Sweden's outstanding STOL attack aircraft. Back in 1967 it was not so easy. The prototype had only just been put together, but it is a competitive world and Marsden—in one of the last of the probes—prepared this illustration in a matter of hours. Today new and secret aircraft are scarce, except in the Soviet Union

SPECIFICATIONS

Types AJ37, JA37, SF37, SH37 and Sk37

Engine: one Svenska Flygmotor RM8 (licence-built Pratt & Whitney JT8D two-shaft turbofan redesigned in Sweden for Mach 2 and fitted with SFA afterburner): (AJ, SF, SH and Sk) 25 970 lb (11 790 kg) RM8A; (JA) 28 086 lb (12 750 kg) RM8B.

Dimensions: span of main wing 34 ft 9¼ in (10·6 m); length (53 ft 5¾ in) (16·3 m); JA37 with probe 53 ft 11 ins; height 18 ft 4½ in (5·6 m).

Weights: not disclosed, escept AJ37 'normal armament' gross weight of 35 275 lb (16 000 kg).

Performance: maximum speed (clean) about 1 320 mph (2 135 km/h, Mach II), or Mach 1·1 at sea level; initial climb, about 40 000 ft (12 200 m)/min (time from start of take-off run to 32 800 ft— 10 000 m = 100 sec); service ceiling, over 60 000 ft (18 300 m); tactical radius with external stores (not drop tanks), hi-lo-hi profile, over 620 miles (1 000 km).

Emergency Equipment and Ground Supply
E1 Auxiliary ram-air turbine (drives auxiliary electrical hydraulic pump)
E2 Actuator
E3 Hydraulic bay

Weapons and External Stores
W1 Forward stores pylon
W2 Wing stores pylon
W3 Saab Rb 305A air-to-ground missile

Control System
C1 Stick force transducer on control column
C2 Rudder pedals
C3 Throttle control
C4 Canard flap actuators (used for highlift in take-off and landings only)
C5 Rudder actuator
C6 Inboard elevon actuator
C7 Centre actuator
C8 Outboard elevon actuator
C9 Side air-brake
C10 Supplementary pitot ('Q' feel)

Fuel System
F1, F2, F3, F4 Cell-type fuel tanks
F5 Integral wing tanks
F6 Centre transfer tank (automatically controlled to maintain optimum centre of gravity. Also acts as reservoir in case of fuel system malfunction)
F7 Single refuelling point below wing

Undercarriage
U1 Rudder-pedal-actuated power-steering nose gear
U2 Steering actuator
U3 Forward-retracting nose-leg
U4 High-pressure tandem main wheels incorporating multi-disc Maxaret units
U5 Leg shortens on retraction by compressing shock absorber
U6 Rear stay
U7 Main leg actuator
U8 Main undercarriage bay door, open (normally pre-closing)
U9 Door actuator
U10 Breaker strut

Instruments and Electronics
Is 1 Pitot head
Is 2 Radar scanner
Is 3 Radar package, slides forward on rails for replacing, inspection and automatic testing of units
Is 4 Forward electronics bay
Is 5 Cockpit equipment
Is 6 Head-up display unit
Is 7 Lower electronics bay (digital computer, navigational equipment)
Is 8 Upper electronics bay (air data unit, radar altimeter, gyro platform)
Is 9 ADF aerials
Is 10 Navigation lights
Is 11 Glass-fibre static-discharge wicks

copyright
FLIGHT international
John A Marsden
LINKÖPING '67

159

No air force tries harder to be cost/effective than the Swedish Flygvapen, which has hardly put a foot wrong (in sharpest contrast to most major Western air forces). For 40 years it has practised off-airfield operation, a vital factor that most other air forces (except the Russians) never quite get round to, except with V/STOL aircraft. This AJ37 of attack wing F15 may be found at Soderhamn or almost anywhere in the Swedish countryside

This is an SH37 sea-surveillance Viggen, of F13 at Norrköping. It bristles with sensors and ECM, and can quickly be switched to fly attack missions

The landing needs no flare, the aircraft being slammed down on to its small tandem pairs of wheels, and brought to rest in 500 yards with the use of powerful anti-skid brakes and a thrust reverser. About seven tons of weapons can be hung on seven external pylons, along with extensive ECM and other equipment.

First flown on 8 February 1967, the AJ37 attack Viggen entered service on 21 June 1971. It has since been joined by the SK37 dual trainer, the SF37 for overland reconnaissance and the SH37 for sea surveillance, all having basically the same airframe, engine and systems but quite different equipment. In 1978, came the more extensively altered JA37 fighter version, with more powerful engine, air-to-air radar/computer/weapons and modified airframe. The notion of a fighter version of a bomber is by no means new, and was seen in such machines as the Hawker Demon and de Havilland Mosquito. In the Soviet Union the MiG bureau has developed two related swing-wing tactical machines, the MiG-23 fighter and MiG-27 bomber. And the RAF's replacement for the Vulcan is the Panavia Tornado, which in its fighter version will replace the Lightning and Phantom. In other words, today's bombers look like fighters and sometimes act like them.

Probably there will be no more big bombers. We live in a world of extremely clever automated defence systems, small missiles that can fly a thousand miles, and inflation that makes even small aircraft expensive. Maybe eventually we shall be able to do away with military aircraft. But to do this completely at the present time would be very shortsighted. So there is still room for the bomber to develop. If inflation continues unabated we shall be forced to revert to slings and arrows, and the process will start all over again.